*Firsts, Facts, Feats, & Failures
in the World of Golf*

Firsts,
Facts,
FEATS,
& Failures
in the World of Golf

KEN JANKE

BICENTENNIAL
1807
WILEY
2007
BICENTENNIAL

JOHN WILEY & SONS, INC.

Copyright © 2007 by John Wiley & Sons, Inc. All rights reserved

Published by John Wiley & Sons, Inc., Hoboken, New Jersey
Published simultaneously in Canada

For general information about our other products and services, please contact our Customer Care
Department within the United States at (800) 762-2974, outside the United States at (317) 572-3993
or fax (317) 572-4002.

Wiley also publishes its books in a variety of electronic formats. Some content that appears in print
may not be available in electronic books. For more information about Wiley products, visit our web
site at www.wiley.com.

Library of Congress Cataloging-in-Publication Data:

Janke, Ken, 1934-
 Firsts, facts, feats, and failures in the world of golf / Ken Janke.
  p. cm.
 Includes bibliographical references and index.
 ISBN-13: 978-0-471-96559-6 (cloth)
 ISBN-10: 0-471-96559-6 (cloth)
 1. Golf—Miscellanea. 2. Golf—History. I. Title.
 GV965.J354 2007
 796.352—dc22
                            2006019139

Printed in the United States of America

10 9 8 7 6 5 4 3 2 1

CONTENTS

PREFACE

*P*laying golf is a wonderful experience. Reading and talking about the game is almost as good as the game itself because we can never experience all of the different things that have occurred through the centuries it has been played. I must admit that my normal round of golf lasts about six or seven hours. It lasts that long because I derive so much enjoyment from talking with others about the sport and all of the special incidents that have happened through the years. There is no other game like it. There is no other game that has a longer history.

My golf library consists of more than 2,800 books and I've only scratched the surface. It may seem silly to have another book about golf, but I have found that there are many fascinating stories about the game and they have not all appeared in one place. I have tried to capture those fascinating stories in this book. There's so much to tell about what Jack Nicklaus called the "Greatest game of all."

This book was compiled over many years. I researched the game using the golf books and magazines in my library and in some cases I was lucky enough to hear stories first hand. The bibliography lists the sources. Every effort has been made to be accurate, but I would encourage readers to contact me NAICINVEST@AOL.com if any inaccuracies are spotted.

ACKNOWLEDGMENTS

*M*y family has always been supportive of my golf and my interest in the sport's history. Sally is the most wonderful wife in the world, never complaining about the time I spend at the golf club or doing research. Our children—Ken, Laura and Julie along with Kim and Charlie who have joined our family—are all very special, as are our grandchildren, Paige, Emma, Grant and Lilly. They all anxiously antici-pate each new project I tackle.

The person who really encouraged this book is Mike Black. He has been a partner and friend since our first meeting at Indianwood Golf Club in Lake Orion, Michigan more than 15 years ago. As we shared a golf cart, we discussed many topics. He seemed intrigued by my golf tales and has asked me to repeat them many times. Mike later told me that those stories should be put in writing to share with others.

Mike and I play together just about every weekend and any other day we can get away from the office. He plays golf with a passion but will never break the course record. He does have some accomplishments at Indianwood. Mike is the only person I know who has the distinction of hitting every structure on the course in one round and I was with him when it happened. He was able to carom a golf ball off the halfway house, the golf cart storage building, maintenance shed and clubhouse in one 18-hole round. The 14th hole has a large tree growing to the front and left of the tee. It is known as Black's Tree in honor of the many times he has hit it. At one time, the entire right side of the tree had lost all of the branches. Mike insisted it had a disease that he said was Surlyn poisoning since he always used balls made of that substance.

At other times, he has moments of brilliance and I find myself digging deep into my wallet to pay the bets I've lost to him. Mike has a wonderful sense of humor and keeps me laughing and happy I'm on the golf course, regardless of my score. Mike Black is a special friend who has been the catalyst for this book and I thank him.

CHAPTER ONE

Firsts

*W*alter Hagen had a strong disdain for finishing second. He stated that no one remembers who was second, and that philosophy stayed with him throughout his career. As a young man, he entered the 1913 U.S. Open, which was won by Francis Ouimet. Walter was in the hunt until the final nine holes, finishing only three strokes behind the leaders, placing a joint fourth.

That kind of an accomplishment, a top-ten finish in a major championship, would earn a great deal of ink today, but Walter was disappointed. So discouraged was he, in fact, that he almost gave up the game for baseball and a professional contract with the Philadelphia Phillies. In spite of his showing at The Country Club, in Brookline, Massachusetts, Hagen did not intend to play the following year at Midlothian. Encouraged to enter that championship, Walter won the 1914 U.S. Open, and the golfing world gained one of the most colorful champions in history. In doing so, he became the first champion to lead after every round in the U.S. Open. While that feat has been duplicated by Jim Barnes (1921), Ben Hogan (1953), Tony Jacklin (1970), and Tiger Woods (2000 and 2002), Hagen set the standard.

What Hagen said is probably true. Golfers today can usually recall that Jack Nicklaus won 18 major professional tournaments. Little remembered is that Jack was the runner-up in 19 professional majors, and that in itself is a remarkable accomplishment.

Being the first to do anything does not necessarily mean that that person is the best, but it does indicate that he or she is a trailblazer of some sort. Whether it was as meaningful as Columbus discovering the New World or as insignificant as being the first to win a Professional Golfers' Association (PGA) Tour event using a colored golf ball, it is still a first. Others may later accomplish the same thing, but it will only be a duplication of the original.

For example, when American golfers are asked the name of the best male professional golfer from Sweden, Jesper Parnevik is probably the person most would cite. But Jesper had never won an American PGA Tour event until 1998. The honor of being the first Swede to win an American PGA Tour event went to Gabriel Hjertstedt, who won the 1997 B.C. Open. His win takes nothing away from Parnevik, a member of the victorious 1997 European Ryder Cup team. The talented Parnevik may win more tournaments before his career is over, but he can never replace Hjertstedt as the original Swedish winner on the PGA Tour.

Timing has everything to do with being first. History tells us that Willie Park, Horace Rawlins, Jim Barnes, and Horton Smith were the first to win the four majors now open to professionals. That can never change. Their accomplishments don't diminish the feat of Harry Vardon, who won six British Opens, or of Jack Nicklaus, who garnered six Masters titles. Both of those wonderful champions will always be remembered as long as golf is played. Each was first in winning six major titles in a single professional event, just as Arnold Palmer was the first to win four Masters titles. That Palmer's record was broken doesn't take away from his being the first to win four, just as Jimmy Demaret's record of being the first to win three Masters cannot be taken from him.

The first victory for any golfer, whether it comes in some obscure junior tournament or in the rookie season on the PGA or LPGA tour, is a milestone. It has been said many times that records are made to be broken. However, being first is something that can never be taken away, no matter how insignificant. It means that the man or woman will forever be remembered for accomplishing something that no other person had done up to that time.

Generally considered the first golf professional, Allan Robertson was different than the others who made a living in the game. The others at the time worked primarily as club or ball makers, as well as caddies. Robertson was much more forward thinking. He hired men first to work as apprentices and then as employees, so he could concentrate on his golf game. He was a successful businessman, which allowed him the time and money to do what he liked the most. Many of his matches were with amateurs who would bet heavily on the outcome. Some wanted Allan as their partner, to take advantage of his sterling play. Robertson, of course, would receive his share of the bets, but he was not opposed to backing himself when the opportunity arose.

He basically served as the golf professional for the Royal and Ancient (R&A) Golf Club of St. Andrews, Scotland, but he never had the title because the position really didn't exist in the 1850s. Still, he was always at the disposal of the members of the R&A.

At a time when the best of players could rarely break 100, Robertson was the first to return a score better than 80 on the Old Course at St. Andrews. He shot a world record 79 on September 15, 1858, when the fairways were considerably narrower, the rough rougher, and the greens less manicured than what we experience today.

It was probably natural that Robertson would become involved in golf. His father, David (or Davie), was considered the first caddie, although that was not true since there was a mention of caddies as far back as 1771, and there is even a record of a tournament that was held for ball makers, club makers, and caddies, dating back to 1819. Davie Robertson was immortalized in 1833 in George Carnegie's poem "The Golfiad" and again following his death in 1836.

One of Allan's apprentices was Tom Morris, who would go on to win four British Open championships. They had a falling-out because Morris embraced the new gutta-percha (gutty) golf ball. Robertson made a comfortable living by producing the *featherie* and did not wish to see a new golf ball introduced. In fact, Allan went so far as to purchase as many of the gutta-perchas as he could, destroying them in an effort to keep his dominant position in producing the featherie. Naturally, when the new ball was cheaper than the old and held up better in wet conditions and traveled farther, it was impossible to impede progress. Even Robertson's record score was made with a gutty, so eventually he saw the light.

During their disagreement, Tom decided to look elsewhere for employment, and Morris was offered the position of "keeper of the green" at Prestwick, Scotland. He moved to the west of Scotland from St. Andrews. The relationship between the two was finally over.

Robertson was so dominant a golfer and personality that he was considered the champion of golf. There is speculation that, following his death, the British Open was initiated to find a successor to that title. It became the oldest of all national championships, first held in 1860 at Prestwick, continuing there for 12 years before moving to other venues. The championship became known universally as The Open or, more formally, The Open Golf Championship, and now it is commonly known as the British Open. Morris was the favorite, but the first winner was Willie Park of Musselburgh, Scotland, who went on to win a total of four titles.

In reality, the first championship wasn't actually an "open." It was only open to professionals, and there were a total of eight that entered. Even the term "professional" was a misnomer. The invitation sent to six clubs read, "Please send a respectable caddie." The following year, the committee announced that it would be "open to all the world" and thus paved the way for amateurs to play in the oldest of championships.

"Old" Tom Morris made history himself, although it wasn't because of his victories in the Open, which number four. It happened in 1868 when "Young" Tom won his first championship. They became the first father and son combination to win the British Open, a feat later duplicated in 1887, when Willie Park Jr. joined his father as a champion.

They remain the only father-son combinations to have won a major championship. The Morris family was also the first father-son duo to play in the same Open Championship.

The Park family had another first—Willie's brother Mungo won the Open in 1874. The only other brother combinations to win the same major were Alex and Willie Smith in the U.S. Open and Jay and Lionel Hebert in the PGA Championship.

There are no records as to when scorecards were introduced. As golf was initially a match game, there was probably little need for scorecards. Once stroke-play competition came into vogue, a need did arise. It is possible that a scorecard was used to record Allan Robertson's 79 at St. Andrews. Still, no one really knows the exact date.

It is recorded, however, that the first time official scorecards were used in The Open was in 1866 at Prestwick.

Long before Allan Robertson came on the scene, golf clubs hired what were then referred to as "hole-cutters." They were the first greenkeepers. The earliest mention of a hole-cutter can be found in the records of St. Andrews. In 1764, a notation indicates that a payment of one guinea a year was made to George Mill for cutting new holes, filling in old ones, and repairing rabbit scrapes.

Female golf professionals came on the scene much later. The first woman golf professional in the world is not known; but there is a record of the first in the United States. Willie Campbell was a wonderful professional golfer, who was especially adept at match play. His wife, Georgina Stewart Campbell, was teaching golf as early as 1896 at the Franklin Park Golf Course in Boston, Massachusetts. Willie was the head professional at the course, and when he died in 1900, Mrs. Campbell was appointed a professional golfer by the City of Boston.

While the Old Course at St. Andrews can claim to be the oldest, and thus the first golf course in the world, it was more accurately the first links; the first golf club was the Honourable Company of Edinburgh Golfers, founded in 1744. It wasn't until ten years later that what is now known as the Royal and Ancient Golf Club of St. Andrews was formed.

For the better part of a century, the Honourable Company played its golf at Leith, Scotland, before moving to Musselburgh. The course was used by others, not just the Honourable Company. Wanting a course that was not quite as crowded, the Honourable Company built a new one, and the club moved to Muirfield. The new course opened in May 1891.

During the time the Honourable Company was at Musselburgh, the Open Championship was held regularly on its links; but when the club moved, Musselburgh no longer hosted the championship. In fact, within one year of Muirfield's opening, it was the site of the British Open, which was held there for the first time in 1892.

More than a century before the British Open was held, John Rattray, an Edinburgh surgeon, won the Silver Club in a competition conducted by the Gentlemen Golfers of Edinburgh, which is now the Honourable Company of Edinburgh Golfers. That was in 1744, and because of the victory, Rattray was named the "Captain of the Golf." It was his responsibility to settle disputes and conduct meetings of the club.

While the records have been lost, it can be assumed that Rattray's victory came in what was possibly the first golf tournament conducted at stroke play. Prior to that time, golf was a series of matches, and the winner was the person who won the most holes, regardless of the number of strokes played. For that tournament, the Gentlemen Golfers of Edinburgh wrote a code of rules. They were as follows:

1. You must tee your ball within a club's length of the hole.
2. Your tee must be upon the ground.

3. You are not to change the ball you strike off the tee.

4. You are not to remove stones, bones, or any breakclub for the sake of playing your ball except upon the fair green, and that only within a club's length of your ball.

5. If your ball come among water, or any watery filth, you are at liberty to take out your ball and bringing it behind the hazard, and teeing it, you may play it with any club and allow your adversary a stroke for getting out your ball.

6. If your balls be found anywhere touching one another, you are to lift the first ball, till you play the last.

7. At holing, you are to play your ball honestly for the hole, and not to play on your adversary's ball not lying in your way to the hole.

8. If you should lose your ball by its being taken up, or any other way, you are to go back to the spot where you struck your last and drop another ball and allow your adversary a stroke for the misfortune.

9. No man at holing his ball is to be allowed to mark his way to the hole with his club or anything else.

10. If a ball be stop'd by any person, horse, dog, or anything else, the ball so stop'd must be played where it lyes.

11. If you draw your club in order to stroke, and proceed so far in the stroke as to be bringing down your club—If then your club break in any way, it is to be accounted a stroke.

12. He whose ball lyes farthest from the hole is obliged to play first.

13. Neither trench, ditch or dyke made for the preservation of the links, or the Scholars' holes, or the Soldiers' lines, shall be accounted a hazard, but the ball is to be taken out, teed, and played with any iron club.

*I*n 1754, William Landale won the Silver Club Challenge at St. Andrews. There is no evidence that it was an event solely for the Society of St. Andrews Golfers, which was to become the Royal and Ancient

Golf Club of St. Andrews. Still, Landale is considered the first Captain of the Golf at the cradle of the game.

The Society issued a statement for medal play that is believed to be the first identifying that method of play. It stated that "in order to remove all disputes and inconveniences with regard to the gaining of the Silver Club, it is enacted and agreed by the captain and the gentlemen golfers present that in all time coming whoever puts in the ball at the fewest strokes over the field shall be declared and sustained victor."

*B*eing named the Captain at the R&A has become a great honor. The driving-in ceremony is filled with tradition and takes place at 8 A.M. on the final morning of the Autumn Meeting. Members surround the first tee, while caddies position themselves on the first hole in an effort to be the person who retrieves the ball hit by the captain-elect. The ball is teed up by the honorary professional of the R&A, and with blast of a cannon at the precise moment the ball is struck, the captain-elect plays himself into office.

The caddies are anxious to get the golf ball, since tradition calls for the captain to present the caddie who retrieves it with a gold sovereign. It was only normal that the captains were Scots in the early days of the R&A. That changed in 1908 with the naming of Horace Hutchinson, the first Englishman to hold the honor.

The first American to be named captain was Francis Ouimet in 1951. He broke with tradition in that he presented caddie Arthur Spreight with a U.S. five-dollar gold piece. It was minted in 1913, the year he won the U.S. Open.

*W*hen the British Open began in 1860, a rule stated that the winner would keep possession of the Champion Belt for the year, and if any player could win it three times in succession, he would retain permanent possession. That occurred in 1870 when Young Tom Morris won his third straight title. The following year no championship was held. The belt was then replaced with a silver cup, and the British Open

Championship resumed in 1872. Young Tom won again and was the first to have his name engraved on the claret jug, although that honor had to wait another year when the work on the trophy was completed. No longer could it become the permanent possession of a three-time winner, however.

In retrospect, it was a wise decision to make the change, as Jamie Anderson won in 1877, '78, and '79, followed by Bob Ferguson with consecutive victories in the next three years. Then, seven decades later, it happened again when Peter Thomson won in 1954 and through 1956.

Only one golfer, Willie Anderson, has been able to win three consecutive U.S. Open titles. He turned the trick in 1903, '04, and '05. There is a footnote, though. Ben Hogan was the U.S. Open champion in 1948. Because of his auto accident, he could not defend the title in 1949, which was won by Cary Middlecoff. Hogan then captured the 1950 and 1951 championships. Thus, Hogan won the three in a row in which he was able to compete.

"HOYLAKE" MASSY

The first foreign-born winner of the Open Championship (the British Open) was Arnaud Massy of France, taking the championship in 1907. The importance of the Open at the time made it the "championship of the world." Massy was so proud of his accomplishment that he named his daughter Hoylake, after the course on which he won the Open.

Massy added another distinction when he wrote an instruction book on the game. It was the first golf book written in a language other than English, and it also became the first golf book to be translated into English from another language.

*R*ain has caused countless cancellations of rounds and even short-ened some tournaments through the years. That was not always the case in Great Britain, where the weather was considered part of the game. The first time a day's play was canceled at the British Open was in 1910, with James Braid going on to win his fifth and final championship.

*W*eather also had a hand in the 1988 British Open Championship. It marked the first time that the championship was completed on a Monday, as Severiano Ballesteros fired a 65 at Royal Lytham in win-ning his third title.

*P*rior to 1962, except for the early championships, every contestant had to qualify to play in the British Open, even the defending cham-pion. A list of exempt golfers was created. From that time on, no golfer who had to go through qualifying ever won the championship until 1999. Then Paul Lawrie became the first to accomplish the feat, and he did it in style. He came from ten strokes back in the final round to capture the title following a play-off with Justin Leonard and Jean Van de Velde.

*I*t wasn't until 1895 that the United States held its open championship, the U.S. Open. The first winner was Horace Rawlins, who was the assistant professional at the Newport Golf Club in Rhode Island, site of the first championship, serving under head professional W. F. Davis. Born on the Isle of Wight in 1874, he learned to play golf as a caddie. His rounds of 91 and 82 bested Willie Dunn by two strokes to gain the championship. The next year Horace signed a contract to become the professional at Sadaquada Golf Club in Whitesboro, New York, having benefited from winning the first U.S. Open. After holding the same position at Waumbek Golf Club in New Hampshire, Springhaven Golf Club in suburban

Philadelphia, Pennsylvania, and Wykagyl in New York, he settled at Ekwanok Golf Club in Manchester, Vermont, for seven seasons.

Rawlins spent 19 years in the United States before returning to England in 1913, because his mother was ill. Following her death, Horace became a clothing merchant, inheriting the family business. He gave up professional golf at that time. Rawlins played in the U.S. Open 16 times. His only other top-ten finish came in 1896 as runner-up to James Foulis.

One year before the "official" first U.S. Open, the St. Andrews Golf Club invited professionals to compete in a match-play event that they called the Open Championship. Four golfers participated, with Willie Dunn defeating Willie Campbell in the final. Dunn received $100 as well as a gold medal, which he proudly wore until he died, always proclaiming that he was the *first* United States Open golf champion. However, the United States Golf Association (USGA) still does not recognize Dunn's accomplishment.

That first official U.S. Open in 1895 had a field of 11 golfers. The first shot hit was not made by a competitor but by Dr. E. C. Rushmore, who was playing as a marker, since there weren't enough golfers to make proper pairings.

Counting Rawlins, five players have won the U.S. Open in their first attempt. Others were Fred Herd in 1898; Harry Vardon, 1900; George Sargent, 1909; and Francis Ouimet in 1913.

Until 1913, anyone who entered the U.S. Open could play in the championship. Then, because of the number of participants, the field had to be narrowed and a 36-hole qualifier was held at the championship site. In 1924, the USGA determined that it was very expensive for golfers to travel to the U.S. Open site without the assurance of a spot, so regional qualifying was adopted across the country for the first time. With Ouimet's victory, it also became the first time an amateur won the U.S. Open.

*T*he oldest instruction book was actually a handwritten journal compiled in 1687 by Thomas Kincaid of Edinburgh; the journal offers Kincaid's thoughts and advice on, for example, how to swing a club: "The ball must be straight before your breast, a little towards the left foot."

Some 170 years later, in 1857, the first golf instruction book was actually published. H. B. Farnie was the author of *The Golfer's Manual,* using the pen name "A Keen Hand." The first golf instruction book published in America was *How to Play Golf* (1898) by H. J. Whigham. It was also the first golf book to include action photographs of the golf swing.

*W*illie Park Jr. became the first golf professional to write a book, *The Game of Golf* (1896).

*T*hat same year, in 1896, Mrs. Edward Kinnard wrote *The Sorrows of a Golfer's Wife,* becoming the first woman to write a book about golf.

*L*ost in golf history, except to those who truly follow the game, is the name of Freddie Tait. The two-time British Amateur champion had his career cut short when he was killed at the age of 30 during the Boer War, where he served as an officer. Despite his young age, Freddie was a hero among the Scots. Great throngs of people would show up whenever he played a match. The St. Andrews amateur was the subject of the first golf biography ever written, when, in 1900, John Laing Low chronicled Tait's life. In 1925, Freddy was recognized with the introduction of the Freddie Tait Cup, an award given annually to the low amateur in the South African Open.

*T*he first known written mention of golf in what was to become the United States was in an edict by Dutch officials in Fort Orange, present-day Albany, New York. On December 10, 1659, they outlawed playing golf in the streets. A fine of 25 florin was imposed for anyone breaking the law.

*A*nother wonderful golfer who is often overlooked is Harold Hilton; he was one of only three amateurs to win the Open, and he did it twice. He was also able to win three British Amateur titles. In 1911, Hilton decided to travel to America and give the U.S. Amateur Championship a try, which was held at Apawamis in New York.

After some lopsided victories, he gained the final against Fred Herreshoff, a former national collegiate champion. It appeared that Hilton had the match well in hand when he was six up at the end of 21 holes. Then Fred began to eat away at the lead, and they finished the 36 holes all even.

Hitting first to the 37th green, all seemed lost for Hilton, as his approach headed for a mound at the right of the green that was dotted with rocks. The ball had a mind of its own, as it missed all of the rocks, bounced, and trickled down the hill and onto the putting surface. Obviously shaken, Herreshoff flubbed his shot, and Hilton became the first to win both the British and U.S. amateur titles in the same year.

*T*he first left-hander to win a major professional championship was Bob Charles of New Zealand, who captured the 1963 Open Championship at Royal Lytham, England. He was also the first left-hander to win a PGA Tour event, the 1963 Houston Classic, and the first golfer from New Zealand to win on the PGA Tour and to capture a major title.

The next left-hander to win a major was Mike Weir, taking the 2003 Masters Tournament. He also became the first Canadian to win a major. When the Sarnia, Ontario, native was 13 years old, he wrote to Jack Nicklaus, seeking advice on whether he should continue to play golf left-handed or switch and become a right-hander. Nicklaus wrote that Mike should continue as a southpaw, encouraging him to use his natural swing. The rest is history.

*T*he first left-handed winner on the Ladies Professional Golf Association (LPGA) Tour was Bonnie Bryant. She won the 1974 Bill Branch Classic in Fort Myers, Florida. It was her lone victory, and Bonnie is still the only left-handed winner in LPGA history.

*W*hen Phil Mickelson qualified for the U.S. Ryder Cup team, in 1995, it was thought that he was the first left-hander to play in that event. He was only the first American left-hander. The honor of being the *first* left-hander on the Ryder Cup team goes to Peter Dawson who represented Great Britain and Ireland in 1977.

*M*ickelson wasn't the first left-hander to win a championship sponsored by the USGA either, although he did capture the 1990 U.S. Amateur. The distinction belongs to Ralph Howe III, winner of the 1988 U.S. Public Links.

With Mickelson's victory in the 2004 Masters, he set a record of sorts. It marked the first time that left-handers won the same major two consecutive years, as he followed Weir's win the previous year. Holing an 18-foot putt on the final green for a birdie, Phil edged Ernie Els by one stroke.

His triumph also set a new record, one that dates from 1860 and the inaugural Open at Prestwick. It was the first time that a first-timer won in six consecutive majors. The streak began in the 2002 PGA Championship, claimed by Rich Beem. In 2003, Weir won the Masters, Jim Furyk the U.S. Open, Ben Curtis the Open, and Shaun Micheel the PGA Championship. Phil took the total to a half-dozen.

*I*n 2002, Katherine Hull became the first woman to attempt to qualify for the U.S. Amateur Public Links Championship.

IN OVER HER HEAD

*P*erhaps the first woman golfer was Mary, Queen of Scots. At least she was the first mentioned in print. When her husband was murdered, she was observed playing golf in the fields beside Seton a few days after his death. That fact was brought out at her trial, and she was later beheaded. She really lost her head over the game.

*T*hat year also marked the first time a Russian native tried to qualify for the U.S. Women's Open Championship. Although Svetlana Goundina failed in her attempt, it was an indication of how popular the sport had become in all parts of the globe.

*T*he name Lian-Wei Zhang is not well known to most golf fans. But the native of Shenzen, China, turned professional in 1995, and in 2003, he became the first Chinese golfer to win on the European Tour with a birdie on the final hole to take the Caltex Masters. He was rewarded with an invitation to play in the 2004 Masters, another first, and shot 77-72. While he missed the cut by a single stroke, he collected a pair of crystal goblets for making an eagle on the 13th hole.

*F*or a great many years, golfers used only six or seven clubs. Caddies would carry them under an arm so that they could quickly hand the proper implement to the golfer. The exact date is not recorded, but it is believed that the first golf bag, known as Dr. Trails Canvas Container, was introduced to the Old Course at St. Andrews in 1890. It came about because golfers began to use more and more clubs instead of the traditional six or seven.

Some of the experienced caddies were reluctant to use them and referred to those who did carry the bags in a derogatory manner as "bag toters."

Golf is an honorable game, or it's supposed to be. Unlike other sports, seldom do fans hoot and boo, although there are some incidents that have marred the good behavior of most galleries. For example, the galleries of some Ryder Cup matches in recent years have seen behavior similar to that seen among spectators at football games. One early example of poor sportsmanship occurred in Hot Springs, Virginia, during the 1967 U.S. Women's Open. Catherine Lacoste, an outstanding amateur from France, was leading the championship, but partisan American fans didn't want to see her win. It didn't make much difference to them who won, as long as it wasn't a foreigner.

Catherine continued to play well in spite of a couple of poor shots that were loudly cheered by the partisan gallery. She held on, however, finishing two strokes better than Beth Stone and Susie Maxwell to become the first non-American and only amateur to ever win the championship.

The first British Amateur Championship was actually an informal tournament instituted by the Royal Liverpool Golf Club in 1885. It proved to be quite successful, so the club suggested that the Royal and Ancient Golf Club sponsor an amateur championship, which they did the following year. A. F. MacFie was the first winner, having defeated Horace Hutchinson, but he was not recognized as the first champion until 1922, when the Royal and Ancient decided to include his name in the official records.

With 24 entrants, setting up the matches proved to be a bit of a challenge for the club. Instead of arranging for some early-round byes, they occurred later in the tournament. For example, three golfers made it to the semifinal, with MacFie given the bye. Hutchinson had to play John Ball in the morning and then face the eventual winner in the afternoon. There was even a one-day delay before the semifinal and final were contested. The club had already scheduled another event the day before the championship was to be decided, and it took precedence. Ball, Hutchinson, and MacFie all participated in the annual club event. Thus, they played in two tournaments in the same week.

*D*uring that first British Amateur competition, matches that were tied were replayed rather than decided in a play-off. Allan MacFie played the same opponent, Walter de Zoete, three times in succession before emerging with a victory.

*O*nly once has the U.S. Women's Amateur Championship been contested at stroke play. It happened at the inaugural event in 1895, which was played at Meadowbrook in New York.

The winner was Mrs. Charles Brown, who shot 132 for 18 holes, nine holes in the morning followed by the second nine in the afternoon. Beginning the next year, the championship was conducted at match play with Beatrice Hoyt the victor at the Morris Country Club, a club founded by women in New Jersey in 1893.

*T*he Shinnecock Hills clubhouse in Southampton, New York, was designed by Stanford White and built for $6,550 in 1892. It was the first American golf club to have a clubhouse. White is best remembered for designing the original Madison Square Garden in New York City, site of numerous sporting events.

*H*aving a clubhouse was not always considered a necessity. The R&A opened its clubhouse, overlooking the first tee of the Old Course, in 1854. The building was much smaller than the one used today and still exists within the walls of the current structure. Prior to that time, the R&A members would meet in the back rooms of the city's taverns, the most popular being the Black Bull Tavern.

WAR GRINDS TO HALT . . . FOR GOLF

*J*oe Kirkwood and Walter Hagen put on a great many exhibitions during the 1930s, including an around-the-world tour. Not all of the tour was spent golfing, as the two thoroughly enjoyed taking in the wonders of the world. Many times they would linger in a city after their scheduled match and the inevitable trick-shot clinic conducted by Kirkwood. They felt the money they earned was meant to be spent, and they, especially Hagen, were champions at that as well.

After a swing from Australia to Singapore and Manila in 1938, they received an invitation to put on their exhibition in Shanghai, China, at the Hung Jao course. Being a bit short of currency, they agreed to make the trip but were wondering how it would be accomplished, since the Sino-Japanese War was being fought and Shanghai was right in the middle of the fighting. Still, it seemed as if it would be a unique experience, so they made the travel plans.

Arriving at the city, they were put up at the Cathay Hotel, one of the only hotels not damaged in the fighting. Most of the city was in shambles, although they discovered that the local golf association was still in existence. However, the Japanese had taken over the club as a command post. The professionals saw an announcement calling for the "Golfers of Shanghai to gather at the Club" and asking the authorities to clear the dead bodies from the course. The war was actually stopped for a day in honor of the exhibition, and while a formal truce had not been signed, there were no hostilities that day.

A bomb had destroyed the 18th green the day before, and it was quickly replaced with a temporary sand green so the match could be completed. As Kirkwood and Hagen played the round, the Chinese and Japanese stood side by side, being more cordial to each other than anyone might expect. Following the match, refreshments were served, at which time the ladies arrived: the Japanese in lovely kimonos, the Chinese in beautiful silk gowns, and the Westerners dressed to the nines. Once the refreshments had been served, it was time for Kirkwood to give his performance.

When he finished, the senior Japanese officer asked if he would repeat the last part of the exhibition where he had hit golf balls at a caddie who was downrange and had to duck and scatter as Joe hit a number of low-trajectory shots. Kirkwood agreed, and the officers gave a number of commands. What the Japanese did was to dress some enlisted men in Chinese uniforms and sent them down the fairway to await the shots. They had their rifles at port arms, with fixed bayonets, and they were ordered to charge toward Kirkwood. The shots came close, and the soldiers dodged and fell to the ground before eventually turning tail and running. Later, Joe and Walter discovered that the officers had made a movie of the soldiers that was used as propaganda in Japan to show the cowardice of the Chinese— that they would even run from golf balls. Of course, the golfers were unaware of the part they were asked to play in the film.

It was, perhaps, the only and certainly the first time in history that a war was halted for a round of golf.

*T*he oldest golf club outside the British Isles is Royal Calcutta, established in 1829, in India.

*I*n July 1895, the Van Cortland Golf Course opened in Bronx, New York, as the first public course built in the United States. It was originally a nine-hole layout named The Meadows; but in 1899, the original course was replaced with an 18-hole layout on land adjacent to the first course.

From 1895 through 2001, the U.S. Open was never played on a true public golf course. The first public course to host the championship was the Black Course at Bethpage State Park in Farmingdale, New York, on Long Island, in 2002.

Another first was established in the 2002 U.S. Open. In previous championships, all golfers began the round on the first tee. This marked the beginning of starting times on both the first and tenth tees. Dudley Hart became the first golfer to start on the 10th hole in a U.S. Open, and he recorded a bogey.

When Pebble Beach Golf Links was built in 1916, an underground irrigation system was installed. It became the first golf course in the country to be built with underground irrigation from tee to green.

Founded in 1873, Royal Montreal, Quebec, is the oldest golf club in North America. Not only is it the oldest, but it also had the first golf professional on the continent, an Englishman by the name of Willie Davis, and it also became the first club to admit women members (in 1891).

Laying claim to being the first golf club in the Western Hemisphere is the San Martin y Flores Golf Club, established in 1871, in Argentina. It was later named the Buenos Aires Golf Club and then the San Andrés Golf Club.

Proud of its many fine golf courses, Japan didn't have a layout until 1903, when Arthur Groom, a merchant from England, designed the Kobe Golf Club, which consisted of nine holes on the slopes of Mount Rokko.

On the European continent, the oldest club is Pau, in the French Pyrenees. It was organized in 1856, although some Scottish officers played there three years earlier on a makeshift course.

Arguments abound, but staking claim as the oldest golf club in Australia is Royal Adelaide. It was founded in 1871.

Following a trip to Alaska in 1923, President Warren Harding became ill and died of a cerebral hemorrhage after returning to San Francisco. The city honored the memory of one of the most enthusiastic of presidential golfers by naming a public golf course, Harding Park, after him. It was the first golf course to be named for a president.

Home of three U.S. Open championships, the Walker Cup, and the Ryder Cup, The Country Club in Brookline, Massachusetts, did not have a golf course until 1892. The interests of the original 404 members centered around horses, with such pastimes as racing, fox hunting, and polo.

One of the members, Arthur Hunnewell, was introduced to golf by his niece, Florence Boit. Miss Boit, who lived in France, persuaded Hunnewell to lay out a small course on his own property. While he only had one club, a mashie presented to him by Miss Boit, Hunnewell enjoyed his attempts to hit the ball. Eventually he talked the board of directors into adding a golf course to the club's other facilities, and in April 1892, the six holes were ready.

An exhibition was held to introduce the members to the game, and hitting the first ball to the 90-yard par-3 hole was Hunnewell with his mashie. It turned out to be the shot of his life, as the ball found the cup for a hole-in-one. Those watching were not golfers. Since it had been explained to them that the object of the game was to hole the ball in the least number of strokes, there wasn't a murmur from the onlookers after the historic shot. In fact, they were quite disappointed that the feat was not duplicated on the remaining holes. Never again was Hunnewell able to make a hole-in-one, but he will forever be remembered for making one on the first shot ever hit at The Country Club.

Only once has the British Open been held outside Great Britain, and that was in 1951 at Royal Portrush Golf Club in Ireland. The winner was Max Faulkner. The same course was also the first venue outside Great Britain for the Ladies' Championship, which took place in 1898.

Called the toughest test in professional golf, the PGA Tour Qualifying School now consists of 108 holes for those wishing to make it to the PGA Tour. There are seldom as many places available for tour aspirants as contestants would like. One bad round can mean the "minor leagues" or even the dreaded minitours.

When it was originally played, most of the entrants were young players hoping to get their card. Over the years, however, it had come to include not only those who had never played professionally but, even more, those who had lost their cards by not finishing high enough on the money list the previous year. Competition has always been fierce, but qualifying became more difficult as the years went by.

In 2002, one of the competitors in the Q School was Scott Simpson, the winner of the 1987 U.S. Open Championship, who ended the year 195th on the money list, even though he had played in 25 events. He is believed to be the first player to have entered the PGA Tour Qualifying School after having won a major title.

Professionalism leaped into the Olympic Games in 1992, when participation in the basketball competition was opened to players from the National Basketball Association. Prior to that time, all events were supposed to be limited to amateur athletes. Still, it was a charade, as the track stars received appearance money to appear in various meets, and the athletes from the Soviet Union and other satellite nations were paid by the government to compete, whether in hockey or gymnastics.

If there was ever one sport where the line drawn between amateur and professional was truly defined, it was golf. But the sport has rarely been a part of the Olympics. That was not always the case. It was an official event in 1900 and 1904, the first in Paris and the last in St. Louis, Missouri. The winner of the gold medal in the ladies competition was Margaret Abbott, who completed nine holes with a 47 and who became the first American to ever win an Olympic medal for the United States. It didn't stop there. Charles E. Sands recorded rounds of 82 and 85 to capture the gold medal among the men.

Miss Abbott not only became the first, but she was the only gold medal winner in women's golf, as there was no competition for the ladies in 1904. Actually, golf played an important part in the Paris Olympics. In addition to the regular competition, the Olympic Committee decided to hold a handicap event as well. The winner was Albert Bond Lambert, putting his 10 handicap to good use. After finishing eighth in the regular competition, he competed in the handicap division. If the name sounds familiar, it is because his father was the founder of the company that made Listerine, Lambert Pharmaceutical, which later became Warner-Lambert. He was a flying enthusiast and the benefactor of Charles Lindbergh's transatlantic flight. He also built the airport in St. Louis, known as Lambert International Field.

Because of Lambert's enthusiasm for the Olympic golf event in Paris, he made plans for golf to be included in the 1904 games. The main competition was the match-play event won by Canadian George Lyon, who defeated H. Chandler Egan, the United States Amateur champion, in the final by a 3 and 2 margin over 36 holes. Lyon should not have been considered a surprise winner. His career included eight Canadian Amateur titles, as well as runner-up finishes in both the U.S. Open and Amateur championships. He was not the favorite, however, primarily because Lyon was 46 years old, while his opponent was just 21.

Another wrinkle was added to the Olympics golf roster—team competition. There were supposed to be six 10-man teams, but only two showed up in St. Louis. One represented the Western Golf Association (WGA) and another the Trans-Mississippi Golf Association. A third team was quickly put together from other golfers present and loosely represented the United States Golf Association. The WGA team won the competition.

That marked the end of golf in the Olympic Games. Competition had been scheduled in 1908 when the games went to England, but the Royal and Ancient got into a hassle about eligibility with the Olympic Organizing Committee and all of the British withdrew. Canadian George Lyon was the only entrant, and the committee offered to give him the gold medal, but he refused. Golf was canceled, never to make a return to the Olympic Games.

In 1979, Ryder Cup eligibility was changed to allow golfers from the European continent to participate on what had been the British team or, more accurately, the team representing Great Britain and Ireland, that combination having been in existence since 1973. The change to a team representing Europe actually was initiated by Jack Nicklaus in a letter to Lord Derby, the president of the British PGA. Jack felt it would make the matches more competitive rather than the fairly one-sided matches of previous years. At the 1977 matches, Don Padgett, president of the PGA of America, and Henry Poe, a former president of the same organization, sought out Lord Derby to also make the proposal. The change was approved by the British PGA, the PGA European Tour, and finally Mrs. Joan Scarfe, who was Samuel Ryder's daughter.

The first Spaniards to participate on a Ryder Cup team were Severiano "Seve" Ballesteros and Antonio Garrido, playing in 1979. The first German was Bernhard Langer, who made the team in 1981. Costantino Rocca became the first Italian when he qualified in 1993, as did Per-Ulrik Johansson, who was the first Swede. Denmark was represented for the first time in 1997 with the addition of Thomas Bjorn, and the first Frenchman was Jean Van de Velde, who played on the 1999 team.

*F*rom 1927 until 1995, every Ryder Cup match was conducted on a course located in Great Britain or the United States. The first to be contested on a layout outside those countries was in 1997, when Valderrama staged the event at Sotogrande, Spain, with Seve Ballesteros serving as captain of the victorious European team.

*I*t is no longer unusual for a golfer to have played on both the Walker Cup and Ryder Cup teams during his career. The first to gain that distinction, however, was Freddie Haas.

*F*reddie has another first. He is remembered for his victory in the 1945 Memphis Open as an amateur, and it brought an end to the longest winning streak in PGA history, the 11 straight by Byron Nelson.

Probably because he was an amateur, few people paid attention to the fact that he wore shorts during the tournament. It remains the only PGA Tour event on record that was won by a golfer wearing shorts.

*W*hile there had been a "Second Tour" in prior years, the beginning of what we now know as the Nationwide Tour began in 1990 as the Ben Hogan Tour, holding its first tournament in Bakersfield, California. The brainchild of Deane Beman, it was originally thought of as a tour for young professionals who wanted experience that might help them gain a spot on the PGA Tour, in addition to those who lost their card, who hoped to get back into the big time. It also turned out that some golfers waiting to play on the Champions Tour (originally named the PGA Senior Tour) decided it would be a good place to hone their game.

Winning the Ben Hogan Bakersfield Open to become the first champion on that circuit was Mike Springer. That experience served as a springboard for Mike. He was later able to win two PGA Tour events as well.

In 1934, the PGA began to keep track of official money won on the tour, and the first to capture the crown was Paul Runyan, who made $6,767 in official money during the year.

The first golfer to win $1 million in official prize money on the PGA Tour during his career was Arnold Palmer, passing the mark in 1968.

Twenty years later, Curtis Strange became the first to win $1 million in a single year on the PGA Tour.

Karrie Webb became the first golfer to pass the million-dollar mark on the LPGA Tour in a single season, in 1996. It also marked the first time the feat was accomplished by a rookie, either man or woman.

It took another five years before a woman earned more than $2 million on the LPGA Tour. Annika Sorenstam made $2,105,868 in 2001, with eight victories and a host of top-ten finishes.

Lee Trevino was the first to win more than $1 million on the Champions Tour in 1992, with $1,027,022 in official money. Hale Irwin raised the bar, earning $2 million in 1997 and then the first $3 million in one season, during 2002.

It is now a common occurrence to see several golfers win that much in a season, but the first time the total prize money on the PGA Tour exceeded $1 million for a year was in 1958.

*I*n 1994, Fuzzy Zoeller won $1,016,804 on the PGA Tour. It marked the first time that a player won more than $1 million without a victory. With purses increasing, it was only a matter of time for the same thing to occur on the Champions Tour, and that happened in 1997. John Bland, the South African who had captured five senior titles in the previous two years, couldn't win in his 35 starts that year, but he was able to pocket $1,169,707. The figure broke the record previously held by J. C. Snead of slightly more than $700,000 in winnings without a victory. With increased purses, it took only five years before the figure earned by Zoeller was surpassed. In 1999, Davis Love III earned $2,475,328 without a single title.

*W*hat a year 1997 was for Hale Irwin. The previous year Hale had seven runner-up finishes on the Champions Tour and was a bit tired of being a bridesmaid. The season began with a win in the Master-Card Championship and ended with a total of nine victories. It tied the record for wins in a single season, which had been previously set by Peter Thomson in 1985. Irwin became the first to win more than $2 million in one season on any U.S. professional tour, with a total of $2,343,364; he had entered 23 events, for an average earnings of more than $100,000 for every week he played.

*W*ith the beginning of the Ryder Cup matches in 1927, there were no set rules as to possession of the cup itself. Naturally, it would go to the winning team, but nothing beyond that had been specified. The United States won, and the team members held a meeting to decide what should be done with the cup.

It was agreed upon that each member would keep it for a period of time with a drawing held to determine the order, which turned out to be Leo Diegel, Joe Turnesa, Johnny Golden, Gene Sarazen, Al Watrous, Al Espinosa, Walter Hagen, Johnny Farrell, and Bill Mehlhorn. After future matches were held, the trophy was kept in the possession of the PGA of the winning team.

*P*art of the tradition of international cup competition is that the matches must be won from the defender for the country to gain possession of the trophy. That is true in the Ryder, Walker, and Curtis cups. Thus when the matches end in a tie, the team who last won keeps the trophy for another two years.

Originally no provision was written in the rules of competition to take care of a tie. The precedent was established in 1936, the first tie in international cup competition, when Doris Chambers, captain of the British Curtis Cup team, declined sharing the trophy following a tie at Gleneagles, Scotland, with the American team. She said her team had not won any claim to it.

*W*hen the Presidents Cup was established in 1994, the same format for a tie was adopted. The Presidents Cup pits golfers from the United States against a team of international players. International was interpreted to mean those golfers not from Europe, so they could have an opportunity to play for a cup in team competition similar to the Ryder Cup.

A decision to have a play-off in the 2003 matches was made, and the procedure was a bit unusual. Each captain would place the name of one member in a sealed envelope. The captains, Jack Nicklaus and Gary Player, actually didn't keep the names secret. Practically everyone knew it would be Tiger Woods and Ernie Els.

The matches did end up in a tie, so the two golfers went to the 18th hole to begin the sudden-death play-off. The hole was tied, as were the next two holes. Both players made pressure putts to keep the match alive. After playing the third play-off hole, the two captains huddled and determined that it was getting too dark to continue. Both Nicklaus and Player agreed that the match should be called a tie.

When it became known that the cup would remain in the Americans' possession, since they had won the previous meeting, Gary Player balked. He met with his team, and they expressed the view that the play-off should continue the next morning. In the meantime, Nicklaus opined that there might be too much pressure on any one golfer and should they continue the following day, perhaps all players should be involved.

When Jack met with the American team, they were of the opinion that the cup should be shared rather than remain in the possession of the United States. That information was relayed to Gary, who then received approval from his team to call the matches a tie. Thus, it was the first time in international cup competition that both teams shared the trophy.

The Curtis family, which gave birth to the Curtis Cup, had a first in major competition for women. In 1907, Harriot and Margaret reached the final of the U.S. Women's Amateur, with Margaret emerging as the winner by a 7 and 6 margin. To this day, it is the only time that sisters met in a final of this prestigious event.

It is still rare to have a golfer on the cover of *Time* magazine. For example, it took three major victories in a single year to gain the honor for Tiger Woods in 2000. However, the first golfer to be pictured on the cover of that magazine was a woman, Edith Cummings, the 1923 U.S. Amateur champion. The Chicago socialite appeared on the *Time* cover in August 1924.

The first victory by a U.S. Ryder Cup team on foreign soil happened in 1937. The European team wasn't able to win in the United States until 1987, when they defeated the Americans at Muirfield Village in Dublin, Ohio.

Upon accepting the trophy, Walter Hagen told the assembled crowd that it was nice to be able to win the cup at home. A patron called out that he was not in the United States but in England; Hagen responded that they were so nice to him there that he thought it was home. That brought a huge round of applause.

O nly one golfer in history has won the money title on two tours in the same year. Annika Sorenstam of Sweden split her time between the LPGA Tour and the WPG (Women Professional Golfers) European Tour in 1995, capturing money honors in both.

W ith the success of the Swedes in women's golf, it's a bit of a surprise that the first male from Sweden didn't win on the American tour until 1997, when Gabriel Hjertstedt took the B.C. Open in Endicott, New York. His final round 70 gave him a one-stroke victory.

M ickey Wright was the first to successfully defend her U.S. Women's Open title, winning in 1958 and again the following year. She was also the first to capture both the U.S. Women's Open and LPGA Championship in the same year—1958.

T he only time a reigning monarch played in a national golf championship occurred in 1939 at Le Zoute Golf Club in the Belgian Amateur, with King Leopold as the competitor. Later, in exile, he reached the quarterfinal of the 1949 French Amateur.

H ollis Stacy became the first golfer to win three consecutive USGA Junior titles when she captured the championships in 1969 through 1971. The only boy to have accomplished it was Tiger Woods in 1991–93.

*N*o one had ever had to go through qualifying rounds for the U.S. Women's Open and then won that championship until 2003. Playing at Pumpkin Ridge, North Plains, Oregon, Hilary Lunke found herself in a play-off with Kelly Robbins and Angela Stanford after regulation play. Hilary, who had played collegiate golf at Stanford University and was once a member of the U.S. Curtis Cup team, was a short hitter. She carried woods 6, 7, 9, and 11 in her bag and made use of all of them.

When she posted a 1-under 70 in the play-off, Lunke made history as the first qualifier to win the most prestigious of all women's golf titles.

*S*am Snead holds many golf records, but possibly one of his finest accomplishments was to become the first golfer to ever score better than his age in a PGA Tour event. Sam, at the age of 67, scored a 66 in the 1979 Quad Cities Open. He also had a 67 in the same tournament. With the advent of the PGA Champions Tour for golfers over 50, some felt that record might never again be duplicated, but leave it to "the King." In the fourth round of the 2001 Bob Hope Chrysler Classic, Arnold Palmer shot 71 to equal his age, becoming the oldest to shoot his age on the PGA Tour.

*T*iming is everything. The first Intercollegiate Golf Association champion was Louis P. Bayard Jr., who played for Princeton University. He toured Ardsley Casino in 91 strokes back in 1897, slightly higher than Jack Nicklaus, Ben Crenshaw, and Tom Kite scored in later years when they won the collegiate individual title.

Now, the winner of the National Collegiate Athletic Association (NCAA), in most cases, becomes a professional in search of the large amount of money available on the various tours. Somehow we forget that university golf was played long before it became popular in the United States. The first match involving two universities was held in 1878—March 6, to be exact—and it was between Oxford and Cambridge.

The victors, led by Horace Hutchinson, won in convincing style by 24 to 0. When taken into consideration that the first Amateur Championship wasn't held until 1885, it means that the Varsity Match is the oldest amateur event in golf history.

*T*he first golfer to win both the NCAA and U.S. Amateur in the same year was Jack Nicklaus. Only Phil Mickelson and Tiger Woods have been able to accomplish that double since Jack's initial success.

*W*inning the 1974 Tucson Open added some icing to the cake for Johnny Miller. His victory enabled him to become the first and only golfer to win the first three events of the year on the PGA Tour. Johnny began 1974 with wins in the Bing Crosby National Pro-Am in Monterey, California, and the Phoenix Open before moving south to the Tucson Open.

*W*hen Denny Shute won the 1936 PGA Championship, he became the first son of a golf professional to win that title. Since then Jack Burke Jr. (1956), Dave Marr (1965), Davis Love III (1997), and Rich Beem (2002) joined Burke, since their fathers were also golf professionals.

WHIFFS IN SPACE

*O*n no particular golf course, history was made on February 6, 1971, by a golfer from Houston, although the shot wasn't made there. It wasn't even made in the United States or anyplace on the planet. There were several million people, certainly the largest gallery assembled at that time, watching Captain Alan B. Shepard Jr. on television.

He said, "Houston, you might recognize what I have in my hand as the handle for the contingency return sample. It just so happens to have a genuine 6-iron head on the bottom of it. In my left hand I have a little white pellet that's familiar to millions of Americans. I'll drop it down. Unfortunately, the suit is so stiff I can't do this with two hands, but I'm going to try a little sand trap shot here."

With that, he dropped the ball, took a swing, and missed. With him on the mission was Commander Edgar D. Mitchell. He observed, "You got more dirt than ball that time."

Shepard dropped another ball and made contact on his next swing. Thus, golf became the first game played on the moon.

The Royal and Ancient immediately sent a telegram reminding the commander of Apollo 14 that "before leaving a bunker a player should carefully fill up and smooth over all holes and footprints made by him."

Spalding jumped at the opportunity of issuing a commemorative "moon ball" with a picture of an astronaut hitting a shot on it. While Shepard didn't divulge the make of the ball he used, word leaked that Jack Harden, the professional at River Oaks Country Club where Alan played, had supplied the balls. It turned out that they were his Spalding range balls, which could be used on the moon's surface and withstand the extreme temperature changes.

*H*istory was also made in 1995 during the Bob Hope Chrysler Classic. It marked the first time that three presidents of the United States played golf together. Bill Clinton was joined by Gerald Ford and George H. W. Bush in a round that took almost six hours to complete. In addition to the "First Golfers," Bob Hope teed it up, along with golf professional Scott Hoch. It also marked the first time that a serving president played in a PGA-sponsored event. Just having the Secret Service walking along guaranteed a large gallery.

Scott was able to shoot a 70, which was pretty remarkable with all of the distractions. The presidents were given "newspaper scores" that listed Mr. Clinton with a 95, Mr. Bush with 93, and Mr. Ford shooting 103.

Spectators at professional golf tournaments can't help but notice caps, shirts, and golf bags with advertising on them. There is little question that endorsements are important sources of income for touring professionals, in most cases far exceeding money won in tournaments.

The first golfer to endorse products was Harry Vardon. After winning the Open in 1899 in Sandwich, England, for the third time, Vardon was approached by various companies. He agreed to endorse only the products that he actually would consider using, such as tobacco for his ever-present pipe. Ads appeared showing him using "Player's Navy Cut" and wearing a golfing jacket he liked.

Then, A. G. Spalding asked if he would be interested in promoting a golf ball to be named the Vardon Flyer, and he accepted the offer. Vardon shrewdly asked for a lump-sum payment rather than royalties on each ball sold. It proved to be a wise decision since the Vardon Flyer was made of gutta-percha and the introduction of the wound golf ball was just around the corner. It was a huge contract, considering the times and the cost of living. He signed the agreement in 1899, and the amount he received would be the equivalent of $1 million today.

Possibly the first golfer to have a racehorse named after him was Gene Sarazen. Mrs. William K. Vanderbilt owned the horse, which, like its namesake, was a champion.

The Champions Tour has been called the "Greatest Mulligan in Golf" for former PGA Tour players. Winners of the various tournaments have generally been those who were also winners when they were younger. The first winner, for example, was Don January, a past PGA champion who captured the 1980 Atlantic City Senior International. It was one of only four senior events held that year now recognized by the PGA as official events. Other winners in 1980 were Roberto De Vicenzo, Charlie Sifford, and Arnold Palmer.

That changed in later years with club professionals rising to the top to challenge the former PGA Tour players. First to win a Champions Tour event without having won on the regular tour was Walt Zembriski, when he took the title in the 1988 Newport Cup Tournament in Newport, Rhode Island.

With the Champions Tour becoming more and more popular, it was finally decided to open the door to weekly qualifying for some of the contestants wanting to make it into the tournament proper. It wasn't easy to gain one of the few spots available, and to follow up the qualifying with a victory was even more difficult.

The first qualifier to win a tournament was Larry Mowry in the 1987 Crestar Classic.

Recording a double eagle in the 1982 Peter Jackson Championship, Al Balding became the first to accomplish that rarest of feats on the Champions Tour.

Winning the 1991 Syracuse Senior Classic broke a streak of 611 professional tournaments without a victory for Rocky Thompson. At least that's the figure quoted by Rocky. Guess what happened after he recorded his first win? The next year the tournament was canceled. When he found out about the cancellation, the always-optimistic Thompson said, "At least now, I'll be the defending champ every year."

*T*he first U.S. Senior Open was held at Winged Foot in Mamaroneck, New York, in 1980 with Roberto De Vicenzo gaining a four-stroke victory over amateur Bill Campbell for the title. In that championship, participants had to be at least 55 years old. The USGA lowered eligibility to 50 the next year, and there was talk that it was done to assure participation by some of the better-known golfers. The other senior events already had a 50-year-old threshold. It worked, as two legends—Arnold Palmer and Billy Casper—were in the field.

Contested on the South Course at Oakland Hills in Birmingham, Michigan, the two didn't disappoint their golf fans when they finished regulation play at 289, along with Bob Stone. Palmer won the 18-hole play-off by four strokes and became the first golfer to win the U.S. Amateur, U.S. Open, and U.S. Senior Open in his career. Ten years later Jack Nicklaus duplicated the feat, and his senior title also came at Oakland Hills following a play-off.

*N*icklaus also went on to win The Tradition, the PGA Seniors' Championship, and the Senior Tournament Players Championship on the Champions Tour, becoming the first to win all four designated major titles for seniors.

*A*bsent from the list of designated major events for seniors was the Senior British Open. Actually, it didn't become an official event for the Champions Tour until 2003, and that year it was also declared a major. In its history, which began in 1987, there have been three golfers who have won both the British Open and the Senior British Open—Gary Player, Bob Charles, and Tom Watson. The first to accomplish it was Player, when he won the 1988 senior title at Turnberry in Scotland. Unfortunately, the winners from 1987 through 2002 can't claim they won a senior major title; as far as the PGA of America is concerned, they didn't even win an official event. That may change, however. It took the

PGA more than 150 years to acknowledge that the British Open was an official tournament on its tour.

*T*he longest streak of not winning a professional tournament before the first victory belongs to Bobby Wadkins. Lanny Wadkin's younger brother participated in 712 PGA Tour events and 65 on the second tour for a total of 777 professional events without once collecting the top prize. It should be pointed out, however, that Wadkins was able to win some international events during his career but nothing on U.S. soil. Bobby finally broke through in the 2001 Long Island Classic, the first senior PGA tournament he entered.

The last time a player had debuted successfully on the Champions Tour was in 2000 at the ACE Group Classic, and it was brother Lanny. It turned out to be Lanny's only victory on the senior circuit.

*A*fter struggling on the minitours for six years, Tom Lehman had a most successful season in 1991. He was able to win the money title on the Nike Tour that year, gaining playing privileges on the PGA Tour for 1992. Having previously played on the regular tour with little to show for it, he made the most of his return to the big leagues. He became the first to win money titles both on the Hogan/Nike Tour and on the PGA Tour when he collected more than $1.7 million in 1996.

*W*ith 73 official PGA Tour victories, Jack Nicklaus trails only Sam Snead in that category. Jack's first start as a professional was in the 1962 Los Angeles Open and came on a sponsor's exemption. His check totaled $33.33.

*I*n 1977, the Boy Scouts of America offered a merit badge in golf for the first time. The pamphlet explaining the qualification standards and the game was produced by Charles C. Hillyer of Jacksonville,

Florida, and consisted of 74 pages. Golf became the 19th sports-oriented merit badge for the organization.

Oscar Cella was given a five-year suspension by the Argentine Golf Association, after being accused of "errors" on the green. He took the case to court and had it overturned. Cella then entered the 1965 Argentina Amateur Championship. The other 31 competitors walked off the course, refusing to play if Cella was allowed in the tournament, and he was declared the winner without hitting a single shot. It marked the first time that a champion was named even though no tournament was held.

Three-putting the second play-off hole in the 1993 PGA Championship cost Greg Norman the title, adding to his reputation of being snakebitten in the majors. He actually was the second golfer to lose all four professional majors in play-offs.

First, Fuzzy Zoeller bested Norman in the 1984 U.S. Open at Winged Foot. Then it was Larry Mize's great chip that did him in at the Masters Tournament in 1987. The other play-off loss was at the hands of Mark Calcavecchia in the 1989 British Open at Royal Troon.

As difficult as it has been for Greg, the first person to hold the record for futility in major championships belongs to Craig Wood. In the 1933 British Open at St. Andrews, Wood and Denny Shute tied after regulation play, with Shute winning the play-off scheduled over 36 holes. The following year, he made it to the final of the PGA Championship, which was then conducted as match play. At the end of the regulation 36 holes in the final, Craig was tied with Paul Runyan, who emerged as the victor on the 38th hole.

Wood's third play-off loss came in 1935 at the Masters. Following the historic double eagle by Gene Sarazen, which enabled the Squire to catch Wood, they covered another 36 holes the following day, with Sarazen winning by five strokes. Gene, of course, became the first golfer to win all four professional majors in a career. The 1939 U.S. Open was the last of Wood's play-off losses. This one was only scheduled over 18 holes. Shute shot 76 to be eliminated, while Craig and Byron Nelson each shot 68. So it was back for another 18, and this time Nelson prevailed with a 70 to Wood's 73.

In 1941, Craig finally got to the winner's circle in a major with victories in the Masters Tournament and the U.S. Open. He won both without a play-off and became the first golfer to win the Masters and U.S. Open in the same year.

The first and only play-off to never happen in a major occurred at the 1876 British Open. David Strath made a double bogey at the final hole, leaving him in a tie with Robert Martin. Some of Martin's backers entered a protest, stating that Strath should have been penalized for having hit into the players in front of him at the 17th hole. It was reported that the ball had struck someone.

Apparently Strath's shot was a good one, and he still needed two putts to hole out. But the committee was asked to make a ruling. They met but came to no conclusion, adjourning the meeting until the next day, when the play-off was to be held. They did make a preliminary ruling that the play-off should proceed "under protest" on Monday afternoon. Strath refused to play unless a ruling was made prior to the beginning of play. Martin was declared the winner when Strath did not appear. The penalty of disqualification apparently was never made since Strath was awarded second-place money in that championship.

There was more to the story, however. It was perhaps the most bizarre Open ever played. Today, we would never dream of holding a championship of such importance and allowing other golfers to interfere with play, but that's what happened in 1876.

The courses at St. Andrews belong to the people. At that time, only the Old Course existed. The R&A was only one club that used the course, and that year they forgot to reserve it for the British Open. The confusion was probably due to the fact that the same day Prince Leopold was to drive himself in as Captain. There was great excitement, since the prince was actually going to be at the course to complete the ceremony at eight in the morning.

Following the ceremony, members of the R&A, along with the townspeople, expected to play golf, and nothing was going to stop them, including the British Open. The solution was to alternate groups, regular golfers along with those participating in the championship. It was also necessary for the Open participants to play two rounds in one day to determine the winner. Professionals had to wait unusually long periods of time between shots, and when the championship ended, it was almost dark.

The first play-off that actually took place in British Open history occurred in 1883 at Musselburgh, Scotland. Willie Fernie was victorious over Bob Ferguson by one stroke in the 36-hole play-off. Had Ferguson prevailed, it would have been his fourth consecutive Open championship, tying the all-time record set by Tom Morris Jr.

Strath's action was more of a protest, but there was a time when the U.S. Open was threatened with a strike. It happened because of two golfers who were entered in the field of 35. John Shippen was a black man and Oscar Bunn a Native American. Both lived at the nearby Shinnecock Reservation (in New York) and were caddies at Shinnecock Hills Golf Club. The other professionals did not want them in the field and said they would withdraw unless something was done. It was a bit ironical, as golf professionals at the time were looked down upon as second-class citizens themselves, and it would seem they could understand prejudice.

The president of the USGA at that time was Theodore Havemeyer, a member of the Newport Golf Club in Rhode Island. The statement attributed to him when confronted by the professionals' demands was, "We will play the Open with you, or without you." The other competitors relented, and the championship went off as scheduled.

How well did John Shippen and Oscar Bunn do? Well, Oscar finished

21st, scoring 89-85 for a 174. John Shippen became the first African American to ever lead the U.S. Open with an opening 78. That score tied him with four others. The second round or, at least, the 13th hole was his undoing. John's ball landed on a sandy road, and he had great difficulty getting it back in play. The errant shot led to an 11 on the hole, seven over par, and the exact number of strokes he finished behind Jim Foulis, the eventual champion. Still, his 159 total was good for fifth place. Shippen was able to play in the U.S. Open on four more occasions and again finished fifth in 1902.

When Shippen played, there was no such thing as a cut. That came later, when the championship was increased to a 72-hole event. The first African American to make the cut was Ted Rhodes in 1948 at the Riveria Country Club in Los Angeles, although he finished out of the money.

There was a time when a play-off wasn't completed. In the 1911 Open at Sandwich, Arnaud Massy and Harry Vardon were tied at the end of regulation play. A 36-hole play-off was scheduled, and Vardon took command early. At the end of the first round, Vardon was five strokes ahead, a lead he increased through the 16th, the 34th hole of the day.

Massy was first on the tee for the 35th hole and hit a fine shot that settled about 12 feet from the cup. His opponent, however, knocked his ball closer than Massy's. The Frenchman turned to Vardon and conceded the entire play-off, not bothering to finish. Vardon did hole out on the 35th before the two men walked off the course.

In American tournament golf, the first play-off took place in 1899 at the Western Open in Midlothian, Chicago. The victor was Willie Smith, who shot a 74 to defeat Laurie Auchterlonie by 10 strokes.

*I*n the U.S. Open, the first play-off occurred in 1901, with Willie Anderson besting Alex Smith by one stroke, 85 to 86. That play-off was contested three days after the final round since Myopia Hunt Club, near Boston, Massachusetts, had been reserved for members over the weekend. Membership play was much more important back then than holding a national golf championship.

Willie won that championship using a gutta-percha golf ball, but he used a wound ball for his other three titles, thus becoming the only golfer to win the U.S. Open using both types of balls.

*A*t one time, play-offs were all conducted at 18 holes or more. The major championships were the last to change their format, although the U.S. Open continues to follow the longer distance, requiring a full round to decide who will be the champion. The first play-off in a major to be determined by sudden death was the 1979 Masters. Fuzzy Zoeller was the winner over Ed Sneed and Tom Watson.

With the U.S. Open deciding the champion over 18 holes, there is no longer a provision to have another play-off using the same number of holes if the competitors are still tied after the one play-off round. Instead, they go on to sudden death. The first time the U.S. Open winner was crowned after a tie following an 18-hole play-off was in the 1990 championship at Medinah Country Club at Medinah, Chicago, Illinois. When Hale Irwin and Mike Donald were tied after the regulation 18 holes, Irwin won on the 19th.

*B*reaking through for his first victory in 1997, David Duval beat Grant Waite and Duffy Waldorf with a birdie on the first extra hole in the Michelob Championship at Kingsmill, Williamsburg, Virginia. The following week Duval also won the Walt Disney World/Oldsmobile Golf Classic in Orlando, Florida, by defeating Dan Forsman in another play-off. It marked the first time in PGA Tour history that the same player won play-offs in consecutive weeks.

The death of the gutta-percha was complete in 1902. That year Laurie Auchterlonie won the U.S. Open title with the Haskell rubber-cored ball. He was the first to break 80 in all four rounds.

Four years before, in the 1898 Open at Prestwick, Scotland, Harry Vardon broke 80 in each round with the gutta-percha ball. It marked the first time that the feat was accomplished in a national championship.

Surlyn covers have become the golf ball covers of choice for most duffers. They don't cut as easily as balata, saving many dollars for the golfer who tops a shot now and then. However, many professionals still prefer the balata covers, stating that they give better feel and control over the Surlyn ball.

The 1971 Bing Crosby National Pro-Am was won by Tom Shaw. What made it historic was Tommy's use of a Golden Ram golf ball with a Surlyn cover, the first time such a ball was used by a winner on the PGA Tour.

Wayne Levi won the 1982 Hawaiian Open using an orange golf ball, which was the first time anyone was victorious on the PGA Tour with anything but a white ball.

Most golfers use a solid-core ball instead of a wound ball. With a great deal of endorsement money available, some golf professionals also switched. The first to win a major with a solid-core ball was Nick Price, when he captured the 1992 PGA Championship using a Precept.

*T*he only time a ball can be placed in a preferred position is on the tee. Today golfers take for granted the wooden pegs on which they place the ball in preparing to make a drive. Golfers carry their own tees, but that was not always the case.

For a great many years, each teeing area had two buckets. One was filled with water, while the other contained sand. A golfer, or usually the caddie, took a pinch of sand, dampened it in the water, and created a tee from which to hit. It was molded to the proper height and the ball placed on top of the mound. One man, George F. Grant, thought there must be a better way. Grant was a dentist and the first African American to graduate from the Harvard Dental School. Being a dentist, he probably was concerned about the damage done to his hands in the process of molding the sand mounds.

After many experiments, Dr. Grant applied for and received a patent for his wood golf tee on December 12, 1899. Unfortunately, it was not a commercial success for him. Others found ways around the patented invention, creating competition for the golf accessory.

It was in 1923 that another dentist, William Lowell, made an improved golf tee. After some tinkering, he eventually painted the little pegs, made from white birch, red. They became known as "Reddy Tees," a name that had two meanings. Walter Hagen adopted the Reddy Tees, enticed with a bit of cash for his endorsement, and they became very popular. Walter would have a pocketful and leave them on the tee after every drive. It was not unusual to see both youngsters and adults scramble after the tees.

Like Dr. Grant, Dr. Lowell's patent had some holes in it. Others marketed golf tees, and Lowell never realized the riches he had anticipated.

*E*nglewood Golf Club, New Jersey, had the distinction of yielding the first score in the 60s for a U.S. Open. David Hunter, representing

Essex Country Club, Boston, shot 68 in the first round. Unfortunately, the magic was gone after he set the record, and Hunter finished with a 313 total and in a tie for 30th place.

Myopia Hunt Club, near Boston, was the site of four U.S. Open championships. The course is little remembered now, except for those who live in the area and are privileged to play it. The layout is still a stern test of a player's golf. Around the turn of the century, it might have been the most difficult course in the country. The many pot bunkers and sloping greens caused players some agonizing moments.

During the last round of the 1898 U.S. Open, Burt Whittmore was on the front part of the third green, his 12th hole in the nine-hole layout that was in use at that time. The hole was cut in the back of the green, and Burt hit his putt a bit too firmly, so firmly that it rolled down a bank and off the green into the rough. He searched for the ball along with his fellow competitors and the caddies. No luck. It was a lost ball, marking the first and only time a golfer had a lost-ball penalty on a putt in the U.S. Open.

*A*ttire for golfers has changed through the years. Even after jackets were no longer being worn, most golfers wore long-sleeved white shirts and ties on the course. The first U.S. Open champion to break that tradition was Byron Nelson in 1939, when he wore a short-sleeved, open-necked shirt, the accepted norm for today's golfer. Paul Runyan may have influenced him. There are pictures that show Runyan wearing a shirt without a tie in accepting the 1938 Wannamaker Trophy for winning the PGA Championship.

*I*t took longer for the tradition to be broken in the United Kingdom. In 1984, John Behrend drove himself in as the captain of the Royal and Ancient Golf Club of St. Andrews. He was the first in history to do so while not wearing a tie.

*W*illiam Wright of Seattle became the first African American golfer to win a USGA title when he captured the 1959 Public Links.

*T*hree years before, Ann Gregory became the first African American woman to compete in a USGA event, participating in the U.S. Women's Open.

A name more associated with tennis than golf comes up as the first African American to play regularly on the LPGA Tour. Althea Gibson, the Wimbledon champion in 1957 and 1958, was a wonderful athlete. In 1963, she began her professional golfing career with the LPGA, eventually playing in 171 events.

While she wasn't victorious, Althea came close. In 1970, she was in a three-way play-off at the Len Immke Buick Open in Columbus, Ohio, where Mary Mills was the victor.

*T*he first African American golfer to win the Vardon Trophy was Calvin Peete, in 1984.

*Q*ualifying for the 1948 U.S. Open at Riviera were two Hawaiians, Toyo Shirai and Guinea Kop. They became the first Asian Americans to compete in the American championship.

*J*erry Pate turned professional shortly after his victory in the U.S. Amateur. The 1976 U.S. Open was the first major he entered as a pro, and he won it in grand style at the Atlanta Athletic Club Country Club, Georgia. It marked the first time that a man won a major in his first attempt as a professional, other than the inaugural events. That feat was not duplicated until Tiger Woods took the 1997 Masters. It was another six years before the third golfer was able to match the accomplishment, when Ben Curtis stunned the golf world with a victory in the 2003 Open at Royal St. George's, Kent, England.

*A*fter an outstanding amateur career and a great showing in the 1967 U.S. Open at Baltusrol, where he led after three rounds, Marty Fleckman turned professional. In his first tournament, Marty captured the Cajun Classic, but he never again won on the PGA Tour.

*W*ith one official PGA Tour victory, the 1988 Deposit Guaranty Classic in Hattiesburg, Mississippi, Frank Connor never had any real dreams of making golf history. He made history, however, three years later, when he took the Knoxville Open in Knoxville, Tennessee. It was a Nike Tour event, and he became the first golfer to win titles on both tours.

*S*cioto Country Club in Columbus, Ohio, became the first golf course in the country to require all golfers to wear spikeless golf shoes. The club gained fame when Bobby Jones won the 1926 U.S. Open there and again as a young Jack Nicklaus honed his talents on the course.

It wasn't until the 1997 MasterCard Colonial in Fort Worth, Texas, that a PGA-sponsored tournament was won by a golfer using spikeless golf shoes. The victor was David Frost.

*A*lthough several nations had used golf as a subject for postage stamps, it wasn't until 1981 that the U.S. Postal Service first honored a golfer with a stamp, and they issued two that year. The golfers were Bobby Jones and Babe Zaharias. The only other golfer to be placed on a stamp in the United States was Francis Ouimet. The first golfer to be featured on a postage stamp in the world was Gary Player, who appeared on a South African stamp in 1976.

*J*oan Harris of Clearwater, Florida, became the first woman to ever shoot her age when she scored 72 at the Hound Ears Lodge Country Club in Blowing Rock, North Carolina. Mrs. Harris accomplished the feat on October 14, 1972.

A tradition at the Karsten Manufacturing Company is to gold-plate two Ping putters whenever a golfer wins a tournament using one of the company's models. One is given to the golfer as a memento of the victory, while the other is placed in a rack at corporate headquarters.

The first golfer to ever win a PGA Tour event using a Ping model putter was John Barnum in the 1962 Cajun Classic in New Orleans. John became the oldest first-time winner on the PGA Tour at age 51. The original putter, not the gold-plated model, is on display at the Michigan Golf Hall of Fame in Farmington Hills.

*M*etalwoods are the rule rather than the exception for most golfers. That was not always the case. They were introduced in the 1980s, becoming standard for professionals and amateurs alike.

Prior to the 1980s, metalwoods could be found at driving ranges because of their durability, although no real golfer would carry one in the bag for a regular round of golf. Some people felt that they had been around since at least the 1940s, so they really weren't new. Actually, the metalwood predated that estimate of its introduction. The Currie Metalwood was produced in Scotland and given a British patent in 1891, which was the first time that type of club was made.

It wasn't until the early '80s that the metalwood was finally accepted, mainly because some golf professionals embraced the driver. The first to win a PGA Tour event using the implement was Jim Simons in the 1982

Bing Crosby National Pro-Am. When Lee Trevino took the 1984 PGA Championship using a metalwood, the nation's golfers rushed to have one of their own.

*A*ny first victory is one to be savored and remembered, especially when it happens on one of the professional tours. Sometimes it takes a bit longer for that first win than the golfer would like. Bruce Fleisher got his first PGA Tour win when he was 42 years, 8 months, and 29 days old. By that time, Bruce was a part-time player on the PGA Tour, having taken a club job in the mid-to-late 1980s.

When Bruce began to play on the Champions Tour, he didn't have to wait very long for his first win. Fleisher triumphed in the first two tournaments he was eligible to play in, with victories in the 1999 Royal Caribbean at Crandon Park Golf Club in Key Biscayne, Florida, and the American Express Invitational at TPC at Prestancia in Sarasota, Florida, the following week. His accomplishments didn't stop there. Fleisher won seven official events that year and became the leading money winner. He was named Rookie of the Year and Player of the Year and won the Byron Nelson Trophy for the lowest scoring average. Sometimes fine wine gets better with age.

*V*oted the greatest woman athlete in history, Mildred Zaharias was given the nickname she is most known by, "Babe," after hitting five home runs in a single baseball game, a feat that even Babe Ruth never accomplished. Turning to golf in 1935, she had an amazing career. In 1946–47, she entered 18 amateur events, winning 17 tournaments. Her victory in the 1947 British Amateur was the first by an American in the oldest of women's golf championships.

*F*or perhaps the first time in history, a dead man won a golf tournament when Kerry Packer teamed with Greg Norman to capture the AT&T Pebble Beach Pro-Am in 1992. Packer, a 16-handicap player from

Australia, was declared dead two years before when he suffered a heart attack. He was kept alive with an artificial respirator and recovered. He and Norman teamed for a 42-under par total of 246, breaking the old tournament record by six strokes.

Now, Kerry was no average golfer in spite of his handicap. Eleven years earlier, he flew Phil Rodgers to Australia to give him golf lessons. Phil would probably be better remembered if he had won the play-off for the 1962 Open instead of losing to Bob Charles. Still, Rodgers enjoyed a reputation as an outstanding teacher, even giving Jack Nicklaus chipping lessons. Packer paid Phil $50,000 for two weeks and probably flew him first-class as well.

*S*eldom has it been necessary to impose a penalty for slow play; at one time, such an action was unheard of in golf. The first competitor in the U.S. Open to receive such a penalty was Bob Impaglia in 1978. Not that it made much difference; he missed the cut by 16 strokes.

*I*n the long history of the U.S. Open, no one had ever returned a score of fewer than 30 for nine holes until 1995. Neal Lancaster closed out his final round with a 29 at Shinnecock Hills. Then, it happened again the following year at Oakland Hills, during the second round and on the second nine. It was none other than Lancaster, who tied his own record.

*T*he rules for gaining entry into a PGA Tour event have been altered through the years, but sponsors still are given the privilege of inviting a set number of golfers to play in their tournament. The exemptions may be given to just about anyone who the sponsors feel will benefit the event, either by drawing additional spectators or by expressing thanks to a player who was loyal to the tournament when he was a big name.

The sponsors for the Doral Ryder Open used their exemptions in the 1990s to invite sons of famous players. They have included the offspring of Julius Boros, Jack Nicklaus, and Billy Casper. By granting these exemptions, the sponsors were pretty much assured that the fathers would also play.

In the 1993 Doral Ryder Open, Gary Nicklaus made the cut along with his more famous father, causing a quick scramble to see if any father and son had ever made the cut in the same tournament before. It had happened before and more than once.

Joe Kirkwood Sr. and Joe Kirkwood Jr. first completed 72 holes together in the 1946 All-American Golf Tournament at Tam O'Shanter Golf Club in Chicago. Junior finished tied for 19th place, winning $342.13, and his father tied for 34th, worth $216.25. Later in the year, they did it again, in the 1946 Miami Open. Both finished higher than in the All-American Golf Tournament. Junior shot 275 for joint ninth, although the check he cashed was only for $306. Senior was only two strokes behind at 277, finishing in a tie for 19th place, and he pocketed $73.33.

The last time they were both able to accomplish the feat was in the 1950 Miami Open. Senior tied for 45th place, not receiving any money for that finish; but his son was joint fourth and collected $575.

Both were victorious on the PGA Tour as well. Joe Sr. won the Canadian Open twice, in addition to two North and South opens in Pinehurst, North Carolina. Junior won the 1949 Philadelphia Inquirer Open and the 1950 Ozark Open for his Tour victories. In addition, the Kirkwoods were the first father and son to both make the cut in the U.S. Open. Joining them as father-son winners on the PGA Tour were Clayton and Vance Heafner, Julius and Gay Boros, and Al and Brent Geiberger. Julius was a two-time U.S. Open champion, winning also a PGA Championship, while Guy was victorious in the 1996 Greater Vancouver Open. The younger Geiberger, Brent, was able to join his father, a 10-time winner on the PGA Tour, when he captured the 1999 Canon Greater Hartford Open.

When Brent won the 2004 Chrysler Classic at Greensboro, North Carolina, he and his father became the first to win the same tournament on the PGA Tour. Al took the title in the 1976 Greater Greensboro Open. There is a footnote, however. Once the PGA decided to make the Open an official event, two others joined the father-son group. Both Tom

Morris and his son, Tommy, along with Willie Park and Willie Park Jr., were victorious in the oldest of championships.

Claude Harmon was the 1948 Masters champion, and some people have indicated that Claude Harmon Jr., better known as "Butch," was also a winner on the PGA Tour. Butch did win what was to become the B.C. Open in 1971, but it was an 18-hole event that was then known as the Broome County Open. He shot 69 and beat Chuck Courtney, Norman Rail, and Hal Underwood in a play-off. It was not, however, an official event.

Oh, yes, Jack Nicklaus finished tied for 10th in the 1993 Doral Ryder Open in Miami, winning $31,033.33, while Gary tied for 66th and collected $2,996. What a difference 43 years makes in prize money.

When Briny Baird aced the third hole at Warwick Hills during the 2004 Buick Open, he joined his father, Butch, who had made the first hole in one in Buick Open history on the same hole way back in 1962.

The only grandfather-grandson combination to win on the PGA Tour, and thus the first, were Tommy Armour, the 1927 U.S. Open champion, and Tommy Armour III, his initial victory coming in the 1990 Phoenix Open.

In February 1996, a family first occurred. Dave Stockton played in the FHP Health Care Senior Classic, while Dave Stockton Jr. was in the Doral Ryder Open. To top it off, another son, Ron, participated in the Nike Inland Empire Open. It marked the first time that members of the same family played in the regular, Champions, and Nike tours in the same week. Only father Dave made the cut.

*J*erry and Tom Barber became the first father and son to play in the same event on the Champions Tour when they competed in the 1993 GTE West Classic. The 76-year-old father shot 221, one stroke better than his son, who was a mere youngster at 50 years of age.

*A*l and Brent Geiberger finally made history in 1998 at Sahalee. It marked the first time that a father and son played in the same PGA Championship. They weren't paired together, and only Brent made the 36-hole cut.

*O*n March 28, 1999, the ultimate father-son accomplishment happened, as both fashioned victories in the same week. Bob Duval captured the Emerald Coast Classic on the Champions Tour, while David won The Players Championship. Both won in Florida, had a two-stroke victory margin, and played the final round in 1 over par.

*W*ith the inaugural event held in 1976, the Memorial Tournament was the creation of Jack Nicklaus. Played at Muirfield Village Golf Club, it has the unique feature of honoring a different golfing great each year. The Captain's Club selects one person to honor with a plaque in an area near the clubhouse. The first to be named was Robert Tyre Jones Jr.

*G*olf fans take television viewing of majors in stride, but the first televised major didn't occur until 1947, and that airing was local, shown only in St. Louis, Missouri. Lew Worsham won that U.S. Open, defeating Sam Snead in a play-off. It was estimated that only about 500 television sets were tuned in to the championship.

At Oakland Hills in 1951, the first network telecast was handled by NBC for a U.S. Open. It only covered shots at the final green.

*T*he first color telecast of the U.S. Open was in 1965, produced by NBC. Winner Gary Player wore an all-black outfit with a white hat, which might have caused a lot of viewers to try to adjust their sets for some color.

*E*arly telecasts of golf tournaments usually meant covering only the closing holes. The necessity of having a large number of cameras made it virtually impossible to televise much more than that.

For the 1972 U.S. Open at Pebble Beach, the American Broadcasting System decided to use 22 cameras, allowing them to cover each and every hole. It was made possible because Pebble Beach was such a compact course. That championship became the first to have every hole televised, a practice followed today for most major events.

*U*sing radio to broadcast a golf tournament came much earlier. The first known broadcast was the 1929 Los Angeles Open over the Pacific Coast Network.

*T*he first television telecast of the British Open was in 1955, when it was held at St. Andrews, Scotland.

*I*t wasn't until the following year, 1956, that the Masters Tournament was televised with, Jack Burke, Jr. the winner.

*W*omen's golf finally made the scene on national television in 1963, when the final round of the U.S. Women's Open was shown, with Mary Mills winning the championship at Kenwood Country Club in Cincinnati, Ohio.

*T*ony Jacklin made the first hole-in-one captured on British television on the 16th hole at Royal St. George's during the 1967 Dunlop Masters.

W. C. Fields made what is believed to be the first film with a golf theme. In 1915, Fields's popular Ziegfield Follies' golf routine was featured in *His Lordship's Dilemma*.

*T*hrough the years, the French Open had been dominated by British professionals alongside victories by native-born Arnaud Massy. The first American to win the French Open was Walter Hagen; he captured the title in 1920, following a very unsuccessful attempt to win the British Open that same year. Hagen went on to become the first American-born winner of the British Open in 1922, and the year before he was the first American-born winner of the PGA Championship.

*T*he first PGA champion was Jim Barnes, a transplanted Cornishman who defeated Jock Hutchinson, originally from St. Andrews, in the final. The year was 1916.

*I*n 1901, the Professional Golfers' Association was formed in Britain, with much of the credit for the founding of the organization going to J. H. Taylor. The first tournament under its auspices was held at Tooting Bec, a club located in suburban London that no longer exists. It was appropriate that the winner was Taylor, and he took home five sovereigns as well as the trophy.

More accurately, the trophy was the Tooting Bec Cup, and it is still awarded to the player from the British Isles who scores the lowest round in the Open Golf Championship.

*M*any records indicate that by capturing the 1955 Mayfair Inn Open in Long Island, New York, Al Balding became the first Canadian to win on the PGA Tour. In reality, it happened 18 years before that, in the 1937 General Brock Open. The winner was Jules Huot, a French Canadian, who was also successful in his native land with several victories, including three Canadian PGA championships, to his credit.

The confusion is probably because the General Brock Open was played on Canadian soil, even though it was an official PGA Tour event. Thus, Balding became the first Canadian to win on the PGA Tour in the United States.

*A*nother Canadian golfer, Dave Barr, who had been successful on the PGA Tour with two victories in the 1980s, became the first Canadian to win on the Champions Tour. He won the 2003 Royal Caribbean Golf Classic, beating Gil Morgan and Bobby Wadkins by one stroke.

*T*he first printed program produced for a U.S. Open was put together by Herb and Joe Graffis in 1928.

*A*dvertising revenue topped $1 million in a U.S. Open program for the first time in 1980, when the championship was held at Baltusrol. The proximity to New York City likely had something to do with the total advertising income realized.

*P*erhaps the Graffis brothers printed the first U.S. Open program, but the first golf magazine, *Golf,* was produced in Great Britain in September 1890.

*P*rior to 1892, the British Open was contested over 36 holes. In that year, it was lengthened to 72 holes, with two rounds played each day. Horace Hutchinson, a former British Amateur champion, led after the first day, so if the championship had not been extended, he would have been the champion. Another amateur, Harold Hilton, won the title.

*I*n 1968, the Royal and Ancient instituted a 54-hole cut in the British Open for the first time. Two years earlier at Muirfield, Scotland, the championship committee decided to conduct the Open over four days rather than to have 36 holes on the final day. It was patterned after the decision made by the USGA for the U.S. Open. There was a slight difference, though: the British Open began on Wednesday and finished on Saturday rather than the traditional format followed in the United States of Thursday through Sunday.

*T*he first time qualifying was initiated for the British Open was in 1914. The fields had become large, and so two qualifying rounds were held, with 80 participants making it into the Open proper that year at Prestwick, Scotland.

*W*ith the exception of the British Open, golf tournaments for professionals were rare. In Scotland, either the Open or exhibitions were conducted. It appears that the first golf tournament other than a national championship was held in 1867 at Carnoustie, Scotland. The winner was 16-year-old Tommy Morris, victorious after a play-off with Willie Park and Bob Andrew.

The first recorded professional golf tournament, other than the U.S. Open, in the United States took place in 1898 at the Ocean County Hunt and Country Club in Lakewood, New Jersey; it preceded the Western Open by one year. The 36-hole tournament was held on January 1–2, with Val Fitzjohn beating his brother in a play-off to carry off the $75 first-place prize.

*R*eceiving a royal designation is a great honor for any golf club. The first to be so named was the Royal Perth Golfing Society, which King William IV conferred on the club in 1833. The following year he granted the designation to the Royal and Ancient Golf Club of St. Andrews. Prior to that time, it was known as the Society of Golfers of St. Andrews.

*T*he youngest winner of the U.S. Open was Johnny McDermott, at age 19. In winning the 1911 championship, the former Philadelphia caddie also became the first American-born champion. The year before, McDermott came close to winning but lost in a play-off.

*P*rofessional golfers wearing eyeglasses isn't an unusual occurrence today. Two recent U.S. Open champions, Hale Irwin and Tom Kite, wore them. The first to win that championship wearing eyeglasses was Willie Macfarlane in 1925.

*M*acfarlane had another first that year. It marked the first time a golfer won the U.S. Open using steel-shafted golf clubs. They had been approved by the USGA for play the previous year.

*A*ctually, the introduction of steel shafts came much earlier. In 1893, Thomas Horsburgh developed a steel shaft in Scotland. He applied for and received a patent, although commercial production never materialized.

*T*he USGA first began charging admission fees to the U.S. Open in 1922. Prior to that year, anyone wishing to watch the championship simply had to show up and walk the course. Daily passes for the event were $1, and it cost $5 for the entire week.

*I*t was the same story at the British Open, but they didn't begin to charge spectators until 1926. The new charge was due to the vastness of the crowd that showed up the previous year at Prestwick, estimated to be almost 15,000 people. The fee was not necessarily to make money but to control the size of the gallery. At least, that's what the R&A said.

*S*o that competitors and the gallery could better see the holes at the 1964 U.S. Open held at Congressional, organizers decided to paint the top inch of the cups white. This was a first, but painting the cups white became common through the years in practically every golf tournament.

*P*rior to the 1954 U.S. Open at Baltusrol, spectators were free to wander the course and walk right along with the competitors, held back by marshals when a golfer executed a shot. That year all of the fairways and greens were roped for the first time in a U.S. Open.

An incident at Baltusrol in the 1936 U.S. Open might have prompted the change. A California professional, Leslie Madison, had his wallet stolen by a pickpocket during the final round. The culprit wasn't found, and Madison was out $55. To add insult to injury, he finished 55th and received no prize money.

⚑

*F*or many years, the size of golf balls differed between the United States and the rest of the world. In North America, the size could be 1.68 inches in circumference, while the R&A specified that a golf ball was to be 1.62 inches. The size of the golf ball eventually became universal when the R&A and USGA agreed upon the larger size. The bigger ball was made mandatory in the British Open for the first time in 1974.

⚑

*L*aura Davies became the first British golfer to win on the LPGA Tour. She was already an established star in Europe when she took the 1987 U.S. Women's Open. Of course, Laura went on to win and win and win. By 1995, most considered her to be one of the best women golfers in the world.

⚑

A Canadian golf architect, Stanley Thompson, had the distinction of building the first course in the world that cost more than $1 million, Banff Springs, Alberta, in 1927. Compare that with just the first hole at Devil's Pulpit, Toronto, Ontario, which cost an estimated $1.6 million to construct in 1992.

⚑

*O*ne of Jack Nicklaus's lofty goals was to win on the regular and Champions tours in the same year, although he was never able to accomplish the feat. Ray Floyd expressed the same desire, after capturing the 1992 Doral Ryder Open at the age of 49. With a September 4 birthday, he still had some time to wait but not in Japan.

In that country, people are considered a year older on the first day of the New Year, so Ray took off in March to play in the Fuji Electric Grand Slam. He won by seven strokes over Gary Player and thus realized his wish, even though it wasn't an official Champions Tour event.

Raymond made it official when he captured the GTE North Classic, the second event he entered after turning 50. He added to the luster of that victory by graciously donating the winner's check of $67,500 to the Hurricane Andrew relief fund.

The victory presented a problem of sorts. Floyd became eligible to participate in the Infiniti Tournament of Champions at La Costa, Carlsbad, California, both in the regular tournament as well as in the senior segment. One of the snags was that the seniors played off forward markers on some of the holes.

As the Tournament of Champions approached, the policy board made their decision. For 1993, it was decided to have the tee markers in the same positions for both the regular and senior competitors. Since Floyd had qualified for both, he was allowed to compete in each and to collect the prize money from both purses, making it the first time a golfer played in two professional events at the same time. He shot 71-72-73-73 for a 289 total. Ray tied for 22nd in the tournament proper to collect $13,825. His score was good enough for a joint seventh-place finish among the seniors, for an additional $17,500. Had he been able to win both segments, the payoff would have been $196,500.

It was a good opportunity to compare both classes of professionals, even though Ray didn't win. Davis Love III won with a score of 272, while Al Geiberger took the senior event with 280. That would have placed Al ninth in the regular event and netted him a check worth $23,025, less than half of the $52,500 he pocketed playing against the older guys.

Taking it one step further, Craig Stadler captured his first Champions Tour event at the 2003 Ford Senior Players Championship, a designated major for seniors.

The following week Craig entered the B.C. Open, a PGA Tour stop. Coming from eight strokes behind, Stadler closed with a 63 to again reach the winner's circle. It marked the first time that a golfer over 50 won on the Champions Tour and then the PGA Tour in the same year.

*A*ugusta National Golf Club required all contestants to use local caddies during the Masters Tournament until 1983, the first year that players were allowed to bring their regular tour caddies.

The club actually held out longer than the USGA. Local caddies were required in the U.S. Open until 1976; Medinah was the last venue that had local caddies in 1975.

*W*hen Lee Trevino won the 1968 U.S. Open, he did it in style. He became the first golfer in USGA history to play four rounds in the 60s. Lee scored 69-68-69-69 for a 275, which also tied the 72-hole record set the previous year by Jack Nicklaus at Baltusrol.

*F*our years before, Arnold Palmer was the first to record four consecutive rounds in the 60s in the PGA Championship at the Columbus Country Club in Ohio. He scored 68-68-69-69 for 274, but it was only good enough for a second-place tie with Jack Nicklaus. The winner was Bobby Nichols with a then championship record 271.

The next time a golfer played all four rounds in the 60s was in 1984, and the golfer was Lee Trevino. While it wasn't a first for the Merry Mex, he did have one distinction: he used a metalwood, marking the first time it was part of the champion's arsenal in a major event.

*S*hooting all four rounds in the 60s in the British Open didn't occur until 1993. At Royal St. George's, Greg Norman returned scores of 66-68-69-64. His 267 total was also a record, eclipsing the 268 shot by Tom Watson at Turnberry in 1977.

*O*ne of the only titles to be denied to Nancy Lopez was the U.S. Women's Open, although she finished second on four occasions.

Nancy did become the first, however, to post four rounds in the 60s during the 1997 championship. Unfortunately, she finished one stroke behind Alison Nicholas.

*J*oey Sindelar became the only golfer in U.S. Open history to be a first-round leader and then not make the 36-hole cut. In 1993, he scored a 66 at Baltusrol on the first day, but his score ballooned to 79 on Friday to miss the cut by one stroke.

*I*t didn't happen in the Open Championship until 1999, when Rodney Pampling, an Australian, missed the 36-hole cut at Carnoustie. His opening 71 led the field, but a second-round 86 sent him packing.

*I*n 1929, the U.S. Amateur was held at Pebble Beach, which marked the first time the USGA held one of its championships west of the Rocky Mountains.

*B*y 1913, William Howard Taft had left the White House, after his defeat by Woodrow Wilson. One of the reasons for his unsuccessful bid for reelection was a split between him and Theodore Roosevelt, under whom Taft had served as Secretary of War. Roosevelt formed the Bull Moose Party, resulting in Wilson's sweep of most of the Electoral College.

Roosevelt was critical of Taft's golf, often mentioning that it gave the appearance that the President wasn't paying attention to his office. Taft was a dedicated golfer, and after leaving office, he became Professor of Constitutional Law at Yale. It was a fairly easy drive from New Haven, Connecticut, to Brookline, Massachusetts, so Taft decided to see some of the golfers competing in the U.S. Open that year. He became the first President to attend a U.S. Open, although he only stayed one day.

A memorable play-off occurred at the end of regulation play of the 1974 Monsanto Open. It took four extra holes before Lee Elder defeated Peter Oosterhuis, qualifying Elder to play in the Masters. Lee received a telephone call that evening from Clifford Roberts congratulating him and letting him know an invitation would be in the mail. Lee became the first African American to play in the Masters.

F irst to break 300 in a major championship was Jack White in the 1904 Open. Two years later, Alex Smith scored 295 to become the first to break the barrier in the U.S. Open.

The last winner to score higher than 300 in a major was Tommy Armour in the 1927 U.S. Open at Oakmont, Pittsburgh, Pennsylvania.

J ack White's triumph came at Royal St. George's, founded in 1887, which was the first course to host the British Open outside of Scotland when it was the venue in 1894.

B y winning his second Masters title in 1947, Jimmy Demaret became the first player to break par in all four rounds in that tournament. Through 2006, no golfer has ever returned all four rounds in the 60s.

A fter turning professional in 1962, Jack Nicklaus made the cut in 27 straight tournaments. Shooting 79-73 in the 1963 Lucky Invitational, Jack missed his first cut, only to win his next tournament, the Desert Classic in Las Vegas, Nevada.

S hooting a pair of 68s, Jeff Maggert was leading the 1996 AT&T Pebble Beach National Pro-Am when the rains came. This was the tournament once known as "The Crosby," where weather always seemed to be a factor. It had been contested through sleet and snow in prior years.

The big problem in 1996 was that the 16th hole at Spyglass Hill, one of three courses used for the tournament, was unplayable. While champions had been declared in other rain-shortened events, not every competitor had played each of the courses in that year's AT&T, and the layouts varied in difficulty. Officials made a decision to declare it a non-event. Every professional received $5,000 in unofficial prize money, regardless of his score, and no champion was crowned. It marked the first time that a PGA Tour event had been canceled after a portion of it had been played.

*T*he first and only time two members of the same golf club met in the final of the U.S. Amateur occurred in 1925. Bobby Jones and Watts Gunn were members of East Lake, Atlanta, Georgia. Jones emerged as the victor.

*C*hick Evans became the third amateur in four years to win the U.S. Open with his triumph at Minikahda, Minneapolis, in 1916. He did it in style, setting a championship record that stood for 20 years.

Later in the year, Evans reached the final of the U.S. Amateur. His opponent was Bob Gardner, the defending champion. It became the first and only time that the winners of the U.S. Open and U.S. Amateur met in a final. With his victory, Evans also became the first golfer to win both championships in the same year, duplicated only by Bobby Jones in 1930.

*A*s great as Bobby Jones was, the best he could do was string together two straight victories in the U.S. Amateur. The first to win three consecutive titles was Tiger Woods, 1994–96.

During a practice round for the 1925 U.S. Open at Worcester, Massachusetts, Walter Hagen was enjoying play with Tommy Armour, Bobby Jones, and Joe Kirkwood, even though he wasn't playing that well. After Walter cut his ball while trying a shot from a brook, he started looking in his bag for another but without much luck, so Jones tossed him a new ball.

Hagen pulled a 2 iron from the bag, which he intended to use for the 180-yard one-shotter. The iron had a hickory shaft, of course, and Walter began to bend it a little over his knee in an effort to straighten it out. Clubs had a tendency to warp a bit when carried in a bag, and it was not unusual to see someone trying to eliminate the bend in that fashion. As he was working on the club, he heard a crack, so Walter returned it to the bag and pulled out a 1 iron. He opened the face a bit to add a little more loft and make it equal to the club he had originally selected to use. He proceeded to hit it in the hole.

It was an unusual combination, as it was Hagen's first hole-in-one, the first time the hole had been aced, the first time the ball had been hit, and it was accomplished with a 1 iron. Robert Ripley heard about the shot and featured it in *Ripley's Believe It or Not.*

It may have happened before, but the first recorded hole-in-one by a one-armed golfer was made by Lester Edge on the 145-yard 10th hole at Spokane Country Club on May 13, 1927.

In 1934, the first tournament of the winter tour was the Miami Open, held at the Biltmore. The winner was a professional from a municipal golf course in Indianapolis, Indiana, Ralph Stonehouse. No one is absolutely sure why Stonehouse was given the honor, although speculation is that since he won the first tournament of the year, he was designated as the first to tee off in the Masters. Of course, it wasn't called the Masters then; it was the First Annual Invitation Tournament.

His playing partner was Jim Foulis Jr. At precisely 9:45 A.M., Ralph Stonehouse was called to the tee, hit his drive in the fairway, followed with a 5 iron on the green, and two-putted for his regulation par. When the tournament was over, Stonehouse found himself tied for 16th place, earning an invitation to play again in 1935. That proved to be his final Masters, but he will always have the distinction of being the first to ever hit a shot in the now historic tournament.

*H*itting a niblick, C. Ross (Sandy) Sommerville, a six-time Canadian Amateur champion, aced the 145-yard seventh hole during the first Masters Tournament. It was the first recorded hole-in-one in the tournament's history. The hole is now the 16th, since the nines have been reversed. The historic shot occurred during the second round.

*S*ommerville was also the only non-American to be invited to play in the 1934 Masters, thus becoming the first foreigner in the tournament.

*I*n winning the first of four British Opens, Young Tommy Morris also became the first to score a hole-in-one in the championship. There is no record of anyone making an ace in any other medal tournament prior to that time. While it cannot be validated, Tommy's hole-in-one may be the first in any golf tournament.

*I*t wasn't until 1907 that a hole-in-one was made at the U.S. Open. The man who experienced that great thrill was Jack Hobens at the 10th hole, a 147-yarder at the Philadelphia Cricket Club.

*I*n the Ryder Cup, an ace wasn't scored until 1973. Peter Butler made a hole-in-one on the 16th hole at Muirfield during the foursomes. He was partnered by Brian Barnes; Jack Nicklaus and Tom Weiskopf were their opponents.

*G*ertrude Lawrence, a well-known actress, supposedly scored a hole-in-one with her first tee shot in her first round of golf. That record, however, was never authenticated. It did officially happen in 1969, when Dale Dusabellon hit her first shot ever in the cup on a 115-yard hole at the Quarry Hill Golf Club in Burlington, Vermont.

*P*laying in the 2004 Senior British Open at Royal Portrush, Ireland, Graham Marsh aced the 11th hole in the opening round. During the third round, Marsh again recorded a hole-in-one on the same hole. It was the first time in a professional tournament that someone made two holes-in-one on the same hole in the same event.

*T*here have been a great many holes-in-one scored on the PGA Tour. In fact, it has become so commonplace that the accomplishment usually only warrants one line in a newspaper article covering the tournament. However, there was an unusual ace scored in the 2001 Phoenix Open, on January 25, which received a great deal of comment.

Andrew Magee wasn't having the best round of his life on a day when there were several subpar scores being posted. When he got to the 332-yard, par-4 17th hole, it was a matter of getting the round over and hoping for a better score on Friday. His drive rolled on the green just as Gary Nicklaus, Steve Pate, and Tom Byrum were leaving. Magee's ball deflected off Byrum's putter and rolled directly in the hole for the first hole-in-one on a par 4 in PGA Tour history.

Questions immediately were raised about a possible penalty, but the rules clearly state that Byrum and his equipment were considered an "outside agency." Rule 19.3 reads, "If a player's ball is accidentally deflected or stopped by an opponent, his caddie or his equipment, no penalty shall be incurred." It helped Andrew to a 66 and renewed optimism for the next round.

*A*nother tradition at the Masters is the past champions dinner. Ben Hogan initiated the idea in 1952 as the defending champion. He hosted the dinner, and Sam Snead, Henry Picard, Jimmy Demaret, Gene Sarazen, Horton Smith, Claude Harmon, Craig Wood, Bobby Jones, and Clifford Roberts attended. The Champions Club continues to have the dinner each year, with the Masters chairman the only outsider attending. The defending champion selects the menu and pays the tab.

*W*hile the past champions dinner has been an annual event since 1952, no attempt had ever been made for such a gathering at the U.S. Open. That changed in 2000, the year that marked the 100th championship, with Pebble Beach as the venue.

Jerry Pate, the 1976 champion, worked closely with the USGA to coordinate the reception and dinner, the first of its kind. There were 21 past champions in attendance, along with their wives or guests. Tracy Stewart, the widow of Payne Stewart, was invited to attend, as he would have been the defending champion had it not been for the airplane crash that took his life earlier in the year.

Those taking part in the festivities included Tommy Bolt, Ernie Els, Lou Graham, Hale Irwin, Tony Jacklin, Lee Janzen, Steve Jones, Tom Kite, Johnny Miller, Byron Nelson, Larry Nelson, Jack Nicklaus, Andy North, Arnold Palmer, Jerry Pate, Corey Pavin, Scott Simpson, Curtis Strange, Ken Venturi, Tom Watson, and Fuzzy Zoeller.

*T*he first golfer to win a championship of any consequence shooting the same score in all four rounds was Denny Shute. He won the 1933 Open when he fired 73-73-73-73 for a 292 at St. Andrews. That also was the only time it has ever happened in a major.

*G*eorge Smith was the first golfer to have the same score in all four rounds of the U.S. Open when he recorded 77-77-77-77 for a 308 in 1929. Unlike Shute's score, it wasn't good enough to win.

That year also marked the first time that a defending champion failed to make the cut. Johnny Farrell, who won in 1928, scored 167 for 36 holes and wasn't around to see Bobby Jones take home the trophy.

*T*here was no such thing as making the cut in the early years of the U.S. Open. The first time it occurred was in 1904, when the USGA adopted the system used in Great Britain of dropping everyone who was not within 15 strokes of the leader after two rounds.

*B*ecause of the elite, smaller fields in the Masters Tournament, there was no cut of the field after two rounds until 1957,when the field was reduced to the lowest 40 players, plus ties.

*F*ollowing his victory in the 1920 U.S. Open, Ted Ray returned to his home in England to resume duties at Oxhey, England. The members of the club bestowed an honorary membership on Ray. It was the first recorded incidence of such an honor to a golf professional, allowing him the privileges of the "gentlemen golfers."

*K*en Venturi became the first golfer to go through both local and sectional qualifying and then to win the U.S. Open. He accomplished the feat in 1964 at Congressional in Washington, D.C. Five years later, Orville Moody became the second to do so, at Champions Golf Club, Houston, Texas, in 1969.

G ermany wasn't known as a hotbed of golf before Bernhard Langer came on the scene. No German golfer made headlines in international competition. Then, Bernhard turned professional 27 days before his 15th birthday. When he entered his first tournament, at the age of 15, he won it. He went on to become the first German golfer to win a major with his victory in the Masters in 1985.

J udy Bell became the first woman member of the USGA Executive Committee, elected to the position in 1987. Rising through various positions, Judy was elected president in 1996. It has been a custom of the R&A to invite the president of the USGA into their clubhouse when the British Open is held at St. Andrews, where the headquarters is located. However, when Judy was president, she was not invited into the male-only conclave. Judy never complained and refused to comment on the incident.

S till, England had a 73-year jump on the Americans. The first female club official, Mrs. R. P. Graham, was appointed secretary to the Edgward Club in 1914.

I t wasn't until 2000, however, that a British club elected a woman as its Captain. Anita Olrog was given the honor at Foxhills Club and Resort in Surrey, England. Her husband had previously been the Captain at the same club.

T here was never a golf club that was established exclusively for women until 1924. That year Marion Hollins helped to establish the Women's National Golf and Tennis Club on Long Island, New York.

Up to this time, it was the first and only golf club for women. Hollins had won the 1921 U.S. Women's Amateur and went down in golf history because of her involvement with both Cypress Point Club and Pasatiempo Golf Club.

The club stayed in existence until the early 1940s, when the bank sold the property that held the mortgage.

A child prodigy in golf, Betty Jameson won the Texas State Women's Amateur when she was only 13. Later, as a professional, Betty was one of the founders of the LPGA, eventually gaining induction in their Hall of Fame. Her score of 295 in winning the U.S. Women's Open is the first recorded score under 300 by a woman over 72 holes.

*T*he founding of what is now the United States Golf Association (USGA) came into being in part because of a controversy, mainly caused by one man, Charles Blair Macdonald.

In 1894, the Newport Golf Club held a "national championship" conducted at stroke play. Macdonald, who had learned the game as a student at St. Andrews, decided to play and lost by one stroke to W. G. Lawrence of the host club. He immediately expressed his strong opinion that a national champion could not be determined by stroke play. It must be conducted at match play. He didn't say that an event couldn't be considered a "national championship" if it was hosted by one club. That would come later.

Influenced by his opinions and strong personality, St. Andrew's Golf Club held another "national championship" the following month, this time at match play. With 28 entries, the men eliminated one another until Macdonald played L. B. Stoddard in the final. The winner, on the 19th hole, was Stoddard. Still not happy with the result, Macdonald now stated that a national championship could not be determined when it was hosted by only one golf club.

Such a forceful man was Macdonald that others began to think that a governing body had to be organized by the various existing golf clubs to oversee the game in the United States. A dinner meeting was held in New York on December 22, 1894, with representatives from St. Andrew's Golf Club, Newport Golf Club, The Country Club, Chicago Golf Club, and Shinnecock Hills Golf Club, with the USGA the result of the meeting.

The following year, in 1895, the first official U.S. Amateur Championship was held at Newport Golf Club and Macdonald won. This time he offered no protest when he was declared the champion.

*M*acdonald is also credited with building the first 18-hole golf course in the United States. It was the Chicago Golf Club, constructed in 1893. A notorious slicer, Macdonald built the course so the holes followed a clockwise direction. Golfers who hooked the ball flirted with out-of-bounds, but a slice never faced that problem.

*T*he honor of building the first course for women in the United States belongs to Shinnecock Hills, when they laid out the Red Course in 1892.

*W*hen the LPGA was formed, it was supposed to showcase women professionals. The very first tournament held under the new organization's auspices was the 1950 Tampa Open, and the winner was Polly Riley, an amateur from Texas.

Did having an amateur win its first tournament embarrass the LPGA? When the organization held a 50th-anniversary "Night of Champions," Polly wasn't invited, even though she had won the LPGA's inaugural tournament.

*I*n winning the 1965 San Diego Open, Wes Ellis putted cross-handed, the first time a tour event was won with the champion using that style on the greens. Orville Moody became the first to win a U.S. Open putting cross-handed in 1969.

The long putter has become a familiar sight, but at first, it was more generally used on the Champions Tour. It was unusual to see professionals use it on the regular tour. Qualifying for the PGA Tour in 1986, Rocco Mediate used a 49-inch-long putter from the start, although he would switch back and forth with a conventional weapon. He was the first to win using a long putter on the PGA Tour when he captured the 1991 Doral Ryder Open.

Johnny Miller tried one of the long putters in the 1982 Los Angeles Open, and he is believed to be the first to try that type of putter on the PGA Tour.

Youngsters dream of winning major golf tournaments, and for some, the dreams even come true. During the 1979 Southern Open at Green Island Country Club in Columbus, Georgia, Larry Mize caddied for 1969 Masters champion George Archer. Eight years later, Larry won the Masters Tournament himself. He thus became the first and, to this date, only Masters champion to have been a caddie for another Masters champion.

No golfer had ever made a double eagle on a hole in the history of the U.S. Open until 1985 at Oakland Hills. Playing in his first championship, T. C. Chen, a 27-year-old from Taiwan, hit a big drive on the 527-yard second hole, but he still had 240 yards left to the green. His shot rolled directly into the cup; but with only about 20 people standing around the green, the cheering wasn't loud enough for Chen to comprehend what he had accomplished. It wasn't until he arrived at the green that he was told what had happened. The person who informed him was named Ralph Eagle.

*T*wo years later, T. C. Chen became the first Taiwanese to win a PGA Tour event, defeating Ben Crenshaw in a sudden-death play-off to capture the Los Angeles Open.

*N*ot counting New Zealand, the first golfer from a South Pacific island to win on the PGA Tour was Vijay Singh of Fiji. His 1993 Buick Classic victory gave him that distinction. Winning the 1998 PGA Championship also put Vijay in the record books as the first from Fiji to capture a major. Incidentally, his first name means "victory" in Hindi.

*I*t wasn't until 2002 that a Korean was victorious on the PGA Tour. K. J. Choi captured the Compaq Classic of New Orleans by four strokes. He also was the first from Korea to gain a PGA Tour card when he qualified in 2000.

*W*hen asked to rank the majors in order of importance, professional golfers usually rate the U.S. Open on top and the PGA Championship as the laggard. Part of the reason, they say, is the strength of the field. The argument is that many club professionals participate in the PGA, depriving some of the tour regulars of the opportunity to play. That may be, but some club professionals have produced fine performances against their tour brethren.

During the 1993 championship at Inverness, the 515-yard 13th hole proved to be the easiest hole on which to match or better par. It was reachable in two shots, resulting in numerous birdies and some eagles.

It was a club professional, however, who made history on the hole. Darrell Kestner's wife followed him with a video recorder so she could assist the PGA of America with some footage on how a club pro performed in the championship. After nine holes, Darrell was a little concerned about having a battery problem with the recorder, so he suggested to his wife that she not record every shot. She followed orders. Unfortunately, she missed recording his second shot on the 13th. It traveled 222 yards and found the cup for the first double eagle in the 75-year history of the PGA Championship.

*T*he first to record a double eagle on the LPGA Tour was Marilyn Smith. She made the historic shot on the first hole in the 1971 Lady Carling Open at Pine Ridge Golf Club in Baltimore, Maryland, on June 4.

*N*o Japanese golfer had been successful on the American tour until Isao Aoki came through in grand style in 1983. He needed a birdie on the final hole to tie Jack Renner, who had already completed his round in the Hawaiian Open and forced a play-off. Aoki's drive came to rest in the rough on the left side of the fairway, but he was only 128 yards away. Still, the shot was not an easy one. It would be very difficult to make the ball stop coming out of the high grass. Isao hit a sand wedge that found the cup for an eagle, giving him the victory. Incidentally, the following year, Renner won the Hawaiian Open without any heroics from Aoki.

*N*ot only was Aoki the first Japanese golfer to win on the U.S. PGA Tour, but he was also the first to capture a European tour event when he took the 1983 European Open at Sunningdale. Isao did have an unofficial victory in Europe prior to that time, however, as he was the winner of the 1978 World Match Play at Wentworth, near London. Aoki also holds the distinction of being the first Japanese golfer to win on the Champions Tour.

A young man by the name of Casey Martin startled the golf world in 1998 when he sued the PGA of America under the Americans with Disabilities Act of 1990 so that he could use a golf cart when playing on the Nike Tour. Casey has Klippel-Trenauney-Weber syndrome. It slows the blood flow in his right leg and causes swelling, making it extremely difficult to walk a course. Martin won the case and was allowed to use a cart in his attempt to qualify for the U.S. Open at Olympic.

Casey did qualify and became the first golfer to ride a cart in the U.S. Open, making the cut and finishing a very respectable 23rd.

Eventually, the PGA's suit against Martin made it through the judicial system to the Supreme Court, which heard the case in 2001. In a 7–2 decision, the Court ruled in favor of Casey based on the Americans with Disabilities Act.

A t one time, the PGA had a "Caucasian Only" clause in its bylaws that virtually shut out African American golfers from trying to make a living in tournaments. Breaking that barrier was not an easy task. The pioneers were Bill Spiller, Ted Rhodes, Pete Brown, and Charlie Sifford, with help from Joe Louis, the World Heavyweight Boxing Champion. Joe was an enthusiastic golfer who played as an amateur in some PGA Tour events.

The breakthrough came in 1964, when Pete Brown was able to edge Dan Sikes by one stroke in the Waco Turner Open to become the first African American golfer to win on the Tour. As a footnote, Sifford did win the Long Beach Open in 1957, but it was an "unofficial" tournament, since the total prize money was below the minimum established by the PGA.

CHAPTER TWO

Facts

*T*oday everyone considers 18 holes to be a standard round of golf. Naturally, there are some courses consisting of only 9 holes, so two trips around the layout are required to complete a "round." It seems like a strange number. Why doesn't an official round require some more rounded number, such as 10 or 20? The main influence on the golfing world came from St. Andrews, particularly the Old Course, which was *the* course when the standard was set. As the game grew in popularity and as golfers looked more and more to St. Andrews for guidance, the feeling was that whatever was done there must be right. A typical round at the Old Course was 9 holes out and another 9 coming back to the starting point. If 18 holes was good enough for St. Andrews, then it was ideal for every other course.

Golf lore speculates that 18 holes became the norm because of the second most important export from Scotland—Scotch whiskey. Having a drink before, during, or after a round has been a part of the game since it began. The story that is quite popular among the Scots is that every golfer took a bottle with him when the round began. A little nip now and then was certainly in keeping with defenses against the weather. When the bottle was half empty, it was time to head back toward the start. It just so happened, the legend goes, that the bottle got down to that level after 9 holes. It's a wonderful story but certainly not fact.

Still, a round of golf did not always consist of that number. The oldest club in the world where golf is still played is at the Bruntsfield Links, in the heart of Edinburgh, Scotland. Originally it had 6 holes. Prestwick, which hosted the first 12 British Open golf championships, had 12 holes when it welcomed the world's best players. The early championships were over 36 holes in one day, requiring three trips around the course. Wimbledon, a name that is more associated today with tennis than golf, had 7 holes from 1864 until 1870, when it was increased to 19. Blackheath in England, and in Scotland, North Berwick had 9 holes, Musselburgh had five, Gullane 13, and Montrose consisted of 25 holes. St. Andrews in Yonkers, New York, considered by most golf historians to be the beginning of golf in the United States, even though evidence is available to show golf was played elsewhere before its founding, initially consisted of 3 holes. Even the Old Course was not always an 18-hole layout. When the R&A was formed in 1754, there were 22 holes. Records vary, but it appears that St. Andrews, Scotland, took on its present number in 1763, although some reports indicate it was in 1843.

Legends about golf are numerous. It's amazing how many of the stories I hear today are not fact but fiction. Some people insist that Gene Sarazen hit a 3 wood to record his famous double eagle in the 1935 Masters when it was actually a 4 wood. Those same people have said they witnessed the shot, and yet, it was a very sparse gallery, as most of the small group that had assembled at Augusta National that year was watching Craig Wood.

*N*o one knows the origin of golf. In reality, it seems that few even knew how to spell it. In early writings, dating as far back as 1457, it has been spelled *goff, goufe, goofe, goiff, gauff, gowff, goulf, golff, golfe,* and golf.

Originally called the Society of St. Andrews Links Golfers, it became the Royal and Ancient Golf Club of St. Andrews in 1834, 80 years after its first written records. The royal title honor was bestowed by King William IV, and it immediately was recognized as the premier club. Still, the R&A is misunderstood by many, especially Americans.

It is a private club and has a limited membership of 1,800. Approximately two-thirds of the members are residents of Great Britain and Ireland, with the rest coming from overseas. Membership is only by invitation. A member proposes a prospective new member, and it must be seconded. While outsiders do not know the figure, the proposal must be supported by an unspecified number of signatures from other members of the R&A. It is believed that the number of signatures required is fairly substantial.

The R&A does not own a golf course. Instead, the members play courses that are open to the public. The St. Andrews Links Trust controls those courses, and they are run by the Links Management Committee. The R&A contributes a sum negotiated each year to the Trust.

At the request of other golf clubs, the R&A became the official governing body for the Rules of Golf in 1897. Then, in 1919, it was asked to carry out the duties of running both the Amateur and Open championships. Thus, the Royal and Ancient Golf Club of St. Andrews really has three functions: a private club, the governing body of golf, and the operator of the golf championships.

For a while, there was an American course with a 19th hole that could be played with a club and ball, not an elbow. It was the Green Island Country Club in Columbus, Georgia. When the course became the site of the Southern Open, under the leadership of Gumby Jordan, it was discovered that the 10th hole wasn't very challenging for the long-hitting professionals. With a well-aimed tee shot, they could drive the green of the par-4 hole. Consequently, a new hole was constructed next to the old one. Instead of closing the original 10th, the club maintained it for some time and used the hole for the higher-handicap players. The flag flying on the green sported a number 19.

*W*ho won more majors in a single event than any other golfer in history? Names like Nicklaus, Vardon, or Jones immediately come to mind, but they didn't approach the record set by John Ball. The great amateur from Hoylake, England, won eight British Amateur championships. Ball's approach to matches was the same one adopted by Bobby Jones many years later. He played against par, not the opponent.

A modest man, Ball tried to avoid the hero worship that followed him. After one of his titles, the members of the Royal Liverpool Golf Club commissioned a portrait of him to hang in the clubhouse. It is said that he never walked past the painting, which hung on the stairway, always keeping to the first floor. His first championship was in 1888, and his final victory came in 1912, a span of 25 years of championship golf. One surprising fact about Ball's eight victories was that he never successfully defended any of his titles. Nicklaus, incidentally, spread his 20 majors over a period of 28 years, the longest span of any of the multiple winners of major events.

*R*egarded by many as the finest 9-hole course in Great Britain, Royal Worlington, founded in 1893, is the only course with fewer than 18 holes to be given a royal designation.

*A*ugusta National is linked with the Masters. What is little known is that the club also hosted another tournament. Actually, it was a championship. In 1937 and 1938, the Senior PGA Championship was held there, with Jock Hutchinson and Fred McLeod emerging as champions. For years, the two were the honorary starters at the Masters, kicking off the festivities for the opening round.

*H*ole measurements for a green are 4¼ inches in diameter and at least 4 inches deep. Gene Sarazen once opined that too much emphasis was placed on putting and that the hole should be larger. As a result, a tournament was staged in Florida where the hole was increased to 8 inches. It really made no difference, as the better putters still made more putts in the larger hole.

*S*tandards for the golf ball are uniform throughout the world. The ball cannot be smaller than 1.68 inches nor heavier than 1.62 ounces.

*W*ar is hell, even for golfers. Rubber just wasn't available to the public during World War II, since it was so important to the war effort. When balls could be purchased, they usually had "vulcanized" printed on them, whatever that meant. The real finds were the prewar golf balls. It wasn't unusual for someone to pay $100 a dozen for those gems, if they could be located, a princely sum at that time.

Bing Crosby gave Sam Snead an unused Spalding Dot just before the 1945 Los Angeles Open, and Sam played it. And played it. The ball lasted the entire 72 holes, and Snead won the title. "The cover was loose, but it kept going," Sam reported. And remember, Snead was representing Wilson Sporting Goods, not Spalding.

*M*any years before Snead accomplished his marathon with one ball, Alexander "Sandy" Herd did the same and went Sam two better. The new rubber-wound Haskell ball had been introduced in the United States and had made its way across the Atlantic. Sandy found out about it and decided to use the new ball in the 1902 British Open. The other stars of the era—Vardon, Taylor, and Braid—refused to use the Haskell, opting to continue to play with a gutta-percha ball.

It has been reported that Herd used the same ball for the two quali-fying rounds and then the four rounds in the championship proper. Of course, you must remember that Sandy was a Scotsman. At the conclu-sion of the final round, part of the insides were coming through a hole in the cover; but by that time, it didn't make much difference, as Herd was the champion, the only time he was able to win that most important of titles. There was no report of any other golfer using the Haskell in that championship. By the next year, the rubber-wound ball was the rule rather than the exception.

When Bobby Jones won the Grand Slam in 1930, his golf ball of choice was the Spalding Dot.

Obsessed golfers are in a class by themselves among athletes when it comes to doing strange things, such as naming their children. As we learned earlier, Arnaud Massy was so thrilled with his British Open victory that the Frenchman named his daughter Hoylake after the course, which was the site of his triumph. Jesper Parnevik did the same many years later in 2001, naming his son Phoenix in remembrance of his first PGA Tour victory there in 1998.

James Braid, a five-time British Open champion, liked the links at Muirfield so much that he used it as the second name for his son. That course played a role in the naming of another child. A cab driver in London, Michael Everest, told his wife that he wanted to name their soon-expected child after the winner of the Open being played that year at Muirfield. Shortly after Lee Trevino won the champi-onship, their son was born and christened Lee Trevino Everest. Mr. Everest never revealed what the name would have been if the child had been a girl.

A member of Red Run Golf Club in Royal Oak, Michigan, got a great joy out of hitting the ball long off the tee. His name was John Grabicki, but he felt it didn't fit. He legally changed it to John Driver. Jack Fleck, the 1955 U.S. Open champion, suggested to his wife that their newborn son be named Snead Hogan Fleck. She balked at the idea but did accept the name Craig Wood Fleck after the 1941 champion.

The ultimate, however, may belong to a man from Philadelphia, Buddy Lutz. His three sons were named Wedge, Chip, and Putter.

The standard warning for golfers is "Fore," and credit for initiating it is given to Sandy Herd's grandfather, who was a caddie. That was back in 1854, and the custom has continued throughout the golfing world regardless of the language spoken.

In the late 1920s, four golfers played fairly regularly at the St. Lambert Country Club near Montreal, Quebec. Only one of the men had an automobile, and it was his job to drive to the course with the other members of the group. The route included driving over a bridge with cross ties, constructed that way to take care of horse-drawn wagons.

They would rush to the tee upon arrival, but the driver, shaken by crossing the bridge, usually hit a poor shot. Since he was the only one with a car, it was a common practice to allow him to hit a second tee shot. After all, the other golfers didn't want to lose their transportation. The car driver's name was David Mulligan, manager of the Windsor Hotel in Montreal, and the act of hitting a second shot off the first tee became known as "hitting a Mulligan."

The Latin word "par" means equality. It first appeared in the USGA's definitions in 1922 as "Perfect play without flukes and under ordinary weather conditions, always allowing two strokes on each putting green."

"Par" was used long before that, however. It first came into vogue in 1911 and was mentioned by American golfers and officials that year.

$\mathcal{A}$ccording to A. W. Tillinghast, the architect who designed Winged Foot as well as other great courses, the term "birdie" had its beginnings in Atlantic City, New Jersey. A group of Philadelphia golfers would head to the shore during the winter months to play at Northfield Country Club. The temperature was normally a little higher than in Philadelphia, and in most cases, the course was devoid of snow. Among the group were Tillinghast and George Crump, the founder of Pine Valley, Clementon, New Jersey. Since there weren't many golfers on the course, they would play a "gangsome," which they preferred to call a "Philadelphia Ballsome." Normally, bets were made all-around, with the payoffs made in golf balls.

On the long 12th, a normal three-shotter, one of the golfers got off two fine shots, landing on the green. Tillinghast said that it was either Ab Smith, or his brother, Bill, who yelled, "That's a bird." The other immediately said that such a feat, resulting in cutting par by a stroke, should mean winning doubly, and the group agreed that that should be the practice from then on. It was from that start that a birdie has become known as one below par for the hole.

$\mathcal{T}$he longest hole ever played by competitors in the British Open is the sixth at Carnoustie, measuring 578 yards. However, on the original 12-hole layout at Prestwick, the first hole supposedly played to 578 yards. At that time, measurements were not as accurate as they are today, so it is difficult to authenticate the actual distance. Still, it was a very long hole by any standard. In 1870, Young Tom Morris, on his way to a third consecutive British Open title, scored an eagle three on the hole. Of course, the term "eagle" was not in use at that time. With the exception of the score, no more information about the feat is available. It is probably safe to assume Tommy holed an approach shot to record the historic eagle.

*P*laying from the back tees, the International Golf Club in Bolton, Massachusetts, measures 8,325 yards in length, the longest in the world.

*W*hen the 1896 U.S. Open was held at Shinnecock Hills Golf Club, it was played at 4,423 yards, the shortest course ever used for that championship.

*T*he longest course hosting the British Open was Carnoustie in 1968, when it measured 7,252 yards. For the U.S. Open, it was Bethpage Black Course in 2002, at 7,214 yards. Taking all of the majors into consideration, Whistling Straits in Wisconsin was the longest, at 7,514 yards when it was the site of the 2004 PGA Championship. It also had three par-4 holes, measuring more than 500 yards, and the par-5 11th was 618 yards.

*O*akmont hosted its first U.S. Open in 1927. It was 500 yards longer than any U.S. Open course used up to that time, measuring more than 6,900 yards.

*A*t Satsuki Golf Club in Tochigi, Japan, the seventh hole is 964 yards long and plays to a par 7, giving it the distinction of being the longest hole in the world.

*I*n the United States, Meadows Farms Golf Club in Locust Grove, Virginia, lays claim to the longest hole, a par 6 that is stretched to 841 yards.

Southern Hills in Tulsa, Oklahoma, had both the longest par-4 and longest par-5 holes in the history of the U.S. Open. The 16th played to 491 yards, while the 5th was 642 yards. During the 2001 championship, only Steve Lowery was able to reach the 5th green in two shots. After a drive officially measuring 348 yards, he hit a 3 wood 294 yards to the putting surface.

The widest extremes as to the length of holes on the same course probably belongs to Teyateyaneng in South Africa. There is one hole 619 yards long, while another measures only 37 yards.

Possibly the record for the largest number of golfers in a play-off occurred in 1980 at the Channelview Golf Course in Houston, Texas. The course was holding a scramble event with three prizes. Tying for third were four six-man teams, or a total of 24 golfers. Off they went on the first hole, which took about 40 minutes to play, resulting in two teams being eliminated when they couldn't match the birdies of the other two. It only took one more hole to determine the third-place team, but in total time, the play-off lasted for more than an hour. The prize for third place was one golf ball each.

On the LPGA Tour, the largest number of play-off participants was six. In the 1999 Jamie Farr Kroger Classic in Toledo, Ohio, Carin Koch, Kelli Kuehne, Mardi Lunn, Se Ri Pak, Sherri Steinhauer, and Karrie Webb all finished the regulation 72 holes with 276 totals. It didn't take long to determine the champion. Se Ri Pak of South Korea birdied the first sudden-death hole to put an end to the tournament.

Six was the largest number in a play-off on the PGA Tour as well. The occasion happened at the 1994 GTE Byron Nelson Classic. The winner was Neal Lancaster over Tom Byrum, Mark Carnevale, David Edwards, Yoshinori Mizumaki, and David Ogrin.

That number was equaled in the 2001 Nissan Open with Robert Allenby beating Brandel Chamblee, Toshi Izawa, Dennis Paulson, Jeff Sluman, and Bob Tway.

*In major championships, no play-off ever had more than three golfers vying for the title until 2002. That year, in the British Open at Muirfield, four players tied after regulation play: Ernie Els, Stuart Appleby, Steve Elkington, and Thomas Levet. Following the stipulated three-hole play-off, Els and Levet were still tied.

They went back to the 18th hole for the third time that day, with Ernie prevailing.

*If you're playing golf in Japan, chances are pretty good you won't run into someone using a golf ball with the number 4 on it. That's a bad-luck number for the Japanese, and they do not manufacture any for the locals. Instead, a dozen Japanese balls in a box are numbered 1, 2, 3, and 7.

*What's in a name? If it's the PGA European Tour, it can be misleading. In 2001, for example, the Tour began with the Alfred Dunhill Championship in South Africa. Following the South African Open, the next tournament was the Heineken Classic in Perth, Australia. A quick visit to Sydney the following week and it was off to Kuala Lumpur for the Carlsberg Malaysian Open.

After the Singapore Masters, the next event was held in the United Arab Emirates and then on to Qatar. In March, the record shows the next tournament was held in Portugal, but that needs some explaining. It was the Madeira Island Open, and while the volcanic island is a Portuguese possession, it is actually located off the coast of Morocco in Africa.

You might think that would end the globe-trotting, but no. Instead of north, it was southwest for the São Paulo Brazil Open, followed by the Open de Argentina. After Rabat, Morocco, the PGA European Tour finally made it to the Continent for a tournament in Spain, starting on April 19. At least they stayed in Europe for the rest of the year.

*P*erhaps the most common form of betting on a golf course is the Nassau, where there is a set amount wagered on the front nine, back nine, and for the total round. Its origin comes from the Nassau Country Club on Long Island, New York, where it was a popular form of betting among members.

*M*ichigan Meadows, located in Richmond, features an unusual green on the 16th hole. It is shaped like the Lower Peninsula of the state, with sand bunkers representing the Great Lakes. The green superintendent has fun with pin placements, sticking them in spots that represent the location of various cities. The best approach is usually through Ohio, although Indiana is best when the pin placement is in Saginaw. Naturally, you need to know your geography.

*T*he 1931 U.S. Open champion was known as Billy Burke, but his birth name was Burkauskas. Doug Ford, who won both the PGA and Masters events, was born Fortinaci. Gene Sarazen changed his name from Eugenio Saraceni, because he felt it sounded too much like a violinist.

*O*nly one golfer has ever been captain of the U.S. Walker Cup team who never played on any of the teams. Lew Oehmig was given the honor in 1977. He was a three-time U.S. Senior Amateur champion and was the oldest to ever win a USGA championship when he captured that event in 1985 at the age of 69.

*T*he courses at St. Andrews in Scotland belong to the people of the town. It is not unusual to see them strolling on the land while golfers are trying to play, as it is their right to do so. A charter was written in 1552 by Archbishop John Hamilton reserving the right of access to the links for "golfe, futeball, shuting and all games." One place the townspeople like to walk is on the road that runs across the 1st and 18th fairways. It's called Granny Clark's Wynd, and the traffic got so heavy, the St. Andrews Links Committee decided to control it by installing a traffic light in 1969. Golfers beginning their round had to wait for a green light controlled from the starter's box. There was a sign on the road that warned pedestrians not to cross the fairways when it was yellow or red.

During the 1800s, it was common for people to use the Swilcan Burn, which cuts across the 1st and 18th holes, to wash clothes. They were then often spread on the grass for drying or until the washing was complete. In 1851, a local rule read, "When a ball is on clothes or within a club-length of a washing-tub the clothes may be drawn from under the ball and the tub may be removed."

The rule was changed in 1888, stating, "When a ball lies on clothes the ball may be lifted and dropped behind without penalty."

*T*he Swilcan Bridge over the burn on the 18th hole at the Old Course is over 800 years old. It was originally used by traders who brought their goods from the harbor into St. Andrews.

A tradition at the Old Course is to play it backward occasionally. For example, the golfer tees off from the 1st hole and plays to the 17th green, then from the 2nd tee to the 16th. That format continues until the round is complete. It is known as the "left-hand course." It was actually the original routing, but it was changed in the late 1800s because the course was becoming worn from overuse.

The "right-hand course" became the accepted routing and was known as the medal course. The left-hand course was the way the British Open was played in 1873, '76, '79, and '81.

*T*he last time the British Open was contested at 36 holes was in 1891 at St. Andrews. There was no loitering on the course. The draw sheet for that Open indicated, "Play will commence at 9 A.M. and the second round at 12:15 P.M." It meant the contestants had approximately three hours to complete the first round. That's quite different than the four- to five-hour rounds we now experience in the majors.

*W*hen Edward VIII was the Prince of Wales, he was a contestant in the Royal and Ancient Autumn Medal at St. Andrews in 1922. His brother, later King George VI, competed in the Autumn Meeting of the Royal and Ancient when he was the Duke of York in 1930, following the formality of playing himself in as captain of the club.

*T*he record for the longest play-off in Great Britain, outside of those scheduled over 18 or 36 holes, occurred in 1960. W. S. Collins defeated W. J. Branch at the 31st hole in the News of the World Match Play Championship at Turnberry, which translates into the 13th play-off hole. The record was matched the very next year in the same event—this time played at Walton Heath, with Harold Henning beating Peter Alliss on the 31st hole.

*O*nly one Irishman, Fred Daly, has been able to win the British Open, capturing the title in 1947 at Hoylake. The medal he received was given to the Royal Portrush Golf Club and is proudly displayed in the clubhouse. In honor of his accomplishment, the fourth hole at Royal Portrush is named after Daly.

*T*here have been many golfers and golf historians who consider Bobby Locke the greatest putter of all time, among them Gary Player. Locke said that he patterned his putting technique on that of Walter Hagen, whom he watched play an exhibition in South Africa as a youngster. Bobby's putting technique allowed him to get maximum topspin on the ball, moving smoothly from the time it left the putter blade.

*M*erion, in Ardmore, PA, had its beginnings as a cricket club in 1865. It was 31 years later that golf was introduced. The East Course, where championships are played, had its birth in 1912. Never lengthy, even when it was first opened, it is thought of as short by modern standards. But yardage alone does not tell the story. The greens are slick and difficult targets, and heaven help the golfer who strays off the fairway when the rough is allowed to grow.

At first glance, the 11th is an unassuming hole as measured by distance. Only 370 yards, the main obstacle is Cobb's Creek, which protects the green in front, back, and to the right. It actually forms a fork in the driving area, making it a hazard for the errant tee shot. Even though it is officially Cobb's Creek, it is better known as the Baffling Brook, probably named by members who tried to maneuver a short iron over it to the green. While many of Merion's holes are considered classics, this is one of Hugh Wilson's masterpieces.

The 11th hole gained prominence in 1930 when Merion was the venue for the U.S. Amateur Championship. That year the championship took on a special meaning. Bob Jones had previously won the British Amateur and Open, along with the U.S. Open. If he could capture the U.S. Amateur, he would win the four major championships in which he was eligible to play in the same year—the Grand Slam.

Jones began by equaling the existing record for a qualifying score, with 142 over 36 holes. He had two concerns when it came to the U.S.

Amateur. First, he did not like to win the qualifying medal, because he had not been successful in the championship proper when he won it before. Second, he worried about the first two matches, which were 18-hole affairs instead of the 36 holes he preferred. He felt it was such a short distance that any golfer good enough to qualify could defeat any other opponent. Jones's morning match was against Ross "Sandy" Sommerville, the Canadian champion and a very underrated player. Bobby was on his game, disposing of Sommerville by 5 and 4, then duplicated the margin in the afternoon match against another Canadian, Fred Hoblitzel. Next came the 36-hole matches, and Jones defeated Fay Coleman 6 and 5 and then Jess Sweetser 9 and 8 to reach the final.

The last match was against Gene Homans, with Jones speeding off to a 7-up lead after the morning round. In the next 10 holes, Bobby picked up one more to become dormie at the 11th hole. Both hit the green in regulation, with Jones about 20 feet away and Homans a bit closer at 15 feet. Bobby's putt rolled to within 10 inches of the cup. Gene had to make his to keep the match alive, but it was not to be. When it missed, he walked over to Jones and shook his hand, conceding the final putt. Jones had captured the Grand Slam, and the 11th hole at Merion gained its place in golfing history.

The hole's reputation was added to during the 1934 U.S. Open. Tied for the lead when he got to the hole was Bobby Cruickshank. His approach was short, falling right into the middle of the creek with a splash, but then a miracle occurred. Up it came, after hitting a submerged rock, to land on the green. Elated, Bobby threw the club in the air to give thanks to the gods of golf. Unfortunately, the law of gravity took over, with the club coming straight down on Cruickshank's head. Groggy from the blow, he never fully recovered, finishing the championship at 295.

The 11th hole at Merion shows that length is not a requirement for a reputation as a great hole. The same is true of the 8th hole at Royal Troon, known as the "Postage Stamp." It's only 126 yards in length, but it can be either a terror or a pushover. The first British Open champion, Willie Park, apparently gave the hole its name when he described it as "a pitching surface skimmed down to the size of a postage stamp."

A story is often told of a woman who didn't hit the ball very far with any club. Whether the story is true or not makes little difference, because the tale gives some good insight into a golfer's manner of thinking. As she walked on the tee, her caddie pulled out the driver and handed it to her. When she swung and hit the ball in one of the bunkers at the front of the green, she turned to the caddie and said, "You under-clubbed me."

Certainly, that wasn't the club selected by Gene Sarazen when he first played the course. Sarazen had won both the U.S. Open and PGA in 1922. He was going to show the British how a champion played, but he didn't fare too well. Like Walter Hagen before him, Gene said he would be back. True to his word, the Squire continued to return, eventually winning the British Open 10 years later.

When the 50th anniversary of playing in his first British Open came around, Sarazen was invited to return to Troon. He accepted, but by this time, he was a gentleman of 71 and was not considered a threat. Still, it was golf nostalgia at its best. He selected a 5 iron at the Postage Stamp for a shot into the wind and then hit a hole-in-one. Even though Tom Weiskopf was the leader with a 68, the press preferred to talk with Gene. That 5 iron is now on display at the R&A clubhouse. David Russell also scored an ace at the same hole during that Open, but because of Sarazen's hole-in-one, he barely received a mention in the press. Of the two aces recorded on that hole, by Sarazen and Russell, one was made by the oldest competitor and the other by the youngest in the championship that year.

Lest someone get the impression that the Postage Stamp is an easy hole, consider the experience of Hermann Tissies during the 1950 British Open. The young German amateur was a fine player, attested to by his qualifying for the championship proper and winning four Austrian Amateur titles. The Postage Stamp green is guarded by three pot bunkers, each of which can drive fear into the novice but that do not present much of a problem for the accomplished golfer. After all, it's only 126 yards. Hermann, however, will swear that all three bunkers can be difficult. He visited each one. In all, he took nine bunker shots, wasted a couple of others, and then three-putted for a 15, the highest score on any hole, even though it was the shortest, in the championship that year.

A National Golf Foundation study completed in 1985 found that the average golf course covers 133 acres.

T he same organization conducted another study in 1997 to determine the most popular names given to golf courses. It revealed that there were 46 courses named Riverside. Other frequently used names were Lakeview (40), Rolling Hills (38), and Hillcrest and Lakeside (tied at 37).

H onolulu boasts only one municipal golf course, Ala Wai, built in 1931. With the wonderful weather in Hawaii, golf is enjoyed year-round. On average, more than 500 rounds of golf are played there each day, with the total exceeding 175,000 per year.

M uch was made of the fact that the finishing hole for the 1997 U.S. Open at Congressional Country Club was a par 3. Most finishing holes are longer in length. Unlike the 1964 U.S. Open, which was held at the same course when the layout was altered, officials decided that the course would be played just the way it was intended for members rather than changing the route.

Perhaps more unusual, however, is beginning with a par-3 hole. That is the case at Royal Lytham & St. Annes, site of many British Open championships through the years. It is the only course in the Open rota that starts with a par-3 hole.

Because of that starting hole, history was made in 1988, when Lanny Wadkins made a hole in one with his first shot in the British Open Championship. He became the first and only golfer to start a major with an ace.

T here was speculation that President Bill Clinton might present the winner's trophy at Congressional that year, but it did not happen for security reasons. Only one champion ever received the trophy from a U.S. president. President Warren Harding awarded Jim Barnes the prize when he won at Columbia Country Club in 1921.

*W*eather and commitments to be at a different location have caused some PGA Tour events to declare cochampions at times. In most cases, two golfers have split the title. That was not what happened in the 1950 Bing Crosby National Pro-Am. The championship was shared by four golfers—Jack Burke Jr., Dave Douglas, Smiley Quick, and Sam Snead.

*A*t the New Grampians Inn course in Victoria, Australia, one local rule specifies that a penalty of one stroke is added if the golfer hits a kangaroo.

*T*hey're a little more lenient at the Santa Rita Golf Club in Tucson, Arizona, and for good reason. The rule reads, "Live rattlers—2 club lengths—no penalty."

*B*ecause of the location of Bjorkiden Arctic Golf Course, situated 150 miles north of the Arctic Circle, there are three special local rules:

1. If a reindeer moves your ball on the fairway, it can be replaced without penalty.
2. If a reindeer eats your ball, drop a new one where the incident occurred.
3. If your ball lands in the snow, play it from where it landed.

*T*he longest reign as a champion in any major event is held by Richard Burton. He won the 1939 British Open and held that title until the championship was resumed in 1946, following World War II. That's a total of seven years as defending champion for winning one tournament.

Only two golfers have been able to win the same major four times in succession. Young Tom Morris was the first to accomplish the feat, when he won the Open Championship in 1868–70 and 1872. The championship was not held in 1871. Walter Hagen won the PGA Championship in 1924 through 1927 when it was contested at match play.

While not a major, Gene Sarazen also won the same tournament four consecutive times. He was the master of the Miami Open from 1926 through 1930; no tournament was held in 1927. Tiger Woods captured the Bay Hill Invitational from 2000 through 2003.

On the LPGA Tour, the only player to win four consecutive titles in the same event was Laura Davies, taking the Standard Register Ping 1994–97.

The man who holds the record worldwide is Mohamed Said Moussa, who won the Egyptian Open eight straight times from 1969 through 1976.

There is always a great deal of discussion and speculation about the captain's selections to the Ryder Cup team. In recent years, the top-10 golfers, according to the points amassed in both the U.S. and European tours, are automatic selections. The captains then have the opportunity to select two additional team members. Selection wasn't always structured in this manner. In the early years, Hagen was the captain of the American team and picked the golfers he wanted on the squad. Gene Sarazen said that most were his buddies.

*N*ick Faldo played on 11 Ryder Cup teams, which is a record. In addition, he has the all-time winning percentage lead, with 46 matches played and 23 matches won. Nick was also the youngest ever to play in the Ryder Cup at the age of 20 years, 1 month, and 28 days. He did not qualify to be on the European team in 1999 and failed to be named as a wild-card selection by the captain that year to break the streak that began in 1977.

THE MAJORS (BASEBALL, THAT IS) AND THE MAJOR (THE MASTERS, THAT IS)

*T*here has been just one golfer to compete in major golf championships and also be a member of a victorious World Series team. Sam Byrd played with the 1932 New York Yankees, appearing in one game of the Fall Classic, while also participating in the Masters, PGA Championship, and U.S. Open. His best finish in a major was runner-up to Byron Nelson in the 1945 PGA Championship. A couple of his teammates on the Yankees were Babe Ruth and Lou Gehrig.

A giant tree stands near the eighth green at the Olympic Club's Lake Course. It is so large that it must be regularly cut back. In 1976, it was trimmed by the greens crew, and once the cutting began, balls started to drop out of the tree. By the time the chore was finished, the men had dodged 105 golf balls.

*T*he originator of the Stableford System of scoring was Dr. Frank Barney Gorton Stableford. It is the only scoring system outside of counting strokes, either in match or medal play, that is covered in the

Rules of Golf. He invented the scoring system after playing a round of golf in which some bad holes ruined an otherwise good score. Originally, the scoring system called for gaining three points for a birdie, two for par, and one for a bogey. If the score for the hole was higher, no points were gained or lost. Records indicate that the inaugural Stableford competition, called the Frank Stableford Open Amateur, was played on May 16, 1932, at Wallasey, England. That scoring system is now used in any number of member-guest and member-member events at country clubs, and a modified version is in place on the PGA Tour for The International.

*L*ong before there were tournaments, most of the best golfers were amateurs. It was not too surprising to see amateurs compete on an even level with professionals, both in Great Britain and in the United States. Not counting the U.S. Open, which was won by five different amateurs, there were a few other amateur winners in events that were either regular PGA Tour events or later deemed to be official.

The first such amateur winner was Chick Evans, when he captured the 1910 Western Open. Next came Bobby Jones, who won the Southern Open in 1930. Both of those tournaments were virtually held in the golfers' backyard, since Evans was a Chicago resident and Bobby was from Georgia. The war years accounted for some other amateur champions. But it wasn't until 1942 that another amateur broke through. While it was only a 36-hole event at the time, it was counted as an official PGA Tour stop, and Johnny Dawson took the Bing Crosby National Pro-Am that year. Records still list him as the champion. Fred Haas Jr. won the 1945 Memphis Invitational. Later in the same year, Cary Middlecoff won the North and South Open, followed by Frank Stranahan's victory in the Durham Open the very next week. It marked the only time that amateurs won PGA Tour events consecutively. Stranahan was able to win four times as an amateur.

Next came hometown hero Gene Littler, who captured the 1954 San Diego Open, followed by Doug Sander's win at the 1956 Canadian Open. The amateurs weren't able to break into the winner's circle again until Scott Verplank took the 1985 Western Open. The last amateur winner was Phil Mickelson, who was successful in the 1991 Tucson Open.

*T*here is one male golfer listed as a winner when the history of the LPGA is reviewed, not including mixed-team events with men and women as partners. It didn't have anything to do with a sex-change operation or a lawsuit enabling men to play in a women's tournament.

Men were invited to participate in the 1962 Royal Poinciana Plaza Invitational, held at the Palm Beach Country Club's par-3 course, described by Mickey Wright as possibly the toughest par-3 layout in the country. For the first time, the men and women competed against each other from the same tees. The winner was Sam Snead, with Mickey finishing second.

*T*he 1901 U.S. Amateur Championship was delayed a week because of the assassination of President McKinley.

*O*riginally scheduled to be played on June 4 and 5, the 1913 U.S. Open was changed to the third week in September to accommodate the entry of Harry Vardon and Ted Ray. The two British golfers would be completing their American tour, and the timing would be convenient for them to compete. It was the first and only time the American championship was changed for two golfers.

*A*nother delay in a major occurred in 1896 at Muirfield, following regulation play in the Open. Harry Vardon and J. H. Taylor had tied, but they were both scheduled to participate in a tournament at North Berwick, Scotland. After they concluded that event, they returned to Muirfield the following day, where Vardon defeated Taylor by four strokes.

Christie's had a special auction in 1993 offering a number of items that had belonged to Bobby Locke, including the four Open medals he had won. The medal from his 1949 victory brought approximately $34,000, and the total for all of his medals exceeded $115,000. That $34,000 was about 80 times more than Locke had received in prize money for winning his first Open.

Sitting atop the famous Ryder Cup trophy is a male golf figure. That is not unusual, as a great many trophies have used such a figure to adorn the top. In this case, it was fashioned after Abe Mitchell, a well-known British golfer who won several tournaments, although he came up short in the Open.

Mitchell was Samuel Ryder's personal golf instructor, and the donor insisted his likeness be used for the trophy. Mitchell did play on three British Ryder Cup teams beginning in 1929.

An innovation introduced in 1974 was the Titleist DT, a three-piece Surlyn-covered ball. DT stands for "Durable Titleist."

Winning the national golf championship of your own country is a great accomplishment, even if it's only once. No one has been able to win more than four U.S. Opens, and Harry Vardon won six British Open titles. Mohamed Said Moussa holds the record number in a single national championship. He won 15 Egyptian Open titles during his career. Gary Player is next, with 13 South African Open victories.

When it comes to winning national amateur titles, it's difficult to come up with any record better than Henri de Lamaze. The Frenchman was able to capture 14 French Native Amateurs and had 11 French Amateur Open victories. It might be argued that the native championship didn't have much competition, but the Open Amateur always drew some fine players. Henri defeated such stellar players in the final as Tim Holland and John Dawson.

A statistical study taken in 1980 came up with the following odds on making a hole-in-one: 3,708-to-1 for a male professional or an expert amateur, 4,658-to-1 for a female professional or talented amateur, and for the average golfer, it was 42,952 to 1. An update of that study was completed in 1987 by *Golf Digest*. Using statistics from their Hole-in-One Clearing House, the magazine determined that on any one hole, the odds were still the same for a male or female professional, but they were 33,676 to 1 for the average golfer. The average golfer apparently got better, or luckier, in those seven years between studies.

S o unimportant was the U.S. Open in its formative years that when the 1901 championship resulted in a tie at the end of regulation play on Saturday, the play-off was scheduled for the following Monday. The reason for the delay was because the course had been reserved for the Myopia members on Sunday. They weren't about to give up their rounds for some professionals.

The first championship was held in 1895 at Newport Country Club, and it was an afterthought. The main event was the first U.S. Amateur, with the U.S. Open held the following day. It was 36 holes over a 9-hole course, played in one day. There were only 11 competitors.

The U.S. Open took on more meaning after a former caddie, Francis Ouimet, won in 1913. Golf became front-page news and the champion an American sports hero. In spite of the stature gained by that win and subsequent champions such as Bobby Jones, Walter Hagen, and Gene Sarazen, who captured the imagination of the public, things hadn't changed much by 1929. In that U.S. Open, which was held on Winged Foot's West Course, members were playing the East Course during the championship. Naturally, the members used the locker facilities and clubhouse, as they would at any other time of the year.

*W*illiam Howard Taft served as president of Chevy Chase Golf Club in 1911 while he was president of the United States.

*T*aft's successor, Woodrow Wilson, was the only president to have played a round of golf on inauguration day. His second wife, Edith Bolling, remains the only First Lady who was a golfer.

*C*omedian Buddy Hackett was an avid golfer who had a strange sense of humor. Playing with Jimmy Demaret, fellow entertainer Jan Murray, and another golfer whose name has been lost through the years, the foursome arrived at the 12th hole at the Concord International Golf Course in the Catskill Mountains.

Each of the other golfers hit drives into the fairway, while Hackett sliced into the trees lining the hole. Buddy went into the woods to search for his ball, as the others walked along the fairway. An idea struck, and Hackett proceeded to disrobe. Then he began to call out, "Help." His playing partners started running toward the shouts just as Buddy emerged from the trees, completely naked, yelling, "Locusts, locusts."

*A*nyone fortunate enough to get a ticket to the Masters is not satisfied with being there without a trip to the 11th, 12th, and 13th holes, commonly referred to as "Amen Corner." It was not always called that. The name was created by Herbert Warren Wind, one of the finest golf writers in history. He dubbed the three holes "Amen Corner" in his article about the Masters Tournament in 1958, which appeared in *Sports Illustrated*. It actually came from a Dixieland song, "Shouting at the Amen Corner," and it is a name that has remained with the course and tournament since that year.

DEAR ANN LANDERS . . .

*A*nn Landers once received a letter from a golfer's wife who complained that her husband took his putter to bed with him the night before he had an important match. The syndicated columnist responded, "Be thankful he's not a jockey."

*I*n the history of the Walker Cup, only one match has ever been decided at extra holes. In 1922 at the National Golf Links, C. V. L. Hooman of Great Britain defeated Jess Sweetser on the 37th hole. It was then agreed that matches tied at the end of a regular round would be halved.

*T*he 1966 PGA Championship at Firestone proved to be the last tournament in which Tony Lema would ever compete. Leaving Akron, Ohio, Tony died in a plane crash in Illinois. Lema was best known as Champagne Tony, since he would treat the press with that liquid when he won an event. He also wrote a book, *Golfer's Gold*, and carried gold-colored tees that helped identify him, as if such a popular golfer needed any further identification.

Tony wasn't in the hunt for the title as he got to the 18th tee. In fact, he finished a distant 34th to Al Geiberger. When he hit the drive, the tee flew in the air near two young boys, who argued about who would get to have the wonderful souvenir. Observing the dispute, Tony walked over, reached into his pocket and emptied the gold tees he had left. The boys were excited about their good fortune. A spectator mentioned to Lema that it was a nice gesture, and Tony said, "They're only kids. Besides, this is my last hole." Sadly, the statement proved to be true, as he perished when the private plane went down shortly after leaving the tournament.

Oldest winner of the U.S. Open was Hale Irwin, at age 45, when he won the 1990 championship at Medinah for his third victory in that tournament.

In the British Open, the oldest winner was Roberto De Vicenzo, who was 46 when he captured the title in 1967—a full 100 years after Tom Morris had won the championship at the same age.

The youngest participant in the history of the U.S. Open was Tyrell Garth at the age of 14 playing in the 1941 championship at Colonial.

Young Tom Morris was also 14 when he played in the British Open in 1865. He then became the youngest winner at the age of 17 in 1868. Following his tragic death, there were at least 60 golfing societies that contributed to the monument that was placed at his grave in St. Andrews Cathedral yard. It depicted the famous stance that Tommy took when playing a stroke and stated: "He thrice in succession won the Championship Belt and held it without rivalry and yet without envy, his many amiable qualities being no less acknowledged than his golfing achievements."

The record for the youngest to ever play in a national championship was lowered in 2002. Jae An, a 13-year-old, became a participant in the New Zealand Open by shooting a 65 in the qualifying round. His accomplishments didn't stop there. An then became the youngest to ever make the cut in a tournament open to professionals, as he tied for 62nd place with rounds of 71-75-71-79.

*A*t age 19, Sergio Garcia of Spain became the youngest player in the Ryder Cup when he made the European team in 1999. He lowered the record that had been set by Nick Faldo in 1977.

*T*en golfers have had the distinction of winning both the U.S. Amateur and U.S. Open during their careers. The first was Francis Ouimet, followed by Jerome Travers, Chick Evans, Bobby Jones, Johnny Goodman, Arnold Palmer, Gene Littler, Jack Nicklaus, Jerry Pate, and Tiger Woods.

Only three golfers have won both the British Amateur and Open—John Ball, Harold Hilton, and Bobby Jones. All three remained amateurs throughout their careers.

*I*nitially, the U.S. Open was a 36-hole championship played in one day. That lasted three years, and then the championship was contested over 72 holes. From 1898 until 1924, competitors completed the championship in two days.

It was then changed to 18 holes the first two days and a 36-hole finale. In 1965, the competition adopted the current format of 18 holes each day over four days, beginning on Thursday and finishing on Sunday, unless the weather interfered. There was speculation that the last change was made because of the intense heat and potential health problems during the 1964 championship at Congressional.

In that championship, Ken Venturi almost didn't make it through the final round, as he fought the heat and was near exhaustion. The more logical explanation is that golf was gaining in popularity and television came into play. Another day of being able to televise the championship meant more money in advertising and a larger payday for the USGA.

*B*eginning in 1987, the Champions Tour initiated a competition within a competition; now named the Grand Champions, it was for competitors over 60 years of age. Little is reported in the press about the results, but it can be lucrative to those who participate. That year Howie Johnson pocketed an extra $84,158 for his showing in the Grand Champions.

It wasn't long before the leading money winner was taking home six figures. By 1999, Tom Shaw earned more than $300,000 for the tournament within a tournament.

*T*he oldest competitor in a Ryder Cup match was Raymond Floyd, who was 51 when he played on the 1993 American team. Only two other professionals were "seniors" when they participated—Ted Ray, at age 50, in 1927 and Jay Haas in 2004.

*O*ldest to win a Champions Tour event was Mike Fetchick, who captured the 1985 Hilton Head Seniors Invitational on his 63rd birthday.

*W*hile Sam Snead was just two months shy of his 53rd birthday when he won the 1965 Greater Greensboro Open to set the record for the oldest winner in PGA Tour history, he didn't come close to the world record for important events open to all ages, though. Alex Herd, better known as Sandy, captured the 1926 News of the World Match Play Championship when he was 58 years old.

That wasn't just another tournament either. The News of the World was considered the second most important golf event open to professionals in the world at one time, attracting an extremely strong field. If anyone had been designating majors back then, it most certainly would have been considered one. It served as the model for the American PGA Championship.

*U*ntil September 10, 1972, every hole on the Old Course (at St. Andrews) had a name, except one—the 10th. That day the St. Andrews Town Council officially named it "Bobby Jones." Only one other hole on the famed course is named after a golfer. The 18th is the "Tom Morris Hole."

St. Andrews hosted both the British Open and Amateur within a month during 1895, resulting in heavy play on the Old Course. Tom Morris decided that the course needed some rest and closed it for about 10 days, much to the dismay of the regular golfers. He accomplished it in a unique way, filling in the holes on each of the greens.

*O*nly five golfers have led, or been tied for the lead, after each round in winning the U.S. Open: Walter Hagen in 1914, Jim Barnes in 1921, Ben Hogan in 1953, Tony Jacklin in 1970, and Tiger Woods did it twice, in 2000 and again in 2002.

*S*ince the Claret Jug replaced the Championship Belt in 1872 as the prize for the British Open, only one golfer has been able to have his name engraved three times as a winner at the same venue. Harry Vardon won three of his six titles at Prestwick.

The list of those winning twice at the same course is also small. Vardon accomplished it at Sandwich, or Royal St. George's, as did Walter Hagen. James Braid was able to pull it off on two separate sites—St. Andrews and Muirfield. The other member of the triumvirate, J. H. Taylor, was a two-time champion at St. Andrews.

Since the end of World War II, Peter Thomson captured two of his five at Royal Birkdale, Jack Nicklaus won two at St. Andrews, and Nick Faldo was twice successful at Muirfield.

In the U.S. Open, the list is even more exclusive. Willie Anderson won twice at Myopia, while Nicklaus garnered two of his four victories at Baltusrol.

The highest opening round for a champion at the Masters is 75, and it only happened once. Craig Stadler was able to play the next three rounds in 7-under par for his victory in 1982.

When the World Golf Hall of Fame was opened in 1974 at Pinehurst, there were 13 golfers enshrined—Patty Berg, Walter Hagen, Ben Hogan, Bobby Jones, Byron Nelson, Jack Nicklaus, Francis Ouimet, Arnold Palmer, Gary Player, Gene Sarazen, Sam Snead, Harry Vardon, and Babe Zaharias. Not one of the 13 was a unanimous selection. Ben Hogan was near perfection, with only one golf writer leaving him off the ballot.

The first golf hall of fame, however, was founded by the PGA of America in 1940, due largely to the efforts of Grantland Rice, the popular sports writer. Original inductees were Willie Anderson, Tommy Armour, Jim Barnes, Chick Evans, Walter Hagen, Bobby Jones, John McDermott, Francis Ouimet, Gene Sarazen, Alex Smith, Jerry Travers, and Walter Travis.

Founding members of the LPGA were Alice Bauer, Patty Berg, Bettye Danoff, Helen Dettweiler, Marlene Hagge, Helen Hicks, Opal Hill, Betty Jameson, Sally Sessions, Marilyn Smith, Shirley Spork, Louise Suggs, and Babe Zaharias.

Muirfield is generally ranked among the top-10 golf courses in the world on most lists, and there are some that feel it is the best links anywhere. The scorecard does not list par for each hole, as it is felt that weather conditions can alter the standard score expected to be recorded by a scratch player. It has neither a professional nor a pro shop.

Members of the Honourable Company have to go elsewhere to have a golf lesson.

*W*ith its beginnings in 1927, the Ryder Cup has become one of the premier events in golf. In all its history, only two father-son combinations have participated in the matches. Percy Alliss played on the 1929, 1933, 1935, and 1937 British teams, while Peter Alliss was a member in 1953, 1957, 1959, 1961, 1963, 1967, and 1969. The other was Antonio Garrido in 1979 and Ignacio Garrido in 1997.

There have been brothers named to the team as well. Lionel and Jay Hebert, along with Joe and Jim Turnesa, played for the United States, while Bernard and Geoff Hunt represented the British. The record, however, belongs to Charles, Ernest, and Reg Whitcombe. The three brothers were all on the 1935 team, with Charles and Ernest partnering each other in the foursomes.

*T*here have been only three U.S. Open champions eligible to play on the American Ryder Cup team who were never included up to 2002. Jack Fleck, Orville Moody, and Steve Jones failed to play in the biennial matches. Every other American-born professional who won the U.S. Open was named to at least one Ryder Cup team since the matches began in 1927.

*G*eorge S. May was a golf innovator. The tournaments he sponsored included the Chicago Open, the All American, and the World Championship. He identified golfers by asking them to wear their names on their backs, and while some professionals balked, most wanted to compete for the richest purses on tour and complied. The innovation led to what is now a common sight—the golfers' names on the backs of their caddies.

He once hired a taxi to drive him from Chicago to Cleveland, Ohio, to see the 1940 U.S. Open at Canterbury. Since he was holding the

Chicago Open later that year, May wanted to see a national championship firsthand and didn't worry too much about the expense. He made an inquiry as to the largest purse in golf. When informed it was $10,000, he immediately made his tournament an $11,000 event.

There was only one winner of the U.S. Open who was employed by a municipal course when he captured the title—Jack Fleck in 1955. His victory in the championship was one of the great upsets of all time. Fleck needed to play the final four holes in 2-under par to tie Ben Hogan and did just that. The smart money was on Hogan to prevail in the play-off, but Fleck emerged victorious. The municipal course professional used Ben Hogan model golf clubs.

When Hogan won his third major in 1953, the British Open at Carnoustie, a ticker-tape parade was quickly arranged in New York. Ben's ride was in a Chrysler convertible.

Four-time U.S. Women's Open champion and member of the LPGA Hall of Fame, Betsy Rawls, earned her degrees in mathematics and physics. She was a member of Phi Beta Kappa at the University of Texas before embarking on a career as a golf professional.

Playing in the U.S. Women's Open, Lori Garbacz was a bit upset over the length of time it was taking to complete the round. She wasn't the only competitor who thought it was taking too long. Most finished in five hours and 20 minutes, which is more time than it usually takes at the local municipal course on a Saturday afternoon.

While waiting on the 14th tee, Lori sent her caddie to make a telephone call to Domino's, ordering a large cheese pizza for delivery on the 17th tee. Sure enough, when the three golfers arrived at the designated spot, there was the delivery boy waiting with the pizza. Lori, Lynn Connelly, and Deb Richard, along with the threesome in front of them, who were also waiting to hit, were all able to have some of their dinner a bit early that day.

*W*inning the 1937 Masters was just one of many great accomplishments by Byron Nelson. It was after that win that he received the nickname "Lord Byron." A noted sportswriter, O. B. Keeler, was covering the tournament for the Associated Press. Keeler had followed the career of Bobby Jones, and he wrote excellent articles and a book about Jones's victories.

During the interview following Nelson's win, he commented to Byron that his play on the final nine reminded Keeler of a poem Lord Byron had written about Napoleon's defeat at Waterloo. The next day, when the article appeared, the headline read, "Lord Byron Wins Masters."

*I*n addition to Byron Nelson, there have been a number of golfers through the years who have been assigned different monikers, either by sportswriters or by their peers. They include:

Harry Vardon	The Greyhound
Walter Travis	The Old Man
Jim Barnes	Long Jim
Walter Hagen	The Haig, Sir Walter
Gene Sarazen	The Squire
Bobby Jones	The Emperor
Bill Mehlhorn	Wild Bill
Tommy Armour	The Silver Scot
Harry Cooper	Lighthorse Harry
Horton Smith	The Joplin Ghost
Henry Picard	The Chocolate Soldier
Paul Runyan	Little Poison

E. J. "Dutch" Harrison	The Arkansas Traveler
Ky Laffoon	The Chief
Sam Snead	Slammin' Sammy
Ben Hogan	Bantam Ben, The Hawk, The Wee Ice Mon
Jimmy Demaret	Dapper Jimmy
Ed Oliver	Porky
Lew Worsham	Chin
Henry Cotton	Maestro
Bobby Locke	Old Muffin Face
Ed Furgol	Wingy
Tommy Bolt	Thunder Bolt, Terrible Tempered Tommy
Lloyd Mangrum	The Riverboat Gambler
Arnold Palmer	The King
Jack Nicklaus	Ohio Fats, The Golden Bear
Gene Littler	Gene the Machine
Gary Player	The Black Knight
Billy Casper	Buffalo Bill
Tony Lema	Champagne Tony
Lee Trevino	Merry Mex
Miller Barber	Mr. X
Orville Moody	Sarge
Graham Marsh	Swampy
Al Geiberger	Mr. 59
Greg Norman	Great White Shark, Shark
Fred Couples	Boom Boom
Craig Stadler	The Walrus
Ben Crenshaw	Gentle Ben
Mike Reid	Radar
Loren Roberts	Boss of the Moss
Ernie Els	Big Easy
Craig Parry	Popeye
Tim Herron	Lumpy
Shigeki Maruyama	The Smilin' Assassin
Sergio Garcia	El Niño

🚩

*T*he longtime caddy master at Augusta National was a man named John Henry Williams. He was better known by his nickname, "Leven," because he was the 11th child in his family.

🚩

*B*uilt in 1958, the Par Three Course at Augusta National soon gained a reputation for being one of the finest in the world. Organizers decided to have a Par 3 Contest to be held on the Wednesday before the Masters got under way beginning in 1960. In all of the years it has been held, the winner has never gone on to capture the Masters in the same year.

Masters champions have won the Par 3 Contest, however. They include Sam Snead, Art Wall, Gay Brewer, Tom Watson, Tommy Aaron, Ben Crenshaw, Ray Floyd, Vijay Singh, and Sandy Lyle. Snead and Lyle won the event twice.

Art Wall set the record with a 20 in 1965, which was equaled by Brewer eight years later. Only once has the contest had cochampions. Rain prevented a play-off in 2003, so Padraig Harrington and David Toms shared the title.

🚩

*I*f you really hurry when you play the 125-yard, ninth hole at Portal Golf Club, you still can't complete play on it in less than an hour, at least in the summer. The reason it cannot be accomplished is because the tee is in North Portal, Saskatchewan, and the green is in Portal, North Dakota, and the folks in North Dakota observe daylight savings time and eastern Saskatchewan does not. Presumably the golf committee has never assessed a penalty for slow play.

On that hole, George Wegener once scored a hole-in-one, accomplishing a couple of unusual golf feats. He teed off in one country and scored an ace in another. George also holed out more than an hour after he hit his shot.

A legend in the investment community was Peter Lynch, the man who guided Fidelity's Magellan Fund from 1977 until his retirement in 1990. It became the largest mutual fund in the world when measured by total assets.

As a youngster, Peter was a caddie at Brae Burn, and one of the men he regularly worked for was D. George Sullivan, president of Fidelity. That helped lead to his employment with the firm after he received his MBA from the Wharton School of the University of Pennsylvania, largely paid with his caddie fees, which he had invested in the common stocks he heard about as he toted the bag for Mr. Sullivan.

A long with the Old Course, Augusta National would probably rank very high on any golfer's list of courses he or she most wanted to play. The beautiful layout was created by Alister Mackenzie. But Mackenzie never had the opportunity to play his masterpiece. The enthusiastic 12-handicapper left Augusta National for the last time in 1932, and it still was not fully grassed. He died in 1934.

W hen the Masters is over, the champion is interviewed in the Butler Cabin. It is one of 10 cabins on club property, and the term "cabin" doesn't do justice to the structures that house members and guests on trips to Augusta National. Each contains beautiful sleeping rooms and facilities, with a bar and golf library that would be the envy of those staying at the Plaza Hotel in New York.

E astern schools dominated golf in the early years, which is probably not too much of a surprise, since the majority of golf courses were in that part of the country. From 1905 through 1913, Yale won nine consecutive intercollegiate championships.

Coming to the final hole of the 1957 British Open at the Old Course at St. Andrews, Bobby Locke had a three-stroke lead. After a good drive, Bobby lofted an iron that settled four feet from the hole. It was merely a formality for him to claim his fourth Open title. He marked the ball, and then it came time for Locke to finish. The ball was replaced, putted, and missed. No matter, he tapped it in for a 279 total, three better than Peter Thomson.

A protest was presented to the Championship Committee much later. It seems that Locke had marked his ball, then moved the mark a couple of putter-heads away to make sure it wasn't in anyone's way. In the excitement of the moment, Bobby replaced the ball in front of the coin without returning it to its original position. That was all caught on film.

It was clearly an infraction, but the championship was over, and the check had been cashed and the winner's name engraved on the silver claret jug. No one has revealed who made the protest. Some have indicated it was Thomson, who could have benefited by being declared the champion, while others speculated it had been Henry Cotton. That the R&A didn't make the person's name public is a credit to the organization.

The committee met. They reached the decision that there had been no advantage given to Locke by putting from the different position, since the ball was not closer to the hole and the margin of victory was sufficient not to have altered the outcome. For once, the rules of golf were sensibly interpreted, and a fine champion retained his title.

There was a time when a scheduling conflict made it impossible to play in the U.S. and British opens the same year, even if jets had been available for travel. That was in 1907. Both were contested during the same week, and champions were crowned on the same day—June 21. Arnaud Massy won at Hoylake and Alex Ross at the Philadelphia Cricket Club.

On the Champions Tour, the youngest golfer to shoot or better his age was Walter Morgan, who recorded a 60 at Essex Golf Club during the 2002 Canadian Senior Open, when he was 61 years old.

The oldest golfer to shoot or better his age on the Champions Tour was Jug McSpaden. The former "Gold Dust Twin," as he was called along with Byron Nelson, returned an 81 in the 1994 Senior PGA Championship at the age of 84.

Jerry Barber holds the record for the most strokes shot under his age in a PGA-sponsored event. When he was 78, the former PGA champion shot 69 at the 1994 Kroger Classic on the Champions Tour.

The year before was also one in which Barber made golf news. He had lost his exemption on the Champions Tour, but he still wanted to play tournament golf. As the 1961 PGA champion, Jerry had a lifetime exemption on the regular circuit. He took advantage of it by entering the Phoenix Open to become the oldest golfer to ever play on the PGA Tour at the age of 77.

Gene Sarazen is the oldest to ever play in the Open. Returning to Troon in 1973, he was 71 years old. He was given an exemption, because it marked the 50th anniversary of his first start in the Open, also at Troon.

A three-time winner of the PGA Championship, Sarazen was also one of the organization's greatest boosters. He holds the record for longevity as a member of the PGA of America, some 78 years.

The use of steel-shafted clubs was first authorized by the Royal and Ancient in 1929, five years after the USGA had approved them. The announcement stated, "The Rules of Golf Committee have decided that steel shafts, as approved by the Rules of Golf Committee, are declared to conform with the requirements of the clause in the rules of golf on the form and make of golf clubs."

The last national championship won by a golfer using hickory shafts was the 1936 U.S. Amateur, taken by Johnny Fischer.

In 1938, the USGA passed a rule limiting the number of clubs a golfer could carry to 14. Prior to that time, it was not unusual for some golfers to have several extra clubs, just in case they were needed. Walter Hagen, for example, carried a left-handed club that he used effectively, since he was ambidextrous.

A story was told of Henry Picard hitting a 2 iron on the range, replacing it, and hitting another 2 iron. When a spectator asked the difference between the two clubs, Henry replied, "Two yards." Perhaps the record was set by Lawson Little, who at one time had 31 clubs in his bag.

The Tuctu Golf Club in Morococha, Peru, is 14,335 feet above sea level.

Highest golf course in terms of elevation in the United States is the Mount Massive Golf Club in Leadville, Colorado. It's 10,200 feet above sea level.

*L*ocated 50 miles south of the Arctic Circle is the Green Zone Golf Course in Tornio, Finland, and Haparanda, Sweden. Yes, the course is located in both countries. A putt on the sixth hole can actually pass through different time zones.

There is also a requirement for non-Scandinavians that they carry a "borderline passport" with them at all times so they won't be violating any laws when they cross between the two nations.

*I*n terms of elevation, the world's lowest golf course is the Furnace Creek Golf Club, located in Death Valley, California. It is 214 feet below sea level. There once was a golf course at Kallia, south of Jericho, which was 1,250 feet below sea level. It ran along the northeastern shore of the Dead Sea.

*I*n 1911, the fifth hole at Annandale Golf Club in Pasadena, California, was called "La Canvada." Of course, it is not unusual for golf holes to have names. The surprising thing is that the scorecard listed the 409-yarder as a par 4½. It wasn't the only one on the course. The 8th and 13th holes were both listed as 3½ and the 16th as 5½. Would a 4 on the 5th be a birdie-par, a half-birdie, or a birdie-and-a-half?

*A*ugusta National golf holes also have names. It should probably not be a surprise that the names are of trees and flowers, since the land on which the course is built was originally a nursery. The 13th is the Azalea Hole, and it is estimated that 1,600 azaleas border the par 5.

*W*ith Bobby Jones retiring at the age of 28, following his great year of 1930, there was the question of who might follow in his footsteps. During the playing of the U.S. Open the next year, it appeared that it might not be anyone. At the end of regulation play, Billy Burke and George Von Elm were deadlocked at 292.

Von Elm had made his mark as a golfer, twice defeating Jones in the U.S. Amateur, but he had since turned professional, although he referred to himself as a "businessman golfer."

Both the 1928 and 1929 championships had ended in a tie, and those play-offs were set for 36 holes. This one was scheduled for the same distance. Burke shot 73 in the morning to take a two-stroke lead, but when he had a 76 in the afternoon, the golfers were still tied.

Off they went the following day for 36 more, and this time, Burke was successful, earning a one-stroke victory, 148 to 149. It took 144 holes to determine who would be the first U.S. Open champion after Jones. The USGA decided on 18-hole play-offs after 1931.

*D*uring the 1926 British Open, Jones forgot his contestant's badge, which allowed him to enter the grounds. Following the third round, Jones invited Al Watrous to join him for lunch and to relax in his room at the Majestic Hotel. Jones was one stroke behind Al with the final round to be played that afternoon. When the two golfers returned, a gate official refused him entrance, obviously not knowing the name of the contestants or recognizing the golf legend. Even though Watrous, who had his badge, vouched for Jones, the official wouldn't budge. Jones simply went to the public entrance, stood in line behind some spectators, and purchased a ticket for five shillings. Naturally, he won the championship.

*R*obert T. Jones III played as an amateur in the 1950 Empire State Open, a PGA Tour event, making the cut and scoring 76-77-73-88 for a 314.

*A*fter Harry Vardon became the first professional to sign an endorsement contract, others followed, not always using the products. Byron Nelson, for example, was embarrassed that ads appeared with him endorsing cigarettes and tried to give the money back, to no avail.

In the days before the 14-club limit, Walter Hagen carried as many as 24 different implements, mainly because he endorsed them. It didn't mean that Walter used them, but they were in the golf bag in case anyone looked.

*A*ny person who has worked as a volunteer for a championship probably knows the amount of thought that goes into the placement of the cups each day. Both the R&A and the USGA go to great lengths to make sure the proper number of hard-, easy-, and medium-pin placements are used. That wasn't always the case.

As late as the 1949 British Open at Sandwich, England, the same hole positions were used all four rounds of the championship proper. It wasn't until Bobby Locke, who was to be in a play-off with Harry Bradshaw, threatened not to play that the committee agreed to change the positions.

*W*hen a pond on a par-3 hole at the Eisenhower Golf Course in Annapolis, Maryland, was dredged in 1971, over 600 golf balls were recovered from the water. Of those, more than 200 were range balls with head pro Al Green's name on them.

*T*aking into account that the best-selling books by category in Great Britain were sports, pets, and World War II, an author decided to take advantage of those facts. In 1975, Alan Coren penned *Golfing for Cats* and placed a swastika on the dust cover.

*F*ive amateurs have won the U.S. Open. They are Francis Ouimet, Jerome Travers, Chick Evans, Bobby Jones, and Johnny Goodman. From 1913 through 1919, the only professional to win the U.S. crown was Walter Hagen, with Ouimet the 1913 champion, Travers winning in 1915, and Evans in 1916.

*O*nly one man has been able to win the U.S. Amateur and U.S. Open on the same course. Jack Nicklaus accomplished it when he won the 1982 U.S. Open at Pebble Beach. With the ladies, it was Julie Inkster, who duplicated the feat with her victory in the U.S. Women's Open at Prairie Dunes, Hutchinson, Kansas, in 2002, the same course on which she won the U.S. Women's Amateur in 1980.

*I*n the LPGA Tour, four amateurs have been able to win tournaments since it was founded in 1950. The first winner was Polly Riley in the 1950 Tampa Open; then Pat O'Sullivan, the long-driving golfer, captured the 1951 Titleholders Championship; Catherine La Coste won the 1967 U.S. Women's Open; and JoAnne Carner took the 1969 Burdine's Invitational. JoAnne turned professional the next year, winning enough tournaments to qualify for the LPGA Hall of Fame.

*N*o amateur has ever won the Masters.

*O*nly Jack Nicklaus, Nick Faldo, and Tiger Woods have been able to repeat as Masters champions.

*T*ommy Aaron became the oldest to ever make the cut at the Masters when he played all four rounds in 2000 at the age of 63.

*F*or professionals, prize money is always important. At the Masters, the amateurs are also rewarded if they complete 72 holes. The low amateur receives a sterling silver cup, while the amateur runner-up takes home a silver medal. Winning, whether as a professional or an amateur, results in a gold medal and a sterling silver Masters' trophy replica, with the runner-up winning a silver medal and a sterling silver salver.

Other golfers are able to collect items that are greatly treasurered, even without finishing first or second. Any golfer making an eagle receives a pair of crystal goblets, and a hole-in-one is commemorated with a crystal bowl. The golfer returning the low round of the day is presented with a crystal vase.

*W*ith the exception of the majors, there are no 36-hole cuts on the Champions Tour. When Jack Nicklaus began playing with the seniors in 1990, he was able to make the cut in 43 straight majors. That streak came to an end in the 2003 Senior PGA Championship at Aronimink Golf Club, Newtown Square, Pennsylvania, when he shot 150 to miss by three strokes. During that run, Jack won eight senior majors.

*S*even golfers did not defend their U.S. Open titles: Harry Vardon in 1901; Alex Smith, 1907; Jerome Travers, 1916; Ted Ray, 1921; Bobby Jones, 1931; Ben Hogan, 1949; and Payne Stewart, 2000.

Hogan was, of course, involved in an auto accident, which prevented his participation in 1949, while Stewart lost his life in an airplane crash in 1999.

*W*hen Walter Hagen won his first British Open at Sandwich in 1922, he endorsed his winning check over to his caddie. Walter's interest was in the title and the exhibitions it would bring, not the prize money. Of course, the Haig never did worry too much about money. His concern was what the money could bring in comforts. He did the same thing after his 1929 victory at Muirfield.

Arnold Palmer almost did Walter one better, although that wasn't his intent. Winning the 1958 Masters gave Arnold his first major as a professional. In all the excitement, he asked his wife to write a check in the amount of $1,400 for his caddie, Nathaniel "Iron Man" Avery. Winnie was a little caught up in what had just happened and, in her haste, added a zero to the check, making it out for $14,000.

Since the first-place check was for $11,200, it was a net loss to Palmer. The mistake was cleared up on Sunday evening when Iron Man was trying to cash the check at Augusta National Golf Club. Arnold received a call to verify the amount. Avery received a check the following morning with the correct total.

*A*nother golfer surprised his caddie with an unusual tip. In 1933, George Dunlap participated in the British Amateur at Hoylake in the Liverpool area. He made it to the semifinal round, losing to Michael Scott. Following the championship, Dunlap bought a used car to drive to St. Andrews, where he played in the British Open.

It wasn't much of an automobile, breaking down twice along the route. But when he finished the Open, he gave the car to his caddie, who was only too pleased to receive such a gift.

*P*laying golf has become common among U.S. presidents. Jimmy Carter was the lone exception in recent years. The only golfing president who was once a caddie was Bill Clinton; he toted bags in his native Arkansas during the 1960s. Gerald Ford had also been a caddie but just for his grandfather, not as a regular.

GEORGE HERBERT WALKER BUSH

*P*resident George Herbert Walker Bush came from a strong golfing background. His father, Prescott S. Bush, was president of the USGA in 1935, and his uncle, George Herbert Walker, also held that position in 1920. If the name sounds familiar, it's because he donated the Walker Cup, which is competed for biennially in matches between amateur teams from the United States and Great Britain.

*C*hi Chi Rodriguez has told stories about his caddie days many times, but little known is that he also played another sport. In 1953, Chi Chi was a baseball player with the Saballana Start, a Class A minor-league team. Another member of that team was Hall of Famer Roberto Clemente.

*M*any courses have what is referred to as a "signature" hole. A public facility in Yakima, Washington, was opened in 1992, and they may have taken the meaning to a new dimension. The 17th has an island green in the shape of an apple, complete with a bunker designed to look like a leaf and a bridge constructed to resemble the stem. Not surprisingly, the name of the course is Apple Tree. The putting surface isn't red, however. It's a little green apple or, more accurately, a big green apple.

*W*hen you think of golf courses that have hosted the U.S. Open and that would have yielded the most consecutive birdies, Pebble Beach would probably not top the list. There are so many difficult holes there, and to make a birdie on just about any of them, perfect shots must be hit.

Still, the record for the most consecutive birdies in that championship is six, and it's held by two golfers. The first was George Burns, with Andy Dillard duplicating it. Both set the standard at Pebble Beach, Burns in 1982 and Dillard 10 years later.

The youngest winner of the U.S. Amateur at one time was Robert A. Gardner, when he took the 1909 championship at the age of 19 years, 5 months. That record lasted until 1994, when Tiger Woods won the title at the age of 18 years, 7 months, and 29 days, when the championship was held at the Tournament Players Club in Ponte Vedra, Florida.

Golf books, especially instruction books, are plentiful. It seems that if a golf professional wins any tournament, a publisher will make a telephone call to propose yet another book that will explain the proper stance, grip, and swing.

The best-selling golf instruction book in history continues to be *Five Lessons: The Modern Fundamentals of Golf*, which was written by Ben Hogan with Herbert Warren Wind, perhaps the best American golf writer of all time.

Not really a golf instruction book, *Harvey Penick's Little Red Book* became the best-selling sports book in history, not just in golf.

Only one non-British golfer had been able to win the British Open prior to 1921, and he was French. The Americans had begun to realize how important the championship was the year before, when Walter Hagen made his first appearance in a very unsuccessful attempt to take the trophy across the Atlantic. Another contingent made its way by ship in 1921 to compete at St. Andrews.

One of those was Jock Hutchison, a naturalized American who had won the PGA Championship the year before. By this time, the Scots were looking for a hero, as the English were dominating the Open. Since Jock was a native of St. Andrews before making his way to America, there were a great many Scots cheering him on. After all, he was still a Scot. Hutchison made many friends and relatives happy when he won the play-off from Roger Wethered, a British amateur.

It was a play-off that might not have occurred for a couple of reasons. The first was an incident that happened in the third round on the 14th hole. Following his drive, Roger walked forward to get a better look at what he was facing for the next shot. Returning, he stepped on his ball by mistake; he received a one-stroke penalty. There is no telling what Wethered might have shot in the final round without that penalty, but it's interesting to speculate.

The British amateur wasn't sure that he wanted to participate in the play-off. He had promised friends that he would play for his hometown in a cricket match the following day and felt very strongly that he should fulfill his commitment. Only at the urging of friends did he decide to participate in the play-off.

In spite of the fact that Jock originally came from Scotland, there were some who were not happy that he took the trophy back to America. It was easy for the R&A to blame a golf club used by Hutchison as part of the reason for his being successful. The culprit seemed to have been a mashie niblick that had large grooves, allowing Jock to put backspin on the ball. The ruling body was quick to act. The same day the final results were announced in the *St. Andrews Citizen*, a notice next to the list advised that the R&A had banned clubs with those types of grooves. It may have been a St. Andrean who won, but he was still an American, and the ruling body tainted his title.

*F*ive golfers have been named "Sportsman of the Year" by *Sports Illustrated*: Arnold Palmer, 1960; Ken Venturi, 1964; Lee Trevino, 1971; Jack Nicklaus, 1978; and Tiger Woods, 1996 and 2000.

Possibly an even greater distinction is being named the Associated Press Male Athlete of the Year. Five golfers have also received that award. The first was Gene Sarazen in 1932, followed by Byron Nelson in 1944 and 1945. Ben Hogan received the distinction in 1953, Lee Trevino in 1971, and Tiger Woods was named three times—1997, 1999, and 2000.

*B*obby Jones officially retired from competition following his great year in 1930. However, he continued to play in the Masters even though he only made the appearances to satisfy the demand of his many fans who turned out to watch the tournament and to be able to enjoy some golf with old friends.

With the exception of the war years, when the event was not held, Jones competed from 1934 until 1948. His final appearance resulted in a tie for 49th place, when he shot 76-81-79-79 for a 315.

*T*here were quite a few rumblings in 1948 when Babe Zaharias indicated she would enjoy playing in the U.S. Open scheduled at Riviera and competing against the men. The USGA rushed to clarify their "men only" policy, which they said was their intention from the beginning.

*T*he Babe had to be content with dominating women's tournaments and beating men in exhibitions. Still, she was the first woman to ever play in a PGA-sponsored event when she entered the 1938 Los Angeles Open at Griffith Park. Unfortunately, Zaharias failed to make the cut, shooting 84-81. She later played in the 1945 Los Angeles Open with scores of 76-81-79. The Babe missed the 54-hole cut that was in place that year.

She also played in the 1945 Phoenix and Tucson opens. The first came on a sponsor's invitation, and she finished 33rd. The Babe had to qualify for Tucson and finished in 42nd place.

*W*hen is a hole in one less than a 1 on the scorecard? When the golfer receives a handicap stroke. In a club event held at the Plainfield Country Club in New Jersey, the format was two best-balls of four. Jack Mayor, a 30-handicapper, was receiving two strokes on the 165-yard 14th hole. He hit a 3 wood and aced the hole for a net minus: -1. His partner, Kermit Dyke, carrying a 17 handicap, made a par for a net 2. The combined score for the team was +1. Even with those heroics, they did not win the competition.

*M*ost Champions Tour events are 54-hole tournaments. The designated majors are usually the exception and are 72-hole events. In the history of the Champions Tour, only the 1999 Tradition, a designated major and a 72-hole tournament, was shortened to 36 holes. The culprit was, of course, weather. In this case, it snowed in Arizona during April, causing officials to declare Graham Marsh the champion of the abbreviated event.

*I*t has been estimated that during an 18-hole round of golf, the ball is in contact with the face of a club for less than one-half second.

CHAPTER THREE

FEATS

Golf has never been a mechanical game in spite of attempts to make it that way by some dedicated people. Ben Hogan was thought of by many as a mechanical golfer. Yet he bristled at the suggestion. Surely, he practiced as much as anyone to get the mechanics of the swing to a point where he could trust in what he was going to do in certain situations. What seems to separate golf from other sports is that there is time to think about what is going to happen next. In other physical games, immediate reaction to the situation at hand becomes the important element. There is little time to adjust to what is happening. Certainly training is necessary to swing at a pitch that is low and away, and the adjustment has to be made immediately so the bat will meet the ball in the proper place. The same is true when a runner is about to be tackled and must cut or go ahead without the benefit of listing all of his options. To paraphrase a Bobby Jones quote, the toughest distance for a golfer is six inches—the length between his two ears.

Thinking about what has to be done makes golf so difficult. Walking from one shot to the next gives a golfer time to think. The thoughts going through the mind can make a simple pitch over water a monumental task. A professional whose name I can no longer remember said that when he was young, he would look at a putt and see three ways to make it and only one way to miss. As he matured, he looked at a putt and saw one way to make it and three ways to miss. It's that six inches between the ears.

We never own the game. It may only be borrowed for a period of time. That time is longer for a Ben Hogan or a Jack Nicklaus, but even they were humbled during their careers. Golf is the only game in which you can lose tournaments more often than win them and still be considered a champion. A defending champion can miss the cut the following year. Ralph Guldahl won the Masters, two U.S. Opens, and three Western Opens over a three-year stretch and then disappeared from the winner's circle. Ian Baker-Finch became the British Open champion and then, inexplicably, couldn't make a 36-hole cut. The swing looked the same, but the results were not.

People will always remember the great shots that settled the majors. Those that immediately come to mind include the 4 wood for a double eagle by Sarazen in the 1935 Masters, perhaps the most famous shot ever struck by a golfer. Watson's chip in at the U.S. Open at Pebble Beach and the chip holed by Larry Mize on the second play-off hole in the Masters Tournament are others. Still, a shot or great accomplishment in some other event is still monumental to that participant. There have been numerous feats by golfers who will never make the pages in any history of golf. That's because they were accomplished in club events or on a Saturday afternoon playing friends for a one-dollar Nassau. Long before I joined Indianwood in Lake Orion, Michigan, there was a member named Ben Jaroslaw. An accomplished golfer, Ben won both the club and senior club championships.

Everyone who knew Ben called him Jaws, his nickname coming from his habit of nonstop talking. For club team events, he would hold trials, inviting a potential team member to play with him so he could observe the member's strengths and weaknesses. One of his finds was John Lathan, a man who could hit the ball tremendous lengths. John qualified for the National Long Drive Championships on a couple of occasions, and Ben wanted to see how far he could hit it. Until Lathan became better known, Ben won a number of scramble events with John on the team.

If I ran into Ben at the men's grill, he would begin to tell me about an event he had recently played in—at length. It would start at the first hole and continue until my only thought was that I hoped the match didn't go into a play-off. I could drink three cups of coffee before he explained how the ninth hole was played. But to Jaws, winning that event was as important as winning the U.S. Open, and the shots he or his opponent hit were memories to be savored.

One of the first inductees into the Michigan Golf Hall of Fame was Chuck Kocsis, a two-time member of the Walker Cup team and the most titled amateur golfer in the state's history. When he was inducted into the Hall of Fame, Chuck was given an honorary membership at Indianwood. While he was a life member at Red Run Golf Club in Royal Oak, Michigan, he could be seen at Indianwood on a fairly regular basis. One evening, Jaws and his wife, Sandy, came into the clubhouse for dinner. While they were escorted to their table in the dining room, Ben noticed that Kocsis was having dinner with his wife and two guests. Jaws immediately went over to Chuck's table and began talking about old times, recalling when he had caddied for Chuck's brother in tournaments. Instead of a brief visit, the conversation continued for close to an hour. During all of it, Sandy sat at the table alone waiting for Ben to join her for their anniversary dinner.

Unknowns have won the major championships and seldom been heard of again. Unlikely champions such as Sam Parks Jr., Jack Fleck, Fred Daly, and Richard Burton had their time in the sun. For one week, they were the best in the field. That they peaked at the right time and became champions is something that can never be taken away from them. They are the exceptions, of course, but they are still remembered for their moments of glory. More often we recall the consistent winners and what they have done. Only a Walter Hagen would have the nerve, when needing a full mashie to hole on the final green to tie Bobby Jones, to ask to have the pin held. That the ball covered the flag all the way is testimony to his ability and self-confidence. When Ben Hogan won the British Open at Carnoustie, those who followed him felt that he would have scored whatever was necessary on the last round to become champion. That round and his 67 at Oakland Hills in 1951 are considered two of the finest final rounds ever played in a men's major championship, not taking anything away from Johnny Miller's closing 63 at Oakmont in 1973. Byron Nelson's streak of 11 consecutive victories on the PGA Tour in 1945 will probably never be duplicated. We may never see anyone win four consecutive Open Championships as did Young Tommy Morris or four straight PGA Championships as Walter Hagen did in the 1920s. Those and other feats on the golf course should never be forgotten.

It is my firm belief that champions of one era would have been champions in another. What they did was play the best golf the world had known at that time, raising the standard for others to follow. I am absolutely convinced that the scores recorded by past champions like Gene Sarazen, Harry Vardon, or others would have been lower if they had been born 50 years later and competed against another group of golfers. They would have adapted to the different equipment and conditions. It was what was in their heart that made them great.

From 1921 until 1934, British golfers had not fared too well in the Open Championship. Only Arthur Havers was able to win during that stretch, which saw the Americans dominate. Henry Cotton changed that. Much in the manner in which Walter Hagen conducted himself, Cotton seemed to have been born to greatness. Henry's confidence in himself probably gave him an advantage over others, and that was especially true on the golf course. So excited were the British when Cotton won the 1934 championship that he immediately became a national sports hero.

That year, he set the championship record at Sandwich with a 65 in the second round. A golf company named a ball after his accomplishment, the "Dunlop 65," which became the best seller in Great Britain for many years and was then renamed the "Maxfli 65."

What Henry accomplished that year was truly amazing. In the first round, he returned a 67, so his 132 total after 36 holes was also a record. The rules for the 36-hole cut used at that time eliminated all golfers who were more than 14 strokes behind the leader. So dominating was Cotton in that Open that if the rule had been followed, only five golfers would have played the final two rounds. The R&A changed the requirement so more players could participate.

Shortly before his death in 1987, Cotton learned that he was to be dubbed a knight, the first golfer so honored. Unfortunately, the ceremony did not take place before he passed away, and T. Henry Cotton was never to hear himself called Sir Henry.

*A*nother historic round played in a national championship was also turned in by Henry Cotton. On his way to the British Open title at Muirfield in 1948, Henry broke the course record with a 66; but what made it very special was that King George VI was in his gallery.

*O*ne of the most demanding golf courses in the world is the Carnoustie Golf Links, Scotland. Golf has been played in the area since before Christopher Columbus first discovered the New World. Allan Robertson, however, designed the first formal layout in 1850. It was then extended to 18 holes by Tom Morris.

Finally, James Braid was hired to redesign the course in 1926, under the watchful eye of James Wright, chairman of the Links Management Committee. Wright was instrumental in bringing the Open Championship to Carnoustie in 1921. The tees, which are normally used by most competitors, are even called the "James Wright Tees."

He was apparently quite a golfer himself, not merely an administrator. Legend has it that Wright played the first three holes in 2-2-1 in 1911, not once but on three separate occasions. With the holes all par 4s and measuring 291, 412, and 316 yards, respectively, at that time, it was quite an accomplishment.

*T*he longest continuous service at one golf club by a British professional was 60 years. Jack Morris, a nephew of Old Tom and Young Tommy's cousin, served in that position at Royal Liverpool from 1869 until 1929.

*P*rofessionals don't have to work at a golf club to set longevity records. When Miller Barber decided to quit competing on the Champions Tour after 2003, he had played in 593 of its tournaments. His success in competing against other seniors can be measured by his 24 victories and the fact that he is only person to win three U.S. Senior Open championships.

When his 689 appearances on the PGA Tour are added, Barber had 1,282 total starts, more than 100 over his nearest challenger. While Miller owns the American record, it is difficult to determine who might hold it worldwide. Both Roberto De Vicenzo and Gary Player have played in numerous tournaments around the globe.

*M*uch had been made of the fact that Ellsworth Vines and Frank Connor, two American golf professionals, were the only two who played in U.S. opens in both golf and tennis. But neither were able to claim victories in the championships. To do so would be an incredible accomplishment.

There was one person who had a double in those different sports— Charlotte Dod. Between 1887 and 1893, she won five Wimbledon singles titles. Turning to golf, she won the British Ladies Championship in 1904 at Troon, becoming the first person to win major titles in two different sports.

*R*anked on the same level as Charlotte Dod would be the accomplishment of Babe Didrikson Zaharias. She won two gold medals at the 1932 Olympics and three U.S. Women's opens.

*E*very golf course has a course record, official or not. In 1987, Curtis Strange shot a 62 during the Dunhill Cup at St. Andrews to break the record for the Old Course. While it may not be the oldest course record, it is on the oldest course.

*T*here were 131,218 rounds of golf played at Rancho Park in Los Angeles during 1976, the most on any single course in a given year in the continental United States. The course goes through 90,000 scorecards annually. While fewer golfers play the Old Course at St. Andrews, their printing run is higher, somewhere in the area of 200,000. It's amazing how many scorecard collectors there must be in this world.

*I*t began in 1919. Up to that time, Ralph Kennedy had played on 176 different golf courses and had the signed scorecards as proof. Kennedy hadn't saved the cards to prove that he had played the courses; it was simply a way of remembering where he had played the game he loved so much.

That year he met a gentleman from England, Charles Leonard Fletcher, who told Ralph that he had played 240 different courses, which he thought might be a world record. Fletcher, too, had kept the cards to authenticate his accomplishment. While there was no authority to verify whether it was indeed a record, Kennedy took it as a challenge. By 1926, he had matched Fletcher's total, which then stood at 445. Ralph wasn't done.

When he turned 50 in 1932, Kennedy reached the 1,000 milestone. He continued to keep the cards, mostly signed by the golf professionals at each site, and carefully placed them in a safe-deposit box.

The big day really came on September 17, 1951. Ralph placed his ball on the first tee of the Old Course. All of the golf he had played through the years didn't help him overcome the jitters he felt as he prepared to hit the drive on his 3,000th different course. Fortunately, because there were newsmen and photographers standing behind him to witness the historic shot, Kennedy hit the ball 180 yards right down the middle of the fairway.

When he finally finished, Ralph had played on 3,035 different courses, each authenticated. His record stands today. Joe Kirkwood estimated that he had played on more than 5,000 courses, but he did not keep scorecards to back the claim.

*D*wight Eisenhower was the head of the European Theater of Operations during World War II and was awarded an honorary membership by the R&A. He decided to play the Old Course, and just like Ralph Kennedy, he had a case of nerves as he stood on the first tee. Word had spread that the general was to play, and a large number of townspeople showed up to see the future president participate in his favorite sport. A bit concerned about embarrassing himself, Ike walked the first hole and hit his opening shot from the second tee.

*S*o dominating was Tiger Woods in winning the 1997 Masters that he set 18 records and tied 6 others for that major event.

*I*n the 1998 Sprint International, Woods made a hole-in-one, an eagle two on a par-4 hole, and an eagle three on a par-5 hole. It is the only time that such a feat was accomplished on the PGA Tour.

*W*hen the ladies have a special fun day at Blythefield Country Club in Grand Rapids, Michigan, the committee sets up the course in such a way that good golf is next to impossible. They even adopt some special rules that must be followed to the letter. On the 120-yard third hole, the women who played right-handed had to use a man's left-handed 2 iron, which was provided at the tee. To make the hole even more difficult, a rope was coiled around the hole.

That didn't stop Sharon Wernstrom. She turned the club over, swinging right-handed, and scored an ace. Sharon carried a 39 handicap.

*O*n July 15, 2003, Aaron Gieseke made a hole-in-one on the fourth hole at Old Hickory Golf Club in the Rochester, New York, area. It was his first ace—and coming on a par-4 hole, measuring 306 yards, made it even more special. Aaron wasn't done.

Playing the same course about six weeks later, he aced another par-4 hole. This time it was the 327-yard ninth hole. Aaron still wasn't done. On October 12, he was back at Old Hickory, and he aced the fourth for the second time. Within a period of less than three months, Gieseke made three holes-in-one on par-4 holes, something that had never been reported before or since.

$\mathcal{A}$s par 5s go, those at Augusta National are not known for their length, although there have been steps taken recently to add yardage. Instead, they are strategic in that a well-struck shot will be rewarded; but if a ball is mishit, disaster surely can result. Only 485 yards long, the 15th hole at Augusta National is that type of a hole. The golfer wishing to reach the green in two must weigh the possibility of being short and ending up in the water.

During the 1935 Masters, Gene Sarazen was faced with such a shot. He was paired with Walter Hagen, who was simply playing out the holes on the final round, anxious to get on with posttournament activities, which included the companionship of a young lady. He was encouraging his friend to get moving so he could begin his evening. Gene, on the other hand, was still in the hunt, although a great roar from the gallery at the 18th made the task at hand formidable. Word spread rapidly, and by the time they reached their drive positions, Sarazen discovered Craig Wood had birdied the final hole for a 282 total.

He turned to his caddie, Stovepipe, asking what he needed to win. At first, Stovepipe was bewildered, then realized Gene was serious and checked the scorecard. He replied, "You need four 3s, Mr. Gene, 3-3-3-3."

To tie, Sarazen would still have to shoot 13 on the final holes, three under regulation figures. Gene looked at his lie, and it was not the most pleasant sight for a golfer. He was 220 yards from the green, and it was tight. Concerned that he couldn't get a 3 wood up from the close lie, Sarazen decided to hit a 4 wood. With the length required, he further felt he would have to hook the club a bit to get the distance necessary to fly the water. There was little question in Gene's mind. He had to go for it. Without a birdie on the 15th, his chance of catching Wood would be next to impossible. Even with a birdie, he would have to make two more on the following three holes.

Then a little superstition crept into the situation. The night before the final round, Sarazen saw an old friend, Bob Davis, who gave him a lucky ring. Davis said he had received it from someone in Mexico City, and it was the ring Juarez was wearing when he was murdered. Gene didn't think that was such a wonderful incident, but Davis insisted it was still a lucky ring and Sarazen should wear it the next day. It was a large, ornate thing, and Gene said it would be a problem for his grip, although he agreed to carry it in his pocket. Before hitting his second, Sarazen remembered the ring, took it out of his pocket, and rubbed it on Stovepipe's head. Later, Davis would confess that the ring was just a little trinket he had bought in Mexico and that he had made up the Juarez story, but for the moment, it may have had a little luck in it. At least it relieved some of the tension.

Sarazen took his stance and laced into the ball. The shot couldn't have come off any better. It headed straight for the flag on a low trajectory, and Gene knew he had hit it hard enough to carry the water. It flew to the green, hopping straight for the cup. There was a small gallery behind the green, and they began to yell and jump. It was a double eagle, the rarest of shots, and he had picked up the three strokes on Wood in one hole. Gene couldn't pick up another needed birdie on the last three holes, but he did par in and then won the play-off the following day. By doing so, he became the first golfer to win all four major titles in a lifetime—the U.S. Open, PGA Championship, British Open, and the Masters. Only Ben Hogan, Gary Player, Jack Nicklaus, and Tiger Woods have been able to match the feat.

Through the years, thousands have told Sarazen they witnessed his double eagle, when, in reality, the gallery was very small. Most were watching the leader, Craig Wood. After his score had been posted for the 15th, many came running to see his final three pars. It was probably the most famous shot ever played in any tournament up to that time, but it would not have had the impact if Gene had faltered the rest of the way or lost the play-off.

What really thrilled Gene, however, was that the shot was witnessed by two of his greatest golfing competitors, Bobby Jones and Walter Hagen.

*H*aving attended Stanford University, Tom Watson played Pebble Beach whenever he had the opportunity, and that was on a fairly regular basis. He loved the course and knew it very well.

So did Jack Nicklaus. Jack had already won both the U.S. Amateur and U.S. Open on the layout. It probably should have come as no surprise that the 1982 U.S. Open would result in the two fighting it out for the championship.

Having completed his round, Nicklaus observed what was happening on television, as Watson came to the 17th hole, a difficult par 3. When Tom hit his tee shot over the green, Jack felt his chances had just improved. Watson's ball settled in the rough above the hole. He faced a next-to-impossible shot. With the green running away from him, the odds of getting the ball near the hole seemed remote. If it could stop within 10 feet of the cup, it would be a great accomplishment. All Bruce Edwards, Watson's caddie, could say was "Get it close."

With supreme confidence, Watson replied, "Get it close, hell, I'm going to make it." He did just that. The chip became one of the most famous shots ever hit in a major, ranking with Sarazen's 4 wood. With another birdie on 18, Tom was victorious in his continuing duel with Nicklaus, costing Jack a record fifth U.S. Open title.

Fast-forward to 2003 and another U.S. Open, this one held at Olympia Fields outside Chicago. Watson was given an exemption by the USGA, along with Hale Irwin and Tom Kite. Bruce Edwards was on his bag, but it was different. Bruce had been diagnosed with Lou Gehrig's disease, or amyotrophic lateral sclerosis (ALS). He had high medical bills, and the disease didn't allow him to function as he once did. Tom never abandoned his caddie of so many years. He did all he could to help Bruce and also led the way in trying to raise funds to find a cure for ALS.

The opening round of that U.S. Open was magic. On his third hole of the championship (the 12th), Tom holed an iron from the fairway for an eagle. When it was over, Watson, now 53 years old, scored a 65, earning a tie for the lead with Brett Quigley. It matched the lowest round that Watson had ever recorded in his 105 rounds in the championship.

It was hard to find a dry eye in the gallery or among the millions watching on television. The round will truly be remembered for many years as one when two friends shared a day of greatness. Sadly, Bruce Edwards passed away just before Watson began his first round in the 2004 Masters.

The longest hole for any U.S. Open at one time was the 17th on the Lower Course at Baltusrol, measuring 630 yards. Back in 1967, it was a mere 610 yards.

One of the qualifiers that year was Billy Farrell, then an assistant at Baltusrol to his father, Johnny, who had won the U.S. Open in 1928. Billy later went on to become the head professional at the Stanwich Club, a fine layout in Greenwich, Connecticut. During the second round, he hit a 3-wood second that reached the putting surface, becoming the only golfer to hit the green in two shots in any Open played on the Lower Course.

John Daly also chose the second round in the 1993 championship for his heroics. Usually there isn't any need for him to carry a fairway wood, so John only carried a driver in his bag, along with an assortment of irons. After driving the ball 320 yards, he pulled out a 1 iron to negotiate the rest of the distance. It carried 302 yards, bounced twice in the rough and onto the green, where it eventually settled about 45 feet past the cup. He thus became the first and only golfer to hit the green in two shots at the longer distance.

Like some other courses scheduled to host the U.S. Open, Baltusrol's Lower Course had a face-lift prior to hosting the 1954 championship. The person called upon to redesign some of the holes was Robert

Trent Jones. His selection came about because of what Jones had accomplished at Oakland Hills when the 1951 championship was held there.

Oakland Hills was dubbed "the Monster" by Ben Hogan, and the USGA was pleased with the changes. The governing body felt the course had been adjusted to be more in line with the changes in equipment and the talents of modern golfers. Quite naturally some of the members of Baltusrol were concerned that changes in their course might make it too difficult.

The one hole that caused a great deal of comment was the fourth, an innocent par 3 until the golf architect got through with it. After the modification, the tee shot had to carry some 190 yards over water, from the championship tee, to reach the green. Even host, professional, and former U.S. Open champion Johnny Farrell criticized the design and difficulty of the hole. On one visit to the club, Jones listened to the concerns and comments. Finally, he sent Frank Duane, his design associate, to fetch a club and ball. Farrell, Duane, and Jones went to the fourth hole, where Trent teed up, swung the iron, and watched as the ball went into the cup for an ace. End of discussion.

*I*nverness Club, in Toledo, Ohio, in 1920 was the first time that Bobby Jones, Johnny Farrell, Tommy Armour, and Gene Sarazen played in the U.S. Open, and it was quite a freshman class. Those four would go on to win 8 of the next 12 championships.

*S*imply qualifying for the U.S. Open is an accomplishment in itself. One man who did that in 1977 was Jeff Coston. He didn't set the bar too high, hoping to break 80 while at Southern Hills, Tulsa, Oklahoma. With a pair of 79s, Jeff was able reach his goal, but he did not make the 36-hole cut. The following year, he was in the field at Cherry Hills, New Jersey. Again, Coston didn't fare too well, finishing last.

It took him another 22 years to make it into the U.S. Open again, this time at Pebble Beach. It may be one of the longest times between appearances. This time the Seattle-area teaching professional made the most of it. Jeff made the cut, shooting 70-77-80-74 for a 301 and pocketing $12,747. More important, he now has memories of playing a full 72 holes in the most important championship in the world.

*P*erhaps the ultimate test of golf in the world is Pine Valley, Clementon, New Jersey. There is no such thing as an easy hole on the course, since it is built on 184 acres of sand that is never raked. The golfer is faced with hitting exact shots from tee to fairway, between pine trees and over scrub and sand that could have slowed down the troops in Operation Desert Storm.

Woody Platt, a fine Philadelphia amateur who not only captured the city championship regularly but also captured the Pennsylvania State Amateur, knew Pine Valley as well as any golfer alive. One day he set off to play and came away from the first green with a birdie after an excellent drive, a 4 iron to the green and a putt. It's not the easiest of starting holes, playing at 427 yards, and any birdie at Pine Valley is usually a reason to celebrate.

The second hole was only 367 yards but still not an easy hole. Woody managed to carry the 180 yards over the scrub and avoided the series of bunkers along the right side. It calls for an accurate drive, requiring an uphill approach to the elevated green. He hit a 7 iron into the hole, making an eagle.

Three-under par thus far, Platt stood on the third tee and looked over the 185 yards necessary to reach the green, again requiring a carry over the sand. The green is 35 yards long, and the wind is always a factor. All he did was knock it in the hole for an ace, his second consecutive eagle.

Quite long for a par 4, the fourth hole measured 461 yards. The drive has to carry over the sand, which is not unique at Pine Valley, as must the second shot. Woody chose a 4 wood for his approach. After the ball stopped 30 feet from the cup, he made the putt to stand six-under par after only four holes. The fourth green comes back near the clubhouse, and Woody decided that was a good time to treat the other golfers, as well as himself, to a drink in honor of his hole-in-one. They never came out of the clubhouse to complete the round.

*D*uring a round of golf at the MacDill Air Force Base Golf Club in Florida, Curley Thatcher had nine straight one-putt greens. This is not an unusual feat, but Curley did it with one arm. He lost his left arm during World War II.

*B*eing on top of the golfing world for seven consecutive years is a truly outstanding accomplishment. Colin Montgomerie won the Order of Merit from 1993 through 1999. The Order of Merit is the PGA European Tour's more genteel equivalent of the PGA Tour's Leading Money Winner.

*A*nother longevity record is one held by Sam Snead. He became the first professional to win a PGA Tour event in four different decades. His first came in 1937 and his last in 1965. Raymond Floyd tied that record when he won the 1992 Doral Ryder Open; his first victory was in 1963 at the St. Petersburg Open Invitational.

*S*am Snead is credited with 82 official PGA Tour titles and more than 100 titles in professional events. Gary Player won 163 tournaments worldwide, and Roberto De Vicenzo is believed to have more than 200 victories in professional events during his lifetime.

*T*asashi "Jumbo" Osaki could have easily played on the Japan Senior Tour in 2002, since he was 55 years of age. Instead, he opted to play on the regular Japan Tour, where the prize money was about 10 times as great.

Amazingly, Jumbo won the ANA Open that year, the eighth time he had captured the tournament during the 30 years he had participated in that event. It marked his 94th title on the Japan Tour.

*J*ay Sigel played on nine U.S. Walker Cup teams, participating in 33 matches, the most by any player from either team. The record for any British or Irish player is 25 matches by Michael Bonallack, who also played on nine Walker Cup teams. The five-time British Amateur champion was knighted in 1998 for his services to golf. He was the secretary of the Royal and Ancient Golf Club of St. Andrews for 17 years.

Joe Carr was probably the best amateur ever to come out of Ireland. He played on a record 11 Walker Cup teams from 1947 until 1967. Joe was awarded the honor of being named captain of the R&A in 1991 and 1992, at the same time Bonallack was serving as secretary.

*F*rom 1913 to 1936, Walter Hagen made the cut 22 consecutive times in the U.S. Open, the all-time record. Gene Sarazen and Gary Player have both been able to match the record. In the Masters, Jack Nicklaus made the cut in 37 of his 44 appearances through 2004.

*E*ven more remarkable was the streak held by Chick Evans. He competed in 50 consecutive U.S. Amateur championships. It began in 1907, and his final appearance was in 1962, when he was 72 years old. There were six years when the championship was not held because of wars.

GENERATIONS IN GEORGIA

*T*he year 2004 marked the 50th straight year that Arnold Palmer played in the Masters. His appearance was celebrated by all who were fortunate enough to be at the invitational that year and was a very emotional one as well, even for those who viewed the walk up the 18th hole on television that Friday, April 9.

In that Masters, there were 92 other starters. Only 11 of them had even been born when Arnold was invited to play in his first Masters in 1955.

When Carol Semple Thompson was named to represent the United States on the Curtis Cup team in 1974, she was a young lady of 25. Her golf was so good that she could easily have made it on the LPGA Tour as a professional. Instead, Carol decided to remain an amateur all of her life.

In total, she played on 12 U.S. Curtis Cup teams, the last in 2002. It is a record for the most appearances in the international competition, and she won more matches than any other golfer in history in the Curtis Cup. When she played in 2002, not one of her teammates was old enough to have been born when Carol made her first appearance in 1974, and yet she was able to win both of her matches that year.

Beginning with the 1942 Texas Open and lasting through the 1946 New Orleans Open, Byron Nelson finished in the top 10 on the PGA Tour a record 65 consecutive times. Ben Hogan was able to put together the next best two streaks of top-10 finishes, totaling 28 and 26 tournaments.

Alice Ritzman had a round of 68 in the 1979 Colgate-European Open, and it didn't include one birdie. Still, it was one of consistency. She turned the front nine even, recording nine consecutive pars. Then she eagled the 10th and followed that up with eagles on the 12th and 16th. Alice parred the other six holes and became the first and only golfer to record three eagles in one round on the LPGA Tour, all of them on the back nine, another record.

Only Bob Charles and Tom Watson have been able to win the British Open and British Senior Open at the same venue. Charles was successful at Royal Lytham & St. Annes, while Watson won at the Ailsa Course at Turnberry in both championships.

*I*n April 2002, the president of the University of Minnesota, Mark Yudof, announced that men's golf, along with women's golf and men's gymnastics, would be dropped by the school. Money was the reason.

The members of the golf team were looking to transfer to other schools that offered golf programs, but they still had the season to finish. Later, the president altered his decision and said if the teams could raise somewhere in the area of $3 million, they could continue to represent the university with a golf team.

Golf was not the most successful program at the school. In fact, the team had not won a Big Ten Championship since 1972. Still, it had an 88-year record of golf and had qualified for the NCAA Championship on 24 occasions. The young men obviously had a mission, and they began to tackle it with a victory in the Big Ten Championships.

In the NCAA Final, the team was in 16th place after 36 holes. Inspired and determined, Matt Anderson, a walk-on, shot 66 the final day, while the leading golfer on the team, Justin Smith, scored a 69. The heroics on the last day enabled the University of Minnesota to be the only team to finish under par and to edge favorite Georgia Tech by four strokes. It marked the first time since 1979 that a school from the north was able to claim the title.

There were no teary eyes when the announcement came that Mark Yudof was leaving Minnesota to become the chancellor of the University of Texas system. The team did have an opportunity to talk about their victory to another president later in the year. They were invited to the White House, where they met President George W. Bush and presented him with a dozen golf balls that had the Minnesota logo imprinted on them.

*A*ttending a Golf Digest Instruction School at Pinehurst, North Carolina, Gordie Franze, a 15-year-old from Rochester, New York, got involved in a putting contest. He drained 354 consecutive four-foot putts. He putted for more than two hours before he finally missed.

*I*f records were kept for the most consecutive times a ball has been bounced on a club face, the winner might have been Michael Drefs of Lake Lawn Lodge in Delavan, Wisconsin. While an assistant professional at the club in 1985, he kept a ball bouncing 1,192 times. It took him about 20 minutes. He didn't have long to savor his ball-bouncing accomplishment.

The very next year the record was broken by Mark Mooney of Hummelstown, Pennsylvania, with 1,764 bounces, using a wedge. Just to make sure there wasn't any question he set the record, Mark had someone tape his feat for posterity. It's doubtful the video will ever be a big seller.

*O*nly 19 days after celebrating her sixth birthday, Brittany Andreas had another reason to have a party. She used a 4 wood on June 5, 1991, to ace the 85-yard second hole at the Jimmy Clay Golf Course in Austin, Texas, and it happened during a tournament, the Pan American Junior Championships. Brittany, from Columbus, Texas, had to compete in the 9- to 10-year-old division. By scoring her hole-in-one, she became the youngest girl in history to accomplish that feat. Seven-year-old record-holder Lynne Radar made her ace on, coincidentally, the second hole at a course in Tennessee. Before Brittany Andreas made her ace, the record had stood for 23 years.

*B*yron Nelson was noted for being one of the great iron players of all time. Perhaps his greatest strength, however, was his ability to place his drives in the proper position on the fairway to set up his second shot. Still, his reputation for precise iron shots continued, and much of that can be attributed to the two play-off rounds he needed to win the 1939 U.S. Open. During those 36 holes against Denny Shute and Craig Wood, he hit six flagsticks with approach shots, using six different irons.

On his way to the 1937 U.S. Open title at Oakland Hills, Ralph Guldahl hit an approach shot on the 15th, and it looked as if he might have a very large problem. His ball was heading toward the next tee when a man in the gallery jumped out, thinking the ball might hit him. It did, on the heel of his shoe, and then it caromed into a greenside bunker. The result was an easier shot for Guldahl than if it had continued on its original path.

The ball came to rest next to a cigar butt. Ralph blasted out of the sand, sending both the ball and the cigar butt on the green. He made his par, but he didn't try to putt the cigar.

When Gary Player won the U.S. Open at Bellerive in St. Louis, Missouri, in 1965, he donated all of his winnings to charities that included cancer research and junior golf. It was something that had never been done before and a wonderful gesture by a true gentleman.

Playing at Balboa Park Municipal Course in San Diego on October 9, 1983, Scott Palmer began a streak on the 260-yard sixth hole that was unprecedented. He holed it with a driver for a double eagle and, of course, a hole-in-one. The next day he recorded another ace on the eighth hole with a 5 iron. Still in the groove, Scott used a wedge to make yet another on the first hole the following day and then made it four in four days when he scored a hole-in-one on the eighth, this time with a 6 iron. He recorded the most aces on consecutive days, and it makes you wonder if he wasn't a distant relative to another Palmer.

Four airline executives decided to have a little fun in 1983 and do something unusual. What they did was play three rounds of golf in one day on three continents. Sherl Folger, Marvin Fritz, Alain Reisco, and Art Sues started at Royal Modammedia near Casablanca, Morocco, at 5:10 A.M. Next it was the Torrequebrada Golf Course in Malaga, Spain, at 1:37 P.M. and finally a 6:35 P.M. starting time at North Hills Country Club in Manhasset, New York. Aren't airline perks wonderful?

GOLFING ACROSS THE U.S.

*T*here's cross-country golf and there's cross-country golf. Floyd Rood began a round on September 14, 1963, and finished on October 3, 1964, without once being penalized for slow play. Floyd hit his first shot from the shores of the Pacific Ocean and didn't stop until he got to the Atlantic, a distance of just under 3,400 miles. He did it in 114,737 strokes and had 3,511 lost balls. At $24 a dozen, that's $7,021.92.

*E*leven years later, two Belgian club professionals decided to make a little history of their own, not on different continents but in five separate countries. Fortunately, most European countries are small, and travel between them can be accomplished in a short period of time.

Simon Clough and Boris Janjic played 18 holes each in France, Luxembourg, Germany, Belgium, and Holland. No electric carts were used either. They walked the entire 90 holes.

*H*enry Longhurst, a noted golf writer and a fixture at the 16th hole during his tenure as an announcer at the Masters, once made a hole-in-one in an unusual manner. During a round at Letchworth, England, Henry had just holed a shot on the sixth with a mashie. Without returning the club to the bag, he holed his tee shot on the short seventh, two consecutive hole-outs, using the same club.

*C*ertainly the most famous golf club at St. Andrews is the Royal and Ancient. In 1843, another golf club was formed there with the name St. Andrews Mechanic's Golf Club, later renamed the St. Andrews Golf Club, made up of citizens who would possibly not have been considered for membership in the R&A. Apparently they knew how to play the game. Thirteen of its members have won 22 Open championships.

*T*wice a member of the British Walker Cup team, Laddie Lucas grew up playing golf at Prince's Golf Club on the English Channel. During World War II, he was a highly decorated fighter pilot in the RAF and later would be elected to Parliament. There are many who consider him the best left-handed golfer to come out of Great Britain.

Returning from a mission over France, his Spitfire was hit by a German plane, and Laddie instinctively knew he would not make it to the base. Flying over the English Channel, he saw a familiar sight—Prince's Golf Club. Using all of his skill as a pilot, Lucas landed the plane to the side of the ninth fairway. When he emerged, he looked at the wreckage in the rough and said, "I never could hit that fairway."

W. Lawson Little Jr. dominated amateur golf in the mid-1930s. The golf world was looking for another Bobby Jones, and Little certainly didn't disappoint. He won the British Amateur and U.S. Amateur in both 1934 and 1935. It was called the "Little Slam," so named in reference to Jones's "Grand Slam" of 1930.

Little was one of the finest match-play golfers in the world. Against stiff international competition, including a singles victory in the Walker Cup, he won 32 consecutive matches. That bettered the record of 22 straight held by Walter Hagen. After turning professional, Little won the 1940 U.S. Open, along with other tour events, but he was never quite the dominating force that was expected of him.

*T*homas Dowd hit a poor drive on the 367-yard 16th hole at Azalea Sands Golf Club in Myrtle Beach, South Carolina, in 1978. His lie was pretty good, so he decided to hit the driver from the fairway for some added distance, and it came to rest eight feet from the cup. A light-bulb lit up in Dowd's head. He used the driver again for the putt and recorded an all-driver birdie.

*P*ossibly the oldest record on the PGA Tour is the one held by J. Douglas Edgar and set in 1919. That year he won the Canadian Open by 16 strokes over Bobby Jones, Jim Barnes, and Karl Keffer. While Keffer is not a well-known name, the other two became hall-of-famers, so the field was certainly a strong one. It was the largest margin of victory up to and since that time. It has been duplicated twice but never beaten. Joe Kirkwood in the 1924 Corpus Christi Open and Bobby Locke in the 1948 Chicago Victory National Championship also finished 16 strokes ahead of their closest competitors.

*O*n the Champions Tour, the largest margin of victory was 12 strokes. Hale Irwin finished well ahead of runners-up Dale Douglass and Jack Nicklaus in the 1997 Senior PGA Championship at PGA National Golf Club.

*K*enny Perry was able to record back-to-back 64s in the 2001 Buick Open at Warwick Hills, Grand Blanc, Michigan. That wasn't a record, but Kenny did enter the record books in another way when he captured his fourth PGA Tour title. He had 29s for nine holes on both Friday and Saturday, the only time in tour history that a golfer was able to score better than 30 for nine holes twice in the same tournament.

It wasn't as if Warwick Hills was a pushover. The course measured 7,105 yards long.

*W*hen he was only 13 years old, Bobby Jones won the club championships at both Druid Hills and East Lake, both in Atlanta

Georgia. A year later he was the Georgia State Amateur champion. Jack Nicklaus was 16 when he captured the Ohio State Amateur.

*A*nother golf legend, Nancy Lopez, was 12 years old when she won the New Mexico Women's Amateur in 1969. She did it in style, winning 10 and 8 in the final against Mary Bryan, who was 23 years old.

*A*t the same age as Lopez, 12, Martha Burkard captured the San Francisco City Women's Amateur in 2000. It's probably no surprise that all of the other contestants were older, some almost double her age. Martha defeated the defending champion in the quarterfinal and a former college golfer in the final.

*S*ergio Garcia was also 12 when he first won the club championship at Club de Golf de Mediterraneo, Spain, where his father was the head professional. By age 15, Sergio captured the European Amateur. It didn't stop there. When he was a 17-year-old amateur, he won the Catalonian Open, a European PGA Tour event, held in Spain.

*Y*outh was served in a big way during the 2001 California Women's Amateur Championship. After five rounds of match play, the finalists were 12-year-olds: Mina Harigae and Sydney Burlison. They were friends who played and practiced together under coach Nick Nelson.

Mina won the title 3 and 2, making her the youngest winner in the championship's history and wiping out the record previously held by Emilee Klein, who was 14 when she triumphed in 1988.

*P*arents, and especially fathers, usually have great dreams for their children. When the children are born, fathers envision their sons and daughters following in their footsteps, becoming leaders of industry, famous entertainers, or sports heroes. That was certainly the case when Beverly Klass was born.

Before she reached her fourth birthday, her father adapted some golf clubs to fit her and had Beverly hitting shots on the beach at Malibu. At that age, simply getting the ball airborne is an accomplishment. The young lady showed promise, and while the ball didn't travel very far, she made great progress and seemed to enjoy the game. All of the practicing and tutoring seemed to pay dividends. Her father thought he might have another Babe Zaharias on his hands. When Beverly was only eight, her father entered her in the National Pee Wee Tournament. With different age-group classifications, she participated in the 8- and 9-year-old division. Actually, she did more than participate. She won the division by an amazing 65 strokes better than her nearest rival over 36 holes.

Beverly continued to improve as she grew older and stronger. Convinced that his daughter was a golf prodigy, her father showed up at the 1967 Women's Civitan Open in Dallas, Texas. It was an official LPGA event with all of the biggest names in women's golf entered. Officials were somewhat baffled by the man who approached the table with a 10-year-old girl in tow, and even a bit more surprised when he requested that she become a competitor in the tournament. At that time, there were no minimum age requirements for the LPGA. It allowed nonmembers to compete if they paid the entry fee of $50 plus $1 for every $1,000 in total prize money. Klass was allowed to enter in spite of some misgivings, and she basically became a professional then and there. Her first round at the Glen Lakes Country Club was an 88, more than a respectable score for someone her age.

Next, she played in the St. Louis Women's Open, in Missouri, and in one round returned an 82 with a 38 on the back nine. She could obviously play, although her scores could not compare with those of the more experienced competitors. Then Beverly entered the U.S. Women's Open and later the Lady Carling Open in Baltimore, Maryland.

By this time, the LPGA was doing whatever it could to keep Beverly off the tour. If Fred Corcoran had still been the commissioner, he might have tried to turn it into a positive; but the membership didn't want to have such a youngster playing in their events. They attempted to bar her from the Lady Carling Open by citing a Maryland law that prohibited hiring children under the age of 14. The state ruled that she was self-employed, so the ban was lifted and she was allowed to play. The LPGA finally acted on its own, amending the organization's constitution to declare a minimum age for competitors of 18.

Still, Beverly Klass played in four tournaments at the age of ten and won $131 in prize money competing with some of the best women golfers in the world.

While Beverly was the youngest to play in the U.S. Women's Open, there was no sectional qualifying in 1957. Once the qualifying became necessary because of the size of the field, a new record was established in 2001. A 12-year-old named Morgan Pressel, a seventh-grader in Boca Raton, Florida, entered the event and surprised everyone when she scored a two-under-par 70. That qualified her to play at Pine Needles with all of the established stars.

By the time the championship rolled around, Morgan had entered her teens, celebrating her birthday two weeks prior to the opening round. She scored a pair of 77s and missed the cut. All in all, it was a wonderful experience for a 13-year-old.

The record for the youngest winner on the LPGA Tour is held by Marlene Bauer, who was only two weeks past her 18th birthday when she captured the 1952 Sarasota Open.

May Hezlet was the youngest to ever win the British Amateur. She was 17 when she was crowned the champion at Newcastle in 1899.

Word spread out of Hawaii that a young girl by the name of Michelle Wie could hit the ball a mile. She was not yet in high school, but she was an accomplished golfer. It wasn't unusual for her to hit drives more than 300 yards.

An invitation to the Nabisco Championships in 2003 proved she could do more that merely hit long drives. Michelle was in the final group, shooting 76 in the last round and finishing in ninth place. Unfortunately, the LPGA still had the rule in effect that required members to be at least 18 years old, so any appearances in the next five years would not result in winning any money.

Shortly after graduating from the eighth grade, Michelle played in the 2003 U.S. Women's Amateur Public Links. Reaching the final, she defeated Virada Nirapathpongporn, a former NCAA champion from Duke University, 1 up to capture the title. She became the youngest to ever win that championship and the youngest player to ever win any adult USGA title. Michelle eclipsed the old record held by Laura Baugh, who was 16 years old when she won the 1971 U.S. Women's Amateur.

*W*hen he was only 14, Bobby Jones qualified for the U.S. Amateur in 1916. That record held for 80 years. Then, the record keepers had to look up birthdays. In 1996, James Oh of Lakewood, California, made it into the championship. Oh was 14 years, 4 months, and 20 days old. That surpassed the record, as Jones had been 14 years, 5 months old.

It only took six years for the record to be broken again. This time it was another Californian, Joseph Bramlett of Saratoga. He lowered the record to 14 years, 4 months, and 12 days. The young man made it to qualifying by shooting 138, six-under par, at Spring Creek Golf and Country Club in Ripon, California. Unfortunately, he did not qualify for the match-play portion of the championship.

*T*he youngest golfer to ever make the cut in a PGA-sponsored tournament was Bob Panasik of Windsor, Ontario. He accomplished that when he was only 15 years old while competing in the 1957 Canadian Open.

*D*uring 2001, the PGA of America adopted a policy that golfers must be at least 18 years old to be a member of that organization. That didn't stop Ty Tryon from trying to earn a PGA Tour card in the qualifying school. Only 17, Ty recorded a 414 total over the six rounds, 18-under par, and made the grade. Some critics felt the high school junior was too young to compete on the regular tour. He had to wait until his 18th birthday in June 2002 to become an official member. Prior to that, time Ty had to rely on sponsors' exemptions to play, and the money earned would not count on the official list until later in the year. Because of health problems, Ty was seldom able to compete, and the PGA granted him exempt status for the 2003 season.

*O*ne of Donald Ross's creations in Michigan is the Dearborn Country Club, after the Henry Ford family donated the land for a course. The tree-lined layout has hosted two LPGA events as well as the 1990 Senior Players Championship. It was also the site of a high school match in 1998 that brought out the best in Scott Strickland, a sophomore on the Cranbrook Upper School team in Bloomfield, Michigan.

Not playing well by his own admission before the match, Scott said he wanted to concentrate on every shot in the nine-hole event, and he must have done just that. Aided by a double eagle on the sixth hole, Scott posted a 28, eight-under par, which helped his team to a 26-stroke victory.

*J*ust a year later a high school junior also made it into the record books. J. D. McNeill of Pinecrest High School toured Southern Pines Country Club in 62 strokes, nine-under par. It broke the course record held by none other than the legendary Sam Snead that had stood for over 40 years.

*N*ovember 1, 1992, will be a date fondly remembered by Jason Bohn, a sophomore at the University of Alabama. He played in a charity event sponsored by the Golfers' Association of Alabama and made a hole-in-one at the 135-yard second hole when he was one of 12 finalists to get one chance to make an ace.

It was worth $50,000 per year for 20 years. That's a lot of money for a college student. In fact, it's a cool $1 million. Jason called his father after the great shot and told him, "I have some good news and some bad news. The bad news is I'm no longer on the golf team. The good news is I'm now the fourth highest money winner on the PGA Tour." In accepting the money, Bohn had to forfeit his amateur status. It didn't take very long for him to make the decision.

*T*here were four men who regularly played together in Louisville, Kentucky. When they finished a round, each would deposit a nickel in a large beer keg for every par 3 they played and failed to make a hole-in-one. The pot was destined to go to the first of the group who made an ace. H. Patt Pope finally accomplished the feat in 1983 and collected 5,574 nickels, or $278.70. There was no report of the USGA taking away his amateur status.

*I*f anyone asked Robert Taylor what was his favorite hole, the answer surely would have been the 16th at the Hunstanton Golf Course in Norfolk, England. On May 31, 1974, he aced the 188-yarder. Then, on June 1, he duplicated the shot. Sure enough, the following day he made his third consecutive hole-in-one on the same hole. His three aces on the same hole on three successive days is the only known occurrence.

*F*rank Cox of New York City and Juno Beach, Florida, played more than 1,500 different golf courses in 76 countries. Perhaps his greatest accomplishment in golf came not on a course but on a wall. In 1979, he hit a golf ball off the Great Wall of China, although he didn't do it with a club. When he tried to bring clubs in, Chinese officials wouldn't allow it. That didn't stop Frank, who turned an umbrella upside down, using the handle for his historic shot.

*O*n July 7, 1977, or 7/7/77, Roland Thompson was playing the Clear Lake Golf Course. It just so happened to be the seventh anniversary of the opening of the course. Roland hit a 7 iron and aced the seventh hole. Apparently nothing too exciting happened to him on August 8, 1988.

*F*or 16 years, Otto Bucher held the record for the oldest man to ever record a hole-in-one. He was 99 when he experienced that great thrill on the 12th hole at La Manga Golf Club. Then, in May 2001, Harold Stilson aced the 16th hole at Deerfield Country Club in Florida to break the record. He had just turned 102 the month before. It was his sixth hole-in-one, the first coming when he was 71 years old.

*T*hought to be the youngest to ever score a hole-in-one is Jake Paine, when he aced the 66-yard sixth hole at Lake Forest Golf and Practice Center in Illinois, in 2001. The three-year-old was rewarded with an appearance on *Good Morning America*.

AWFUL, THEN PERFECT- FOR PAR

*D*uring the first round of the 1999 Players Championship at Sawgrass, Ponte Vedra, Florida, Fred Couples hit a ball in the water on the 17th. He then reteed and knocked a 9 iron into the cup for a very unorthodox par.

*B*efore John Daly and Tiger Woods arrived on the scene, astounding everyone with their drives, there were a number of others who were known for their length. Jimmy Thomson was probably the first to gain a reputation as a "Siege Gun," but there were others. Among the long hitters was Clarence Gamber, sometimes called "Goofy," although not to his face. He gained that moniker by betting he could put five golf balls in his mouth at one time, and he won many bets by being able to do so.

Gamber was featured in Ripley's *Believe It or Not* in July 1942 for driving a green 300 yards on the fly. Besides his tremendous tee shots, Gamber's biggest claim to fame was in the 1930 Miami Four Ball, when he teamed with Cyril Walker, the 1924 U.S. Open champion, to win the title. In Michigan, he was a frequent winner against stiff competition.

During the early 1930s, there was a regular foursome of Al Watrous, the most titled professional golfer in Michigan history; Walter Hagen; Tommy Armour; and Gamber, who played at Indianwood. More than a few dollars were bet on the matches and gin games that followed. The ninth at Indianwood was relatively short, measuring 329 yards, but the hole was not a pushover. The ever-present rough was there to gobble up an errant drive, and with out-of-bounds on the right, many golfers used an iron off the tee. Not Gam.

He knew only one way to play the hole—with a driver. The green sits below the men's locker room, which was a wooden building in those days and is blind from the tee. When Gamber hit, everyone remained quiet until they heard the thud of the ball hitting the locker room and bouncing back toward the green. On one occasion, Gam hit the tee shot, but there was no sound; Al Watrous asked Clarence if he had hit the ball well. Gamber replied in the affirmative. When the group arrived at the green, there was no ball in sight. Gamber had hit it straight and knew he was not out-of-bounds, so the location was a mystery. Eventually, a caddie found the ball, only two feet from the cup. There was only one problem. It had cleared the locker room and was two feet from the pin on the

18th green. Watrous estimated the ball had to have carried about 350 yards to fly over the building. Incidentally, Gam got a free drop, hit over the locker room, and made a bogey.

*W*inning a club championship is a memorable accomplishment for any golfer. It was especially important to President Franklin D. Roosevelt, when he captured the championship at Campobello Golf Club in 1904 shortly after graduating from Harvard University. Polio, of course, ended his golf participation, but FDR must have been an accomplished player in his younger days.

*I*n 1999, The Country Club was host to the 33rd renewal of the Ryder Cup. The storied club had been the site of major championships in the past, but this marked the first time the biennial matches would be held in Massachusetts since the inaugural in 1927. It would be remembered as the most controversial in history.

What had become a "walk in the park" for the American team was now a tightly contested event. Beginning in 1979, the opponent for the United States was made up of players from Europe and not just professionals from Great Britain and Ireland. This change opened the door for players like Seve Ballesteros and Bernhard Langer to join the British stars. The idea was to make the Ryder Cup more competitive than had been experienced in recent history.

Following the change, there were three more successive victories for the United States, but the desired result kicked in with the 1985 renewal. Europe won that year at The Belfry Golf Club in a handy fashion. American golf fans felt it was probably the venue and things would return to normal in 1987. Instead, it was another European victory at Muirfield Village, followed by a tie in 1989, again at The Belfry. The tie meant the cup remained with the European team, since the Americans did not win it back.

Not accustomed to having the cup on display in Europe, the United States team vowed to win it in 1991. The matches became known as the

"War by the Shore" at the Ocean Club in Kiawah, South Carolina. The Americans won but by the slimmest of margins, and two years later they were able to hold on to the cup at The Belfry. In each of the next two matches, the score read 14½ to 13½, both in favor of Europe. America needed a victory badly, and its PGA named Ben Crenshaw as the captain for 1999.

Ben was a golf historian. He knew the story of a previous British invasion in 1913, when Harry Vardon and Ted Ray were the heavy favorites to win the U.S. Open at The Country Club. Their quest was halted by Francis Ouimet, a former caddie at that club, who won the play-off from the two British stars. Ben was an emotional leader and never gave up hope even when the Europeans built a commanding lead going into the singles matches on the final day.

One by one, the Americans began to post victories on the scoreboard. It came down to one match—Justin Leonard against Jose Maria Olazabal of Spain. At one time, the Spaniard was four up, but Leonard fought back to even. Both were on the 17th green in regulation, with Leonard's ball about 35 feet from the hole and Olazabal's slightly closer but still with a formidable putt. If the American could get a half in the match, the Ryder Cup would return to the United States.

Leonard's putt hit the center of the cup and dropped. A celebration ensued. Not only did the gallery erupt but also teammates following the match rushed to congratulate Leonard. There was only one problem, and it was major. Olazabal still had to putt. If he made it, the outcome would still be in doubt and not known until the 18th hole was played.

Depending on which viewpoint was accepted, it still resulted in a controversy. Mark James, captain of the European team, insisted that Tom Lehman jumped in the line of Jose Maria. Lehman never questioned that he ran on the green, but he denied being in Olazabal's path to the hole. Whether he did or not, the long celebration didn't make it easy for Jose Maria. When he missed, the United States was assured of winning the Ryder Cup.

While the Europeans felt the victory was tainted, there is little question that Leonard's putt will go down in history as one of the greatest clutch shots in Ryder Cup history.

*T*alk about swinging with a handicap. Harry Dearth played a match in 1912 at Bushey Hall in England, losing 2 and 1. Dearth played the entire round wearing a heavy suit of armor.

*S*coring a 63 on the front nine didn't exactly put Lawrence Knowles in a good frame of mind when he toured Agawam Hunt in East Providence, Rhode Island, one afternoon. Lawrence wasn't about to walk in and call it a day. He still had another nine to go, and we all know that golfers feel it has to get better. For Knowles, it did. He came in with a 36. The 27-stroke difference is the largest margin of improvement for any golfer breaking 100 in a single round.

*U*ntil 1958, the PGA Championship was conducted at match play. Perhaps the main reason for changing it to a 72-hole medal event was television. Match play doesn't fit into the proper time frame for an industry that measures in seconds. If the final turns out to be one-sided, ending on the 14th hole, for example, there is just too much time left to fill. Viewers will change stations and watch something else.

Another factor leading to the change in format was the quick elimination of name golfers. Take the 1947 championship held at Plum Hollow Golf Club in Southfield, Michigan. At the end of two rounds, Ben Hogan, Sam Snead, Bobby Locke, and Jimmy Demaret were all on the sidelines. The final pitted Jim Ferrier and Chick Harbert. They were both fine golfers, but they were not the names that would normally draw large galleries. Fortunately, Harbert was from Michigan, and many local fans showed up to root for their hometown favorite. The match was well played and produced a memorable shot in the history of golf.

After the morning round, in which both had scored 69, the match was even. The first and second holes were halved. Chick hit his drive on the third in the middle of the fairway while Ferrier pushed his tee shot well off line. Out-of-bounds was on the right, and Jim flirted with it. His ball was located on a tarpaulin hung between two trees not far from the club's maintenance shed, about a foot off the ground.

Byron Nelson was the referee for the match, and he ruled that the ball could be lifted, the tarpaulin removed, and the ball dropped without penalty. The ball was close enough to a bush that Ferrier couldn't take a swing that would enable him to hit it toward the green. It appeared that Jim was in trouble and all he could do was chip it back toward the fairway. That would put him at a great disadvantage, since Harbert was one of the longest drivers in golf and would still be closer to the green.

Ferrier decided to take a chance by playing a big hook over the shed and the out-of-bounds fence with a 5 iron. To further complicate the matter, a wind was coming from the west, and the ball would have to be hooked into the strong breeze. The shot came off better than Jim could ever have envisioned it. The ball came up quickly, cleared the building and trees, and headed over the fence. It then began to hook, and when it was above the green, the wind slowed its flight. The ball almost dropped straight down and very close to the hole. Ferrier made the putt and eventually won the championship. Byron Nelson said it was one of the greatest shots he had ever seen and that he never again expected to see another like it in his lifetime.

Had the PGA Championship been contested at medal play, Jim probably would never have tried such a shot. In match play, if it hadn't hooked, the most Ferrier could have lost was one hole. Under the circumstances, it was worth the risk, and golf was richer for it.

Chick Harbert went on to win the 1954 PGA Championship and a host of other tournaments. He was a fine player as a youngster and even played an exhibition with Chick Evans when he was 6 years old. While his given name was Melvin, Evans's caddie began to call him "Little Chick" and the nickname stuck.

Since Chick grew up in Michigan, his golfing hero was Walter Hagen. His father was the golf professional at Marywood Country Club in Battle Creek, Michigan, and arranged for an exhibition to be given by Walter Hagen a few years later. He told Chick that he could be the local representative in the exhibition. Harbert jumped at the opportunity, anxious to play well in front of the hometown crowd and also to impress Hagen.

The round went off very much to Chick's liking, and when they got to the final hole, the golfers were even. Both hit the green in regulation, about the same distance from the hole, but it was determined that Harbert would putt first. He knew that if he made the putt, it would give him a 71, and the best Hagen could do was tie. If Chick made his and Walter missed, he would beat one of the all-time legends in the game. While he had putted on that green hundreds of times, Harbert was going to make sure of the line on such an important shot. He crouched behind the ball, walked the length of the 20-footer, and looked it over from behind the cup. He got down on his hands and knees and did everything except dig a hole to see how deep the roots were. After he was sure of the line and the speed necessary to make the putt, he took a stance and stroked the ball directly in the middle of the cup.

Hagen, the great showman, observed all of this with much amusement. Now his turn, Walter went through every gyration Harbert had demonstrated with a few extras of his own. Up stepped the Haig; he knocked it in—backhanded.

One of the forgotten major winners is Bob Hamilton, the 1944 PGA champion. Hamilton certainly didn't rank with the other American headliners of the era, such as Byron Nelson and Jug McSpaden, but he could play the game. Proof of that came on June 3, 1975, when he recorded a 58 at age 59 on the Blue Course of the Hamilton Golf Club in Evansville, Indiana, which measured 6,233 yards. It still stands as the lowest score made by someone shooting his age, although Chuck Kocsis had a 59 at Edgewood Country Club in Union Lake, Michigan, in 1972, and Malcolm Miller did the same at Minocqua Country Club in 1977 when they were both that age.

*A*rthur Thompson is thought to be the oldest golfer to shoot his age. The Canadian was 103 years old when he bettered that number at Uplands Golf Club, which measured over 6,000 yards.

*A*s a result of a childhood accident, Ed Furgol had a withered left arm. It was permanently bent so that he couldn't swing in what was considered the normal manner, with a straight left arm at impact. It required a takeaway on the outside of the swing plane, with a loop in the swing that enabled the club to be square to the target when the ball was struck. While it was unorthodox, there was little question that Furgol's position when the club and ball met was excellent. Some students of the swing said Furgol actually had an advantage in hitting against a firm left side on every shot. Still, it took many years of practice to develop a swing that would serve the purpose, especially for someone wishing to compete at the highest level of the game.

In 1954, the U.S. Open was being played at Baltusrol over the Lower Course. Ed needed a 5 on the final hole to record a 284 total. He had been known to hook his drives on occasion at the most inopportune times. One of those times was from the 18th tee at Baltusrol. His tee shot ended in dense woods, so deep he really didn't even have a shot back to the fairway. Furgol did have an opening to the 18th fairway of the Upper Course, a hole that ran parallel to the one he was playing.

Checking with an official, he was assured that the Upper Course was in play and not out-of-bounds. He punched the shot out, hit his third just short of the green, and got down in two for the par that brought him victory by one stroke. It was the only time a U.S. Open was won by a golfer playing the wrong course.

*T*elevision played an important role in the career of Lew Worsham. The first golf tournament aired on TV was the 1947 U.S. Open, held at the St. Louis Country Club, Missouri. It was only shown locally, with an estimate that about 500 sets were tuned in to the telecast, but it was a start. Worsham won the championship in a play-off with Sam Snead.

George May took note and also had his World Championship of Golf televised locally. May always tried to go one better than the next person, and that was evident in his tournaments held at Tam O' Shanter. The key word is "tournaments." He held two in succession. First there was the All American, with separate competition for women and amateurs as well as professionals. The following week the World Championship was held with the largest purse in golf. By 1953, the first-place check had grown to $25,000 with a guarantee of 25 exhibitions at $1,000 each. That was a great deal of money in 1953, and it virtually assured that the victor would be the leading money winner for the year. May also arranged to have the tournament televised nationally, another first.

Anyone who watched the event on TV and didn't know too much about the game might have gone away thinking that heroics happened weekly, such was the ending to the tournament. Chandler Harper was in the clubhouse having shot 279. Most observers felt he had the title in his pocket, or at least there would be a play-off if Lew could get lucky and birdie the final hole.

With cameras rolling, Worsham hit a good drive and had 107 yards to the hole. He pulled a pitching wedge out of the bag and struck the ball. Lew never was able to see the result, because the gallery engulfed the green as soon as the ball landed, but he knew what happened when the cheers rose in volume. He had holed the ball for an eagle and victory. Almost two million people across the country witnessed the shot on television that Worsham couldn't see.

The wife of a Canberra dentist in Australia, Wendy Egan, had a career round, shooting a 35. Like many golfers, she insisted on a shot-by-shot description of the round, not once but with regularity. Her perplexed husband finally ran an advertisement in the personal section of the *Canberra Times* that read, "My wife played her best round of golf last Tuesday. Would those who have not yet heard about it please phone 731103 for full details of every shot. . . . Noel Egan."

The first call came at 7 A.M. on Saturday, and the calls continued through the weekend.

A great deal of emphasis is given to hitting the ball in the fairway. That is especially true when the rough is high as at U.S. Open sites. However, it may not make that much difference at some of the regular tour stops.

Since such records have been kept, only four golfers have hit every fairway in a 72-hole event on the PGA Tour. Three of them occurred in the Memorial Tournament, twice by the same man. Calvin Peete accomplished it in successive years—1986 and 1987. Unfortunately for Calvin, he finished tied for 57th and tied for 48th those years. Drive for show, putt for dough!

S eve Ballesteros was never known as a golfer who hit a lot of fairways from the tee. The question is, did he have to? When Seve played in the 1979 British Open at Royal Lytham, he hit only eight fairways during the first three rounds. It didn't get any better. In the final round, he hit only one fairway, the same as the number of parking lots he hit. Of course, Ballesteros won the championship.

P laying at Chorlton-cum-Hardy, England, in 1920, Fred Garner hit a shot into a bunker. When it landed, it dislodged another ball that had been buried in the sand. Garner wasn't sure which was his ball and didn't want to touch either in the hazard, so he took a swing and hit them both. He holed out his own ball.

O n June 12, 1939, Ernest Smith set out to play golf in five different countries on the same day. He played in Scotland, the Isle of Man, Ireland, England, and Wales. His best round was 68 and his highest a 76.

J. D. and Annette Werley decided to get away for a little vacation, choosing Montego Bay, Jamaica, in 1979. That's not a bad spot to visit when the wind is blowing in Easton, Pennsylvania. Playing a round at Half Moon Rose Hall Golf Club, they invited their caddie, Gary Bernhard, to take a swing. He pulled out Dr. Werley's 5 iron and took a shot at the 173-yard ninth hole, scoring a hole-in-one. It was the only swing he took. It's tough to improve on perfection.

*O*llie Bowers, a retired U.S. Air Force senior master sergeant, reportedly played 9,757 holes of golf in 1969. It amounted to 542 rounds on an 18-hole course, plus one hole. Perhaps he was in a play-off.

*W*hile Ollie played a lot of golf during one year, the record for one week is thought to be held by Colin Young. He played 70 rounds one week in July 1989. That's 180 holes a day, or 1,260 in one week. Apparently he never read a statement made by Horace Hutchinson in 1896. Hutchinson wrote, "Remember that it is always possible to 'overgolf' yourself. Two rounds a day is enough for any man with a week or more of solid golf in front of him."

*C*hi Chi Rodriguez is the only golfer on the Champions Tour to win four consecutive tournaments. He did it in 1987, capturing the Vantage at the Dominion, United Hospitals Classic, Silver Pages Classic, and Senior Players Reunion.

*O*n April 17, 2002, Christopher Cain set the record for the most holes played during a 12-hour period. The professional at the Penn State Golf Courses, he completed 505 holes in that time. It broke the previous record held by Brennan Robertson of Sarasota, Florida, who had played 476 holes in 12 hours on August 19, 2000.

*T*here is an old adage stating, "It never rains on a golf course." It never mentioned typhoons. One had just passed on January 3, 1982, and Chief Petty Officer Kevin Murray decided to play a round at the Guam Navy Golf Club. He was dealing with some pretty strong winds, and the 40-miles-per-hour gusts came in handy on the second hole, measuring 647 yards. With the wind at his back, he hit a drive that was later measured at 387 yards. Murray's second shot with a 4 iron hit short of the green, then made its way into the cup for the longest double eagle ever recorded.

*I*n 1989, Oak Hill, in Rochester, New York, played host to the U.S. Open with some spectacular results. The sixth at the Rochester course measured 167 yards, not necessarily long but a good shot for the average golfer. Of course, the players who qualify for the U.S. Open are not average. They proved it on June 16, when four of them made holes-in-one on the hole. Each used a 7 iron. They were Doug Weaver, Mark Wiebe, Jerry Pate, and Nick Price. Someone who must understand figures stated that the odds of that happening were something like eight million to one.

Two years later the club placed a plaque at the spot where the historical shots had been hit to commemorate the accomplishment. Then officials went one step further in announcing that on each June 16th, the cup would be placed in the same position—the right front portion of the green—and the tee markers would be at exactly 167 yards, so members could try their luck at duplicating the shots.

It took only two years to break that record of four aces on the same hole in the same day. This time, it was five amateur golfers at the Brockway Golf Course in Brockport, Pennsylvania. Not quite as dramatic a setting as a national championship, it was a practice round for the member–guest event that was to begin the next day. Spuck Anderson, Mark Becker, Lindo Cristina, Wayne Horton, and Steve Trout made holes in one on the 113-yard eighth hole. To date, no odds have been quoted for that happening. It probably doesn't make much difference, because someday we'll read that the record has been broken again. Such is golf.

*H*ow long can a champion golfer remain at the top of his or her game? An argument might exist for 17 years, at least when it comes to consecutive years of winning meaningful golf tournaments.

Two giants of the game hold the record for consecutive years of winning at least one PGA Tour event (17 years). It was established first by Arnold Palmer from 1955 through 1971 and later equaled by Jack Nicklaus, beginning in 1962 and lasting until 1978.

On the European Tour, the record holder is Bernhard Langer, who also had 17 straight years with at least one victory, the first one coming in 1978. The best he could do in 1996 was a second-place finish in the French Open, halting the streak.

To add further to the 17-year theory, Kathy Whitworth holds the record on the LPGA Tour, with wins from 1962 through 1978.

*M*iller Barber held the record on the Champions Tour. He won at least one tournament for nine consecutive years, from 1981 through 1989. That record was broken by Hale Irwin, who had victories in 10 consecutive years through 2004.

*M*orris Hatalsky set a record on the Champions Tour in 2003. Beginning at the 12th hole in the second round of the Bayer Advantage Celebrity Pro-Am through the fourth hole in the second round at the Music City Championship, he did not shoot over par for 98 consecutive holes. In between those two tournaments, Morris also completed three bogey-free rounds in the Columbus Southern Open at Green Island, where he won.

The five rounds of golf that did not include a single bogey were 65-66-65-67 and 68. The record eclipsed the previous mark of 97 holes, which had been set in 1994 by Jack Kiefer.

S tanding on the ninth tee in the second round of the 1977 Danny Thomas Memphis Classic, Al Geiberger was on the verge of making golf history. With a birdie, he could become the first golfer to shoot 59 in an official PGA Tour event. He had started the round at the 10th, so it was his final hole, measuring 403 yards.

Playing partner Dave Stockton said, "He got a break on his last drive. It was headed for the finger of a fairway bunker, but hopped over the sand and left him with just a 9 iron to the green." Al hit that 9 iron to within eight feet of the cup. Geiberger remembered thinking, "Whatever you do, don't leave it short. You may never get this chance again." Not to worry, Al hit the putt dead in the center of the hole.

Al only used one ball in the round, and it ended up in the World Golf Hall of Fame, which was then at Pinehurst, North Carolina. He decided to stick with one ball until something went wrong. Geiberger has been know as "Mr. 59" ever since that day—June 10, 1977.

Both Chip Beck in 1991 and David Duval in 1999 have tied the record-low round at 13-under par, but it has not been bettered on the PGA Tour. However, in U.S. Open Sectional Qualifying at Woodmont Country Club in Rockville, Maryland, Shigeki Maruyama of Japan shot 58, scoring 29 on each nine in 2000. While not a PGA Tour record, it is the lowest round ever recorded in USGA competition and the first time that a score in the 50s was made by a competitor.

I t wasn't until 2001 in the Standard Register Ping at Moon Valley Country Club, during the second round, that a woman broke 60. It was none other than Annika Sorenstam, and like Geiberger, she began her round at the 10th hole. She recorded birdies on the first eight holes she played, turning in 28. Birdies followed on the first through fourth before Annika settled for pars on the next three holes. A birdie at the eighth was capped with a par on her final hole to break the LPGA record with a 59.

Ironically, her playing partners were her sister Charlotta and Meg Mallon. Both of them had been paired with Se Ri Pak of South Korea when she had become the first LPGA member in history to score 61 in the 1998 Jamie Farr Kroger Classic, at that time the record.

The young Swede hit every green in regulation and had two two-putt birdies on par 5s. The 59 also helped Annika set the LPGA 72-hole record up to that date with a 27-under par.

A t the 1996 Volvo PGA Championship, Bernhard Langer shot 73-74 and missed the cut. It brought to an end the longest streak of cuts made on the PGA European Tour, a total of 68 consecutive tournaments.

D uring the 1930s and '40s, Byron Nelson played in 113 consecutive tournaments without missing the cut, a PGA Tour record that has since been surpassed by Tiger Woods.

T o illustrate how dominant Mickey Wright was in golf, all you have to do is look at her 1960 record on tour. There were 23 tournaments that year, and she played in 21 of them, missing two because of injury. Mickey never finished higher than ninth in any event, and that happened only one time. In the others, Wright won six events, finished second twice, third five times, fifth three times, seventh three times, and eighth tied once.

Of course, Mickey went on to have one of the most distinguished careers on the LPGA Tour. In 1963, she won 13 events, the record for the most victories in a single year. In total, she won 82 tournaments, including 13 majors.

T iger Woods posted another phenomenal year in 2000. Not only did he win three majors, but he had a total of 11 victories worldwide, nine of them coming on the PGA Tour. He became the first professional to win the Vardon Trophy with an average score of less than 68 when he lowered the standard to 67.79 strokes per round. Worldwide earnings topped $11 million. Tiger won the U.S. Open at Pebble Beach by 15 strokes over Ernie Els, a new record for that championship. In the British Open at St. Andrews, Woods posted a 19-under-par total that set the record for the most strokes under par in any major in history. At the age of 24, he became the youngest to win all four majors in a career.

*A*long with the great year Woods had in 2000, he also matched something only Lee Trevino had been able to do until then. In 1971, at Merion, Lee captured his second U.S. Open title; he then flew to England and won the British Open at Royal Birkdale; and, finally, he returned to North America and won the Canadian Open the following week. In a matter of three weeks, he won three national championships.

Tiger did the same in 2000, becoming only the second golfer to win those three championships in one year. It took Woods a bit longer, since those tournaments were not scheduled as close together as they were in 1971.

*M*ost golfers have putting problems at one time or another during their careers. Ireland's Christy O'Connor Jr. was among them when his stroke went sour during the 1992 season. To make matters worse, Christy was a passenger on a helicopter that crashed. Although he survived with no physical damage, the experience wasn't one he would recommend to soothe the nerves, especially on the putting surface.

Nevertheless, O'Connor played in the Dunhill British Masters the next week. All he did was one-putt the last nine holes to win the tournament.

*A*s far as tournaments go, the Women's Westchester and Fairfield County Match Play Championship would never be listed as a major. Still, the 1999 renewal of the event produced a most remarkable result.

Playing in a second-round match, Donna Lesser and Buffy Ogden came to the seventh hole, where Ogden proceeded to make a hole-in-one. Lesser wanted to concede the hole and move on to the eighth, but she was encouraged to hit by Buffy, who said Donna might hole her tee shot as well. That's exactly what happened, and the hole was halved with aces.

Mitch Voges became the first and, at this time, only U.S. Amateur champion to use a long putter with his win in 1991. That victory qualified Mitch for the U.S. Open the following year, and he continued to use the long putter, except for the final putt in the opening round. His caddie, Christian Voges, Mitch's son, had propped it up against a water cooler on the 18th tee. Neither realized it was missing until Mitch was on the green, facing a 20-footer to save par. No problem. He grabbed a 3 wood, took his normal sidesaddle stance, and ran it home for a 78.

While he missed the cut the next day, there was a bit of a silver lining to the incident. Mitch said he looked forward to the day he could tell his grandchildren about the time he holed a 3 wood on the 18th hole at the U.S. Open.

A doctor, Joseph Boydstone of Bakersfield, California, recorded 11 aces in 1962, the all-time record for a single year. Three of them came pretty quickly—in one round. Actually it was during the space of just seven holes. On October 10, he aced the third, fourth, and ninth holes at the Bakersfield Golf Club. There is no record of any other golfer making three holes-in-one on the same nine.

Chandler Harper set a PGA Tour record in 1954, when his final three rounds in the Texas Open were 63, 63, and 63.

*D*uring the formative years of the LPGA, there was skepticism on the part of male golfers about the ability of the women professionals, with the feeling even more pronounced in Great Britain. The first commissioner was Fred Corcoran, a man of many promotional talents. Even with his enthusiasm, it was difficult to get much exposure for the fledgling organization and players.

On a trip to England, where he was trying to arrange for a match between the American professionals and a group of British women amateurs, he ran into Leonard Crawley, a golf writer and former British Walker Cup team member. Crawley had asked just how good the women professionals were, and throwing caution to the wind, Fred told him they were good enough to beat any team of British male amateurs Leonard might be able to assemble. Not believing him, Crawley agreed to put together a team of six men, and a match was arranged.

Sponsored by the company that manufactured Weathervane clothes, Babe Zaharias, Betty Jameson, Peggy Kirk, Betty Bush, Patty Berg, and Betsy Rawls made the trip to play six former British Walker Cup stars at Wentworth. At the Babe's request, she was matched against Crawley. The ladies defeated the stars 6 to 0, with Zaharias leading the way, scoring a 74 from the back tees on one of the most demanding courses in the country.

*S*enior golfers aren't expected to make headlines at majors. That changed in 2001 at Southern Hills, Tulsa, Oklahoma. Two former U.S. Open champions surprised a lot of people that year. Shooting a 67 in the first round, 56-year-old Hale Irwin recorded the lowest round ever shot by someone over 50 in the U.S. Open. The record lasted only three days. Tom Kite, 51 years old, broke the record on Sunday with a course-record-tying 64. Hale couldn't keep up the torrid pace and finished tied for 52nd, but Tom's heroics earned him 5th place.

Two years later, at Olympia Fields, Matteson, Illinois, Tom Watson shot 65 and became the coleader after one round in the 144th U.S. Open.

*A*t age 60, Bob Charles played all four rounds at Royal Lytham & St. Annes in 1996 to become the oldest to ever make the cut in the Open. He shot 71-72-71-77 for a 291 and pocketed $7,750.

*W*ith most of the golfing world watching, South Korea had a special interest in the 1998 U.S. Women's Open. A young lady by the name of Se Ri Pak was in a play-off for the championship with Jenny Chuasiriporn, an amateur who played for the Duke University golf team. Regardless of who won, a new record was about to be set, because both youngsters were only 20 years old. It took 20 holes, but Se Ri Pak prevailed to become the youngest to ever win that championship.

Actually, 1998 was truly a record year for Pak. Earlier, she had captured the LPGA Championship, setting the age record in that major and becoming the first golfer from South Korea to win on the LPGA Tour. Then, the week following the U.S. Women's Open, she played in the Jamie Farr Kroger Classic. She entered because the sponsors had given her an exemption the year before, one of only two she received before becoming eligible to play the tour full-time. She felt it was a perfect way to thank the sponsors for their previous generosity.

Her opening round of 71 did not necessarily demand headlines, but the next day, it was different. Pak recorded a 61, the lowest round ever returned in LPGA history up to that time. She followed up with a 63 the next round. The 124 for two consecutive rounds also set an LPGA record. It didn't stop there. She had a final-round 66 for a 23-under-par total of 261, both records for a 72-hole event until broken three years later by Annika Sorenstam.

*D*ave Stockton has the record for the shortest time anyone has held a major title. He won the PGA Championship in August 1970 and failed to defend it in February 1971. The change of dates on the schedule was a result of an agreement between the PGA and PGA National Golf

Club, which had a contract to host the championship earlier than the normal schedule, making it the first major of the year.

Denny Shute would only have been PGA champion for six months as well. He won in November 1936, and the next championship was scheduled for May 1937. Shute successfully defended his title, so he remained champion for another year.

*H*itting practice balls was popularized by Ben Hogan. It's no longer unusual to see professionals on the range until the sun goes down, even after they have completed a tournament round. There's no telling how many balls Hogan hit, because he never kept a record. He practiced because he wanted to perfect certain shots. There was a definite reason for his practice routine.

One person who did keep track was another Texan, who actually came from Fort Worth, Hogan's hometown. In 1983, Irvin Hemmle hit 48,265 practice shots, an average of 132 per day.

*O*n May 21, 1988, David Morris decided to do something that might get him into the *Guiness Book of World Records*. He began to hit balls with a driver at the Abergele Golf Club in Clwyd, Wales. In the next hour, he hit 1,290 drives. That's an average of one every three-and-a-half seconds. It appears that he had help, since it would be difficult to bend over, place the ball on a tee, and hit the shot in that period of time.

*D*avid Ogron holds the record for the most golf balls hit during a 24-hour period, with 10,392. He also set the records for the most balls hit in 12 hours, with 6,971, and in one hour, 2,272. All three are recognized as Guinness World Records.

*A*fter Jack Nicklaus II, or Jackie, as he's most often referred to, won the North and South Amateur in 1985, much was made of the fact that his father had also won the same tournament in 1959. Actually, it was the second time a father-and-son tandem won the North and South. Irving Robeson captured the title in 1918; but his son, Fillmore Robeson, beat him to the punch when he won it in 1915.

Perhaps an even better father-and-son accomplishment occurred in 1974, when Wally Sezna won the National Father and Son Championship at the Atlantis Country Club in Lantana, Florida. The West Chester, Pennsylvania, native entered the tournament twice, once with son Davis and again with Ron.

Each team scored 147 over the 36-hole competition conducted as an alternate-shot event. The tournament committee huddled to discuss a play-off, but the committee decided it would be best to declare the two Sezna teams cochampions.

*B*estowing honorary membership to a golf club is usually reserved for those who have done something outstanding, politicians, and long-serving golf professionals. In 1971, members of the Waihi Golf Club in Hamilton, New Zealand, added a new dimension to that practice. Chico was named an honorary member. That was his full name, and he was a dog who had the ability to find lost golf balls, which were then sold to members, with the proceeds put in the club's funds. Regular members didn't have to worry about losing starting times to Chico once he became a member, either.

*O*ld Tom Morris was having his problems on the High Hole at the Old Course, laying two more than his opponent, Captain Broughton, a member of the R&A. The captain suggested that Tom give up the hole, but the St. Andrews professional said he might hole the next one.

The captain said he would give Tom £50 if he could do it, and Morris replied, "Done."

Sure enough, Old Tom holed the shot from a difficult lie in the rough. True to his word, Captain Broughton arrived the next morning with 50 gold sovereigns. "Take it away," said Tom. "I would not have it. We were in fun."

That was a fortune, especially for a golf professional, but Morris was a special person and not about to take advantage of anyone.

*C*onsidered an eccentric by many, Moe Norman was finally recognized by the Royal Canadian Golf Association and named to its Hall of Fame because of his excellent record. Talented golfers who had the opportunity to see Moe play have been almost unanimous in stating that he was one of the finest ball strikers that golf has ever seen. He was a two-time winner of the Canadian Amateur, as well as twice winning the Canadian PGA Championship. Still, his behavior on and off the golf course led to his eccentric reputation. The stigma was unfortunate. Moe had been struck by a truck as a youngster, and that was probably the cause of his reputation for being somewhat unorthodox.

Among his 33 course records was one that stands out above all the rest. At the St. Charles Golf Club in Winnipeg, Manitoba, Moe needed a 4 on the final hole to set the record. Norman asked a member of his group what kind of hole it was, and the reply was "A drive and a 9 iron." He proceeded to hit a 9 iron from the tee and then used his driver from the fairway, knocking the ball close to the hole, where he then made the putt to break the course standard.

A record that will be very difficult to break is the streak of continuous appearances in majors held by Jack Nicklaus. It began with the 1962 Masters and continued through the 1998 U.S. Open, 146 in a row. Jack didn't play in the 1998 championship because of a hip problem, even though he was eligible to compete.

*D*iscussions have taken place since golf began as to who deserved the title of the "greatest golfer who ever lived." There was Young Tom Morris and then Harry Vardon before a young amateur made the scene. To even be compared to those giants was an honor, but Bobby Jones certainly deserved consideration. When he retired from golf at the age of 28, there were few who would have questioned his credentials as the best the game had ever seen.

At the time, amateurs were on the level with professionals, and once Jones began to win, he was usually the favorite for any tournament he entered. It was news when he wasn't the victor. Jones was basically a part-time golfer. As a competitor, he was always an amateur. The strain of championship golf and not having any more worlds to conquer led to his early retirement. Jones hinted at the beginning of the 1930 season that it would probably be his last in competitive golf, and with the year he had, it was an ideal time to hang up his spikes. Shortly after giving up championship golf, he announced that he was turning professional but not to compete in the game. Instead, he cashed in on the offers from manufacturers and promoters to write, make films, and endorse golf equipment. The Robt. T. Jones, Jr. golf clubs produced by Spalding became the most popular clubs ever produced, and the instruction films featuring Jones are still classics today.

The Walker Cup staging in Great Britain afforded Jones the opportunity to enter both the British Open and Amateur events that year. Early in April, he set sail on the *Mauretania* with other members of the American Walker Cup team. Bobby was able to continue his record of not losing in the singles—and, as captain, he led his team to victory.

The Open that year was held at Royal Liverpool, and Jones bested Macdonald Smith and Leo Diegel by two strokes, shooting 291. It marked the third time he won the Open. Next was the Amateur at the Old Course. Since all of the matches were contested at 18 holes except for the final, Bobby was apprehensive. He always worried about the shorter matches, favoring 36 holes to determine the outcome. Besides, it was a strong field, which included all of the American Walker Cup team members in addition to the British stars. In the final, Bobby faced Roger Wethered, winning 7 and 6. It was his first Amateur title and the one he was most concerned about winning.

After returning home, Jones went to Minneapolis, Minnesota, for the U.S. Open at Interlachen. Hot weather took its toll, but Bobby built a five-stroke lead going into the last round. He held on to win with a 75 while Macdonald Smith again trailed by two strokes. It marked his fourth U.S. Open title, and all that was left to win the Grand Slam was the U.S. Amateur at Merion.

He had his first look at Merion as a 14-year-old, when he burst on the national scene. It would prove to be a historic return. Jones was the qualifying medalist, something that scared him. Having been medalist before resulted in losing matches in prior championships, and all golfers have a bit of superstition in them. He shouldn't have worried. His winning margins were 5 and 4, 5 and 4, 6 and 5, 9 and 8 and 7 in the final. Bobby had won all four majors for which he was eligible in one year.

Amateur golf would never quite be the same after his retirement. Only one amateur has ever been able to win either the British Open or the U.S. Open since that time. Johnny Goodman took the 1933 U.S. Open at North Shore, Glenview, Illinois.

The golf world was hopeful that there would be other heroics after Bobby retired and a new slam was invented four years later. In 1934, W. Lawson Little, Jr. captured the attention of everyone when he first won the Amateur at Prestwick. His margin of 14 and 13 over Jack Wallace set a new record in that oldest of amateur championships. Little then captured the U.S. Amateur at The Country Club in a strong field that included nine former champions. His accomplishment was quickly dubbed the "Little Slam."

Little returned to defend his crown at Royal Lytham and did so with a victory over William Tweddell in the final. Later in Cleveland, Ohio, Little successfully defended his American title by beating Walter Emery by 4 and 3 in that final. He scored better than par in every round of the championship. It was the only time in history that a golfer won the amateur titles consecutively in both Britain and the United States.

Winning the Masters and U.S. Open in 1960, Arnold Palmer began to talk about golf history. It, too, centered on the Grand Slam by Bobby Jones, accomplished in 1930. Palmer felt there was an opportunity for another type of slam in professional golf. By winning the Masters, U.S. and British opens, and the PGA Championship in the same year, Palmer thought, a golfer could claim the "Modern Slam," or "Professional Slam." Since golf professionals couldn't compete in the U.S. and British amateurs, he substituted the Masters and PGA Championship in his version.

His quest continued at St. Andrews, but he fell short when Kel Nagle edged him out. Each year thereafter, some golf scribe would mention the new slam once a Masters champion had been crowned. British bookmakers even gave odds and accepted bets on the possibility.

Until 1972, no golfer was able to win the Masters and follow it up with a victory in the U.S. Open. Then Jack Nicklaus headed to Muirfield with a chance to accomplish the feat. It wasn't to be that year either. Lee Trevino won the British Open to stop the bid. Serious talk subsided until Tiger Woods had a most remarkable year in 2000.

Statistics don't always tell the story, but they go a long way in what happened that year. Woods began the season with a victory streak that eventually reached seven in a row, second only to the unbelievable year that Nelson had in 1945. His scoring average was 67.79 for the 20 tournaments in which he competed, easily the best in history. That average earned him the Vardon Trophy. His official winnings, which exceeded $9 million, broke his own record for the most ever won on the PGA Tour during a single season. In abbreviated PGA European Tour appearances, Tiger won more money than did Lee Westwood, the official leader in that category who played the European Tour full-time. Since he was not a member of that organization, he could not claim the official money title, known as the Order of Merit.

Still, professional golfers are measured by the majors won. While Tiger wasn't successful in the Masters that year, he was victorious at

Pebble Beach and St. Andrews and capped the year by successfully defending his PGA Championship title at Valhalla Golf Club. He therefore won three consecutive majors, the only time that had been done since Hogan's great year of 1953.

With the beginning of the 2001 golf season, all eyes were on Woods. There were two camps. Some felt that if Tiger could win the Masters, he would have won the Modern Slam. Others, notably Palmer and Nicklaus, stated that the four victories had to occur in the same year.

Woods came through. His 272 total earned him his second green jacket. Some dubbed it the "Tiger Slam." Regardless of what side of the debate people were on, it could not take away from the fact that he held all four major titles at one time and that Woods had accomplished something no other golfer had in the long history of the game.

*B*en Hogan is the only golfer in history to have won the British Open in his only appearance. After his victory in 1953 at Carnoustie, he informed the championship committee that he would not return to defend the title.

*I*t had been 19 years since Southern Hills, Tulsa, Oklahoma, hosted the U.S. Open. The first time was memorable when Tommy Bolt captured his only major, and the 1977 renewal would go down in history for another reason.

Hubert Green went to the final round with a one-stroke lead over Andy Bean and two strokes ahead of Tom Purtzer. Shooting a 34 on the opening nine, Green was still in the lead, but then the fireworks began. This time it wasn't because of some golfer starting a birdie binge and challenging Green. Approximately when Hubert was making the turn, three USGA officials were being briefed by the chief of security that someone had called to say that Green's life was threatened. The FBI had received a telephone call from a woman who overheard three men talking that they planned to shoot Hubert on the 15th green. That information was forwarded on to the Tulsa, Oklahoma, police. They immediately dispatched additional officers to Southern Hills, both uniformed and plainclothes policemen.

A decision had to be made on whether or not to inform Green, to suspend play, or to take other action. There was a concern that if Hubert was told, it might have a negative effect on his game, altering the outcome of the championship. Harry Easterly, the USGA president, was against talking to Green, but both Sandy Tatum and Bill Williams felt it should be disclosed. ABC Television officials were also aware of the threat, and they used cameras to pan the galleries when not in use for the actual play.

Just after Hubert finished putting out on the 14th green, he was escorted to the side and given the information. There were three alternatives explained to him. He could continue to play, withdraw, or request a suspension of play. Green decided to keep going. With the exception of Lou Graham, the other golfers began to fade from contention, so it wasn't a walk in the park for Hubert. He hung on, however, winning the title by a stroke over Graham.

Later, Hubert joked that the call probably came from one of his old girlfriends.

*M*aking a hole-in-one at the third hole during the 2002 U.S. Open, Andy Miller, the son of former champion Johnny Miller, got himself in the record books. Andy and Johnny became the only father and son to score aces in the championship. The elder Miller made a hole in one on the 12th hole in 1982 at Pebble Beach. Andy's ace, incidentally, came on Father's Day.

*O*n April 24, 1990, Margaret Waldon aced the seventh hole in a round of golf at Fernandina Beach, Florida. What made the shot unique was that she was 74 years old, and it was her second consecutive hole-in-one on the same hole on successive days. One other fact—she was blind.

*P*laying at Boyne in northern Michigan, Mike Black hit a drive on the first hole that traveled about 230 yards. A bit off-line, it hit a pine tree, but Mike didn't see it drop to the ground. He keenly observed the line of the flight and the tree, jumped into the golf cart, and made a direct run to where his tee shot had gone.

When he arrived, Mike got out of the cart, and as he walked to the spot, the ball fell from the tree. Black's accomplishment was that he out-drove his drive.

*T*he rarest of shots is the one that finds the hole for a double eagle. In 2001, Jeff Maggert made one at Royal Lytham & St. Annes in the opening round of the British Open. He became the only golfer to record double eagles in both the British Open and Masters. Jeff made his other historic shot on the 13th at Augusta National in 1994.

*I*n 1916, Chick Evans became the first golfer to win the U.S. Amateur and U.S. Open in the same year, a feat later duplicated only by Bobby Jones. The scoring record Chick set in that open was accomplished with only seven clubs in his bag and was not broken until 1937.

Even though Evans had an outstanding tournament record and easily qualified for the World Golf Hall of Fame because of his playing ability, perhaps his greatest contribution was establishing the Evans Scholar Program through the Western Golf Association. Thousands of caddies have received college educations because of what he initiated in 1929.

Chick was an enthusiastic golfer through all of the years, even when he was past his prime. He played his last round of golf at one of his favorite golf courses, Glen View Club, when he was 84, nearly blind and very weak. It was just two years before his death. On the ninth hole, measuring 340 yards, Evans hit 2 woods and was just short of the green. He then holed a birdie with a 9 iron. It was a fitting final hole for a gentleman, both on and off the course.

THE LONGEST PUTT

*T*he longest known putt holed on a golf course happened at Moon Valley Country Club in Phoenix, Arizona. It measured 127 feet. The lucky golfer was Floyd Slasor, and the term "lucky" seems to fit, as he made it for an eight on the hole.

For a major tournament, the record is held by Nick Price. He made one measured at 110 feet during the PGA Championship in 1992 at Bellerive.

A number of outstanding golfers have come back from injuries or illnesses to resume careers. Perhaps the most celebrated were Ben Hogan following his near-fatal bus accident in 1949 and Babe Zaharias, who won her third U.S. Women's Open after battling cancer.

In March 1972, Gene Littler was informed that cancer had been discovered in lymph nodes under his left arm. When he underwent surgery, a section of his muscle had to be cut away. Gene began an exercise program to regain some of the strength he had lost. It wasn't something that could be accomplished overnight, and he finally played his first round of golf four months later, shooting 79. The next year he went back on tour, and in the fall of 1975, he was victorious, winning the St. Louis Children's Hospital Classic, shooting 268, with all four rounds in the 60s. It didn't stop there, as Gene won three events in 1975, and once he joined the Senior Tour he was able to capture eight individual crowns.

*O*ne of the oldest records on the PGA Tour books was the 257 shot by Mike Souchak in the 1955 Texas Open. It stood until 2001, more than 45 years, before Mark Calcavecchia had 256 at the Phoenix Open. His rounds of 65-60-64-67 also tied the PGA Tour record of 28-under par set by John Huston in the 1998 Hawaiian Open. During the 72 holes, Mark registered 32 birdies, another record. The TPC (Tournament Players Championship) at Scottsdale measured 7,098 yards; it was not a pitch-and-putt course.

Mark's record was also destined to be broken. In the 2003 Texas Open at La Cantera Golf Club, Tommy Armour III reduced the 72-hole total to 254, with rounds of 64-62-63-65. The site had changed from when Souchak set the mark, but the record again belonged to the Texas Open.

The 28-under-par mark by John Huston lasted until the 2003 Mercedes Championships held at the Plantation Course in Kapalua, Hawaii. Ernie Els recorded rounds of 64-65-65-67 for a 261 on the par-73, 7,253-yard-long layout. His margin of victory was eight strokes over Rocco Mediate and K. J. Choi.

Possibly the best performance by a rookie in the Ryder Cup matches was delivered by Larry Nelson in 1979 at The Greenbrier, White Sulphur Springs, West Virginia. Nelson, who won three major events, for some reason, is overlooked as one of the finest golfers of the century. Perhaps it is because of his quiet manner, as he is always low-key and unassuming.

In those matches, he bested Seve Ballesteros four times. He and Lanny Wadkins beat Ballesteros and Antonio Garrido 2 and 1 on the first day in a four-ball match. That afternoon, Nelson again teamed with Wadkins and won 4 and 3 over Bernard Gallagher and Brian Barnes in foursomes.

The next day Nelson and Wadkins twice defeated Ballesteros and Garrido, 3 and 2 in the morning foursomes and 5 and 4 in the afternoon four-ball match. In singles, Larry defeated Ballesteros 3 and 2 to record five victories and no losses, a record that has never been duplicated by a rookie in the Ryder Cup.

*T*elevision doesn't reveal the many contours on the greens at Augusta National Golf Club. While viewers can get an idea of how fast the greens are, it is almost a necessity to see them in person to realize the challenge golfers face on some putts. Being able to complete even one round without a three-putt green is a great accomplishment.

On the first hole in the opening round of the 1998 Masters, Tiger Woods three-putted, and that ended a streak of 113 consecutive holes without a three-putt. The last time he had experienced that misfortune was on the 13th hole of the second round in the 1996 Masters.

*E*ver the sportsman, Bobby Jones decided to attend the 1936 Olympics held in Berlin. A visit to Gleneagles, Scotland, was included in the itinerary for some relaxation. While there, he expressed a desire to play at St. Andrews, and a driver delivered a ballot for a starting time at the Old Course. Typical of the man, it contained no request for special consideration. It was simply made out with "R. T. Jones, Jr., Atlanta, Ga."

Having lunch at the Marine Hotel, he observed that a large crowd had gathered at the Old Course. Such was Jones's modesty that he didn't realize the people had assembled to see him play an informal round. Instead, he was concerned that a competition was being held and that he might somehow interfere with its progress. What he didn't know was that word had spread that he would be playing that day. The town was virtually shut down. Signs were hung in shops stating, "Bobby's Back." It was estimated that at least 4,000 people gathered to see their favorite son.

Despite the fact that he had not been playing competitively for six years, Jones did exceptionally well, recording three birdies on the seven opening holes. On the eighth, his tee shot with a 4 iron landed softly on the green, finishing within 10 feet of the cup for yet another birdie. His caddie, whose name has been lost through the years, expressed what every person following the round felt when he turned to Jones and said, "My, but you're a wonder, sir."

CHAPTER FOUR

Failures

Mishaps on the golf course can happen to anyone, from the beginning duffer to the most talented of professionals. It has been said
many times that golf is a humbling game, and it is that. It is one of a
handful of sports where the champion golfer loses more often than
wins. A tournament player considers it a good year with four or five victories during the season. Even Vardon, Jones, Hogan, and Nicklaus lost
more tournaments than they won, and they may have been the best to
ever play golf.

A very good friend, Greg Ruddy, enjoyed the game immensely and at
one time played to a handicap of two. He was good enough to qualify for
the Michigan State Amateur and to always be a factor in his club championship. While he was competitive, he could laugh at himself when
things went wrong. When some of those failures happened, I was there.
We would put together teams for various events that might be scram-
bles, or best balls, and we were often successful. Our favorite team included Ron Kramer, the former tight end for the Green Bay Packers and
Detroit Lions, who was a magnificent athlete, and Al Wygant, along
with Greg and me. Al was a member of the 350 Club, which meant he
had hit a drive over 350 yards in competition. He called himself "Long

and Wrong," which pretty much sums up the way he would hit off the tee. When he had a pitching wedge in his hand, however, it was as if he were looking at a hooded cobra.

One year we were able to win a local Walter Hagen event, held to benefit the American Cancer Society in honor of The Haig, and to qualify to play in the state tournament. The format was a best ball of the four golfers, and we were in the scratch division. At the state event held at Boyne Highlands, Michigan, we approached the competition as we normally did—in a casual manner. Our practice round wasn't even played at the tournament site; we opted instead to practice at Birchwood Farms, which we had never played, because it had an enjoyable layout. The practice round didn't last long, as we departed after 11 holes, seeking dinner and liquid refreshment at Duffy's, one of the area's better restaurants. We weren't too concerned about when we would get to bed, since our starting time for the first round was one o'clock.

We surprised ourselves by shooting a 67, leaving us only one stroke behind the leaders. Immediately after showering, we headed back to Duffy's. This time, there was a problem. Our starting time for the final round was 8 A.M., and wanting to swell the coffers of the restaurant owner, who had been our host at Birchwood Farms the previous day, we closed the place.

The wake-up call came all too early. I tried to rouse Greg in the next bed but to no avail, and I went to the shower and let the water beat down on me for at least 20 minutes. The telephone rang again, and it was Big Al. He said he couldn't wake Ron either, but we owed it to the tournament for the two of us to play. While I was ready to let them put a "WD" next to our name on the scoreboard, I agreed with Al. Our starting hole was the 14th, and we took our cart there to wait for the shotgun start. Just as the shotgun went off, Kramer showed up, and the three of us began the round. As things sometimes happen, we made five consecutive birdies among ourselves and arrived at the turn. Ron asked me what our room number was and then went into the pro shop and called Greg. It must have taken two or three minutes for Greg to answer the telephone, and when he did come on the line, all Ron said was, "We're doing better without you. Stay in bed." The team didn't keep up the torrid pace; but by some miracle, we added a few more birdies and won the title. Word spread quickly, and when Greg showed up at lunch, other competitors asked him if he was the man who hurt the team by three strokes the day before by playing.

That win qualified us to play in the national Hagen tournament at Disney World in Orlando, Florida, still in the scratch division. We knew we were in trouble when we went back on the course following a practice round to watch some of the other golfers. We stood at a long par 3 as one team hit their shots to the green. During our round, we were happy to have two of our team on the green, but the youngsters we observed were knocking the pin down. In fact, they verbally abused one of their group for having left himself a 25-foot putt while the others were within 10 feet. It turned out that they were the University of Georgia golf team; they qualified by winning their state title. There wasn't much left for us to do but enjoy the surroundings, which included the good restaurants and watering holes.

When the tournament began, teams were assigned scorekeepers who had previous experience in the Walt Disney Classic, a PGA Tour event. There was a difference in that they only had to record one score per hole for our team instead of a score for each competitor. That approach was a little foreign to the lady assigned to our team. She carried her scorecard on a clipboard and had duly recorded how each of us was dressed so she could keep track of each shot. As we hit our tee shots, she dutifully put a hash mark next to each name, indicating we had each taken one stroke. Three of us hit the ball in the fairway, but not Greg. His drive was a towering hook that ended up deep in an area where the animals don't have legs. When we got to our drives, I asked Kramer if we should go over and help Greg find his ball. Ron replied, "Forget it. If he ever finds his ball, he won't have a shot, and one of us should make a three or a four."

We each hit our approaches to the green, and our scorekeeper put down the second hash mark for the three golfers. The three of us recorded pars and began to walk to the next tee just about the time Greg made his way out of the underbrush. The lady came up to us and asked, "I know what to mark down for your scores, but what do I do for Ruddy?"

Ron said, "Give him a BIP."

"What's a BIP?" she queried.

"Ball in Pocket," answered Ron.

When she turned in the scorecard upon the completion of the round, there were seven neat BIPs marked on the card after Greg's name.

Ruddy, as has already been shown, enjoyed some liquid refreshment from time to time. In recent years, the attitude toward drinking and driving has changed, and it is no longer something that is accepted, with good reason. It's nice to know that Greg has changed with the times and his older age. Following the pro-am event at a past Buick Open, Greg attended a party in suburban Flint, Michigan, where he was overserved. The time came to drive home, and he knew that he was going to have a problem. Not wanting to draw attention to himself and with no one to ride with, Greg headed down I-75 to his home. He thought the best thing to do was to make sure he watched the white line painted on the right side of the highway. As long as he was able to concentrate on that line, he felt he would have no problem gaining his destination. The result was that he took every exit along the expressway and back again on each entrance ramp. A trip that would normally take less than a half hour amounted to three hours before he pulled into his driveway.

Whenever I was with Greg, it was virtually impossible to reach in my wallet. He always wanted to pick up the tab and usually did. One of the only ways to solve that was to get him to a place where he could neither pay cash nor sign a chit. It was with that in mind that I invited him and two other men to join me at Wabeek Country Club, Bloomfield Hills, Michigan, for an afternoon round of golf.

Following lunch, we proceeded to the first tee, where our caddies were waiting for us, four young men who had all recently caddied in the PGA Championship at Oakland Hills. They were knowledgeable and courteous, adding to the enjoyment of the game. The usual small bets were made, which included the provision for presses whenever a golfer was two down on a bet. The golf course was really not designed for Greg, at least when he had a driver in his hands. He was long, but the ball didn't always find the short grass. Wabeek was a tight course with much trouble for those who strayed off the fairways. Rather than use an iron off many of the tees, which would have been the prudent approach, Greg preferred to attack the course. He was an early-day John Daly. The result was that Greg was saying "press" to me fairly often.

Standing on the 18th tee, Greg asked me how we stood with our bets, and I informed him that he was $70 down. He asked if he could press for $50, and I accepted, feeling I was really playing with his money anyway.

The 18th hole is a 450-yard dogleg right. The distance is deceiving, since a golfer can decide what line to take over the lake, which begins in front of the tee. Normally it is no problem to hit a 5 iron over the short and safest path, but that leaves a very long second to an elevated green. The brave could hit directly at the green over the water with a carry of 267 yards. Going through the fairway also presented a problem, since there was a hill on the other side covered with knee-high rough.

It was my honor, and my drive came off better than I could have hoped, cutting off quite a bit of the water hazard and then beginning to fade. The ball followed the fairway, and when it came to rest, I judged I would have no more than an 8 iron left to the green. Greg asked the distance to the far end of the lake, and I told him the exact length, since it had been measured by a laser not long before.

He turned to his caddie and said, "There's a dozen MacGregors in the bag. Break open a sleeve and toss me one."

His drive flew straight and high, directly at the green. Unfortunately, it fell about two yards short of dry land. Again he turned to his caddie, saying, "Give me another one."

The second tee shot was almost a duplicate of the first. Another splash, perhaps a yard from the fairway. Greg proceeded through 11 golf balls. Each was hit on line, and each fell between one and five yards short of the water's edge. His 12th tee shot hooked violently, climbing halfway up the hill into the deep rough. The caddies were beside themselves, trying hard not to laugh. Not so with the three golfers. We could hardly stand up.

Following the other two golfers' drives, which found the fairway, we walked across the bridge to begin the search for Greg's final tee shot. Taking at least the allotted five minutes, we gave up trying to locate the ball. By this time, we had been playing the hole for about a half hour, and the group behind us finally walked on the 18th tee.

Here was Greg, lying 23 with a lost ball, and his opponent was about to hit his second shot with an 8 iron. As we walked along the fairway, he put his arm around my shoulder and with great sincerity said, "I concede the hole."

There will always be more failures than feats. It's the nature of the game.

If you have never heard the name David Ayton, it can be blamed on the Road Hole at the Old Course. The hole has been called anything from the most difficult par 4 in the world, although it was once a par 5, to some unprintable names. It measures 461 yards and doglegs to the right. Along that right side is a boundary wall. Most of the time the hole is played into a prevailing wind. After a blind tee shot, the golfer is faced with a long approach to a two-tier green, with the hole usually cut in the top left near the Road Bunker for the final round of tournaments. If the ball slides to the right, it generally ends up on the road, which is in play. The Road Bunker, located on the left side of the green, puts fear in even the most accomplished golfers' hearts.

During the 1885 Open, Ayton stood on the 17th tee in the final round with a five-stroke lead. Being from St. Andrews, winning the championship in front of fellow townsmen would have meant the world to him. David hit a fine drive and followed it with a brassie that left him with a little run-up shot. Even if he didn't get down in two, a five on the hole would have left him in command with the kind of lead he enjoyed, since it was then a par 5.

Ayton chipped a bit too gently. The ball didn't hold its line but caught the slope and finished in front of the bunker. Now he was faced with a pitch instead of a run-up. It didn't hold the green, running onto the road. Another shot was a bit too gentle, and the ball rolled back on the road. Learning his lesson, he was a little bolder on the next shot. Too bold. It went into the bunker. David left two shots in the sand before reaching the green, where he two-putted for an 11. He lost the championship by two strokes. Had Ayton been able to handle the Road Hole on that final round, he would forever be remembered as an Open champion instead of someone now unknown to the golfing world.

Tom Shaw's boyish appearance was either a blessing or a curse, depending on when he was playing tournament golf. Upon joining the PGA Tour, Tommy wasn't against a little imagination when it came to completing the information as to his age on the application. After all, the younger the better, and Tom always looked younger than the actual years he had lived. It came to haunt him later in life when Shaw decided there was a great deal of money to be made playing on the Champions Tour. He had to locate his birth certificate to prove he actually belonged in the over-50 crowd, since the PGA records indicated he wasn't eligible. Tommy could easily have passed for a man of about 35 when he made his debut with the seniors.

He had some success on the regular tour with three victories, two coming on difficult layouts like the Doral Open and the Bing Crosby National Pro-Am over Cypress Point, Pebble Beach, and Spyglass Hill. In capturing the Bing Crosby, all he received was a check, which spent well enough, but there was no trophy to accompany the money. Tom bought a piece of metal art of a cypress tree and created a trophy of his own, so he could always remember the tournament. Such a sentimental golfer should somehow be immortalized in golfing lore. He has been, but not necessarily because of a victory.

During the 1970 Open at St. Andrews, Tommy seemed to have no problem on the first hole, as he hit a nice drive and found the green with his approach shot. That the ball came to rest above the hole didn't present too much of a problem for a professional with his talents. After all, he had successfully negotiated a number of fast greens on the American tour.

His putt was a bit strong, and while Shaw had envisioned the possibility of starting with a birdie, he was a little surprised as it gained speed. The ball continued to roll until it went off the green, eventually stopping in the Swilcan Burn. Undaunted, he dropped a ball on the other side of the water and hit a wedge into the hole for a slightly unorthodox bogey. He went down in British Open history as possibly the only golfer to hit a green in regulation, take only one putt, and still end up 1-over par for the hole.

That same year Lee Trevino was in the hunt during the final round when he walked on the tee for the fifth hole. It is a par 5 and one of the double greens on the Old Course. Actually, there are only four single greens on the course, with seven of them serving two holes each. The pin positions are on the right going out and on the left coming back. The holes are clearly marked by different-colored flags, white on the front nine and red on the back nine.

Lee hit two good wood shots and faced his approach to the fifth green. Hitting his third shot, Trevino immediately knew he had lined up for the wrong flag. It sailed true to the hole being used for the 13th hole, and it was a beauty. Instead of having a short putt for his birdie, Lee faced an 80-footer and proceeded to three-putt for a bogey. That made the deficit too large, and he couldn't catch Jack Nicklaus and Doug Sanders, who went on to tie after regulation play.

Going to the 15th tee on the final round of the 1939 Hershey Open, Byron Nelson was still vying for the title. Nelson hit his drive over a hill and straight down the fairway, although he couldn't see the ball land. When he arrived at the spot where the ball should be, it was nowhere to be found. His golf balls had his name imprinted on them, so there should have been no problem with identification. It was simply a matter of the ball's having disappeared. Everyone in the area was sure that it should have been in the middle of the fairway.

Byron had no choice but to go back to the tee and hit another drive, adding a stroke and distance penalty. He finished in fourth place in spite of the mishap. Following the round, Nelson was interviewed and the penalty was discussed, so the incident was reported by the press the next day.

About 10 days later, Nelson received a letter telling him that the writer had invited a guest to the tournament, a young woman who didn't know a thing about golf. When they were returning to New York after the tournament, she reached in her purse and pulled out the golf ball she had "found" on the course. It wasn't until that time that the man realized what had happened. He explained to Nelson that he felt bad that Byron had lost out on finishing third because of the extra two strokes, and he included money orders totaling $300, the difference in prize money between third and fourth.

The letter was postmarked from the New York Central Post Office and signed John Paul Jones. Byron never found out who the man was, but he greatly appreciated receiving the money at a time when purses were small.

⚑

*H*itting her tee shot during a round at Smithers, British Columbia, Elaine Johnson watched as it bounced off a tree and came directly back at her. The ball struck Elaine for a two-stroke penalty, then lodged in her brassiere for what was apparently an unplayable lie as well.

⚑

*O*ld Warson in St. Louis, Missouri, has had a storied past, even though it is not one of the older established golf clubs in America. Its first professional was E. J. "Dutch" Harrison, the "Arkansas Traveler." Voted by many as one of the best golf courses in the country, Old Warson was selected to host the 1971 Ryder Cup Matches. The United States team won, but that was not unusual in those days. One incident in those matches did stand out, however, and while it didn't lead to changing the Rules of Golf, it went a long way toward pointing out how a rule can be unfair or, at least, not in keeping with the honor of the game.

During the four-ball matches, which Americans refer to as best-ball matches, Arnold Palmer and Gardner Dickinson were pitted against Peter Oosterhuis and Bernard Gallagher. On the fifth tee, the Americans had the honor, and Palmer hit a fine shot on the par 3 that measured slightly more than 200 yards in length.

That year caddies for the Ryder Cup were college students. It was prior to the time that the U.S. and British teams brought their regular tour caddies, and with the dominance shown by the Americans, neither team considered it necessary. Carrying Gallagher's bag was a young man by the name of Jack McLeod, an enthusiastic golfer. He was thrilled to be a caddie in such a prestigious event. He was even more excited to be in the same group with Arnold Palmer.

After hitting his shot, Arnold walked to the side of the tee as Gallagher prepared to hit his ball. Awed by the presence of Palmer and probably realizing he could someday tell his children that he spoke to the legend, McLeod congratulated Arnold on the fine shot, asking what he had hit. "A 5 iron," Palmer responded.

It was an innocent exchange, being of no benefit to Gallagher, who was already at the tee and didn't hear either the question or the reply. One person who did hear it was John Conley, the referee for the match. Conley was a PGA member and a former vice president of the association from Pittsburgh, Pennsylvania. He knew there was a problem, but he wasn't completely sure how a rule was broken, nor the penalty for the infraction. He called for Joe Dey, the PGA commissioner, and Joe Black, who would later be elected the president of the PGA of America.

After the hole was apparently tied with pars, Conley informed the group of the rules infraction and that the British team had lost the hole. Arnold pleaded with the officials to change the decision and not impose the penalty, but to no avail. The Americans went on to win the four-ball match. Perhaps the ruling would not have influenced the outcome, but both sides were not happy with the decision, based on an innocent question from a young man.

Compare that incident with one that happened during the 1953 Walker Cup at Kittansett, Cape Cod. Jimmy Jackson was paired with Gene Littler on the American team and discovered on the third tee that he had mistakenly started the foursomes match with 16 clubs in his bag. That was two over the limit. He immediately reported it, and once the officials from the R&A and the USGA met, it was ruled that the Americans had violated the Rules of Golf and the penalty was disqualification under the rules that then existed.

Noticing some commotion, the captain of the British team, Tony Duncan, went to find out what was happening. When informed of the decision, Tony declared, "This is ridiculous. We haven't come three thousand miles to win a 36-hole match by default on the second hole." After some consultation, it was decided that the American team would be penalized two holes and the match would continue. Jackson and Littler ended up winning the match 3 and 2.

The next morning, a headline stated "Britannia waives the rules." The decision was in keeping with the sportsmanship of international competition.

One of the most difficult tickets to get in golf is for the Masters Tournament. Anyone who is lucky enough to have one usually wants to keep it. Not Garrett Risner Jr. of Stone Mountain, Georgia. In 1980, he tried to give one away. Actually, he was throwing the ticket in as a bonus if a man he approached would buy a candy bar for $225. It turned out the prospective buyer was an undercover policeman. Risner was found guilty of scalping.

Getting a ticket to the Masters is hard enough. Flying or driving there should be easy. Members of the press corps don't have to worry about buying a ticket, but they do have to make some travel arrangements to get to Augusta.

Bob Warters, editor of *Today's Golfer,* a British publication, decided to cover the 1992 Masters Tournament for his magazine. After all, Ian Woosnam was the defending champion and, along with Nick Faldo, a pretournament favorite. A travel agent was called to book the flight, and Warters was on his way. The first leg went fine, with the plane landing in Boston. Warters then found the Northwest Airlines counter so he could continue on to Augusta.

It wasn't until the plane was airborne that Warters began to feel something was wrong. The Atlantic Ocean was on his right, which meant the jet was heading north. Ninety minutes later it landed in

Augusta, Maine, not Augusta, Georgia. Our modern-day Marco Polo quickly bought another ticket, got on the same plane, and returned to Boston. He made it to Georgia 26 hours after leaving London and having boarded five different aircraft.

*E*ven more difficult than finding a ticket is getting an invitation to play in the Masters. While the past champions have lifetime exemptions, the remainder of the invitations are based on ability and especially the past year's performance Loren Roberts qualified for 1998 and was looking forward to competing again.

About a week before he was to go to Augusta, Loren sneezed, causing him to crack a rib, forcing him to withdraw from the tournament.

*C*anterbury, Cleveland, Ohio, was the site of the 1946 U.S. Open and the scene of a penalty that probably cost Byron Nelson a chance at his second national title. At that time, golf fans could walk right along with the contestants and were not relegated to designated areas.

After a shot was hit, the gallery would rush up to within a few feet of where the ball came to rest while marshals would hold up ropes to keep the crowds back. Many times the golfers would have to struggle to get through the gallery to reach the ball. That's exactly what occurred when Nelson and his caddie, Eddie Martin, a soldier home on leave, nudged their way through the crowd. Unfortunately, they emerged only a few feet from Byron's ball. The caddie ducked under the rope, and before he realized where he was, he had kicked the ball a few feet.

The USGA assessed Nelson a one-stroke penalty, leaving him tied with Vic Ghezzi and Lloyd Mangrum at 284. After two 18-hole play-offs, Mangrum won. Without the penalty, there might not have been a play-off and Nelson could possibly have been the champion.

Byron never blamed his caddie, saying it was just some bad luck and if that was the worst thing he ever did in his life, Eddie would be a fine man.

*A*s was the custom, Mangrum took possession of the trophy, and it was placed on display at Tam O'Shanter in Chicago, where he was the head professional. A fire at the club destroyed the cup, and the USGA had to replace it before the next championship.

Fortunately, the exact specifications were on file with the Gorham Company, and it could be reproduced in time to be presented at the 1947 championship. Now, the champion receives a duplicate of the trophy to be held for a year. The winner does have an option of purchasing a smaller version of the trophy to keep permanently. The question is, who would not want to spend the money to have such a valued prize?

*P*laying the Weston Golf Club in Massachusetts, Malcolm Russell hit a pitch shot and lost his ball. It lodged in the branches of a tree. Three days later, as he was walking under the same tree, his ball fell from the branches, landing at his feet.

*S*am Snead's record in the U.S. Open caused him many heartaches through the years. In his very first start at Oakland Hills in 1937, he was congratulated when he concluded the championship with 283, a new record. There was only one problem. Ralph Guldahl was still on the course, and he eventually lowered the standard by two more strokes to become the champion. It was only the beginning of Sam's frustrations in the U.S. Open.

The real backbreaker for Snead came at Spring Mill in Philadelphia two years later. Sam reached the 17th hole thinking he needed two pars to win the championship. He missed a five-footer for par on that hole, but he was still in good shape, especially since the 18th was a par 5, just the kind of hole at which Snead excelled. Communications on a golf course left something to be desired in 1939. Competitors relied on information passed along to them from people in the gallery or from friends who were following along. Playing behind him were Craig Wood and Denny Shute, both very much in the chase for the title. The cheers that he occasionally heard from behind him made him believe they were dropping a few putts for birdies. No one came forward with information as to how he stood in the championship.

Now feeling he needed a birdie on the 18th to tie, Sam set out to do just that. He hit a fairly good drive, but he hooked it slightly, and it found the rough. Sam was about 275 yards from the green with a poor lie. He decided to play a brassie. The shot never got the altitude he was looking for and ended up in a bunker about 100 yards short of the green. It was a steep-faced bunker, probably calling for the shot to be hit with a sand wedge. However, that might not get Sam to the putting surface. Thinking that he still needed a birdie, he chose an 8 iron. It didn't get up quick enough, with the ball lodging in some loose sod that had been placed at the top of the bunker. From there, Snead hit a shot into another bunker at the left of the green, blasted out of that one, and three-putted for an eight. Instead of becoming the U.S. Open champion, he finished fifth.

Years later Snead said if he had known he needed a five to tie, he could have hit three 8 irons and made it to the green. Fred Corcoran, Sam's manager, insisted that the outcome would have been different if he had been standing on the 18th tee with Snead and been able to pass along the correct information as to how he stood in comparison to the other competitors. Sam was destined never to win the U.S. Open, although he later had two more second-place finishes. In fact, Snead played in a total of 31 of the American championships, the most by any golfer without winning a U.S. Open.

There was another time when Sam wished he could have skipped a hole. It occurred in the 1957 Western Open at Plum Hollow, Southfield, Michigan. The course had not exactly been kind to him in the past. During the 1947 PGA Championship, he was one of the favorites. In his first match, Sam faced Gene Sarazen, who was long past his prime.

Sarazen pulled off one of the major upsets by defeating Snead and sending him to the sidelines. The fourth hole at Plum Hollow measures 455 yards and is the most intimidating on the course, with out-of-bounds on the right and trees lining the left side of the fairway. Not only is a long drive required, but the putting surface is slanted so that unless the ball is directly below the hole, any putt can be an adventure.

During the championship, Snead hit two balls out-of-bounds and then took six more strokes for a catastrophic 10. The amazing thing is that Sam had a 25-footer for a birdie on the 72nd hole that hit the cup and lipped out. If it had dropped, he would have tied for the play-off with George Bayer, Doug Ford, Gene Littler, and Billy Maxwell.

Dawson Taylor, a Detroit auto dealer, placed a plaque next to the fourth tee after getting Sam's approval before it was displayed. It read, "Duffers take heart! On this, the fourth hole at Plum Hollow, on June 27, 1957, in the Western Open, Sam Snead took ten strokes. In spite of his disaster he finished with 280, one stroke behind Doug Ford, the winner at 279."

The plaque mysteriously disappeared a couple of years after it had been placed near the tee. No one ever admitted to taking it down, although there was speculation that some of the Plum Hollow members were not happy with the constant reminder of Snead's failure, nor did they want to be reminded how difficult the hole was as they approached the tee.

*D*isaster really struck at Carnoustie in the 1999 Open Championship. The leader by five strokes after the third round was little-known Jean Van de Velde, a Frenchman who was trying to be the first from his country to win the coveted title since Arnaud Massy in 1907. At least he was little-known to Americans. Van de Velde had been victorious once on the European PGA Tour in his 11 years, but his was certainly not a household name to most golfers.

Going to the final hole, all he had to do was make a double bogey, and he would be the champion. His putting had been phenomenal all week, vaulting him into a lead that seemed insurmountable as he stepped on the 18th tee. While many courses claim to have the toughest finishing hole in golf, few would doubt that the honor belongs to the last hole at Carnoustie. It measures 487 yards from the "Tiger Tees" and plays to a par 4. The Barry Burn comes into play the full length of the hole as it crosses the fairway twice and presents a problem on both the right and left sides of the hole at various distances.

The Frenchman probably made his first mistake when he decided to hit a driver from the tee. Being in the final group, he knew that a six on the hole would win the championship; he could easily have hit a 2 iron, followed that with a wedge short of the burn, and had an easy pitch to the green. Even a three-putt would have clinched the victory. His drive just missed the water, but his ball was still resting to the right of the fairway on a grass peninsula, 189 yards from the green.

Mistake number two came when he selected a 2 iron instead of playing short and onto the fairway. Van de Velde pushed the shot to the right, where it hit the grandstand, flew back, and hit the burn's rock wall and dropped into heavy rough. While only 50 yards from the green, it was not an easy third shot. His attempt at hitting a wedge went into the burn on the fly.

Rolling his pants up above his knees, Jean wanted to hit the shot from the water, but it became obvious that the ball was too far below the surface, so he took a drop and was hitting his fifth stroke to the green. That shot found the bunker to the right of the putting surface. Number six was eight feet from the hole. He steadied himself and the putt found the cup for a triple bogey, still enabling him to make the play-off with Justin Leonard and Paul Lawrie.

Lawrie emerged as the champion, which was a story in itself. Paul became the first Scotsman since 1931 to win the Open on Scottish soil. And he came from ten strokes back with a final 67, to record the largest victorious comeback in any major in history.

Much to Jean's credit, he never offered excuses following the Open disaster. He took full responsibility for club selection, not blaming his caddie for the misfortune.

Carnoustie, for that championship, was considered by many to be the most difficult ever played for the British Open. Attesting to that was the fate of Rodney Pampling of Australia. He opened with a 71 to become the first-round leader. The next day wasn't so kind to Rodney. He scored 86 and missed the cut. It marked the only time a first-round leader missed the 36-hole cut in the history of the world's oldest golf championship.

The 132nd British Open Championship at Royal St. George's in 2003 also had its share of disasters. On his opening drive, Tiger Woods hit his ball in the fescue grass rough. After a search, the ball was declared lost, with Tiger making the long walk back to the first tee to strike his second drive of the day. The two strokes it cost him was the exact number he finished behind the winner three days later.

Thomas Bjorn of Denmark also had a Thursday problem. Two-under par at the time, Bjorn was facing a bunker shot on the 17th hole. He left it in the bunker; out of frustration, he banged his wedge in the sand, resulting in a two-stroke penalty.

A bunker was also his undoing in the final round. In the lead by two strokes, he twice failed to reach the putting surface, settling for a double bogey on the 16th. Even with the sand problems, Bjorn finished tied for second, only one stroke behind Ben Curtis.

The final disaster was a disqualification for Mark Roe. He had played superbly following an opening 77 with a 70 on Friday and 67 in the third round. When he was playing with Jesper Parnevik, they forgot to exchange cards on the first tee. The disqualification resulted from Roe's signing the wrong scorecard—Parnevik's instead of his own. Mark would have had a 54-hole total of 214 and tied for third, only two strokes behind the leader. The final round was not to be for Roe.

S pectators at the 1933 Western Open, held at Olympia Fields in sub-urban Chicago, observed something not seen at any other tournament. In the field of 220 golfers, one contestant was registered as Vincent Gebhardi. His entry form indicated he was a professional from the Evergreen Golf Club, Chicago, Illinois. When he arrived at the 18th green, he lined up his putt and hit it in the hole. All of a sudden, the police arrested him. No, he wasn't arrested for playing a bad round of golf. While Gebhardi was the golfer's real name, he was better known as "Machine Gun Jack McGurn," the alleged executioner for the Al Capone gang. Judge Thomas Green had issued the warrant, and the arrest was made by Lt. Frank McGillen, two sergeants, and five other officers. That's two foursomes of law enforcement officials to arrest one golfer.

A W-HOLE-LY MISSED OPPORTUNITY

B ack in 1870, Robert Clark was playing at Musselburgh in a foursome match. It was late and getting dark as they hit the tee shots on the final hole, a par 3. Unable to follow the flight of Clark's ball, the group searched for it but to no avail. He and his partner eventually conceded the hole, which meant the match was lost. As they headed off the green, one of the golfers glanced in the hole, and there was Clark's ball. He had scored a hole-in-one, but according to the rules of golf, the hole had already been conceded. If the ball had been found earlier, the hole and the match would have been won.

E ven though Richard Allen knew he had recorded a hole-in-one on the 13th hole at Barwon Heads Golf Club in Victoria, Australia, he still lost the hole. On a dreaded Friday the 13th in 1990, Richard made his ace, but there was one problem. He gave his opponent, Jason Ennels, a stroke on the par 3, and his opponent also scored a hole in one. To add insult to injury, Jason was his brother-in-law.

During the 1910 British Amateur, Horace Hutchinson and Bernard Darwin were all even after 18 holes of their match. Following drives on the first play-off hole, Hutchinson hit two shots out-of-bounds before knocking the next one on the green. All Darwin had to do was play safe, but he hit three out-of-bounds himself and conceded the hole.

Professor P. G. Tait was a noted mathematician and philosopher at Edinburgh University. Obsessed with golf, he would spend his summers at St. Andrews, with most of his waking hours spent on the links. It was there that his son, Freddie, learned the game well enough to win the British Amateur on two separate occasions.

The professor conducted different experiments on the flight of the golf ball, developing theories as to the spin required to attain distance and the center of gravity in a golf ball. One of his theories was that a ball could only carry about 190 yards. The ball in use at the time was the gutta-percha, which was not as lively as those in use today. That was in 1892, and it was his son who was driving balls at the university in the experiment to prove his father's theory.

That same year Freddie stood on the 13th tee of the Old Course and let one fly. It carried 250 yards, eventually coming to rest 341 yards from where he stood. So much for Dad's theories.

Three years later, incidentally, Edward Blackwell hit what is believed to be the longest recorded drive with a gutta-percha ball on the 17th, or the Road Hole. He hit it 366 yards on a windless day, and it was measured to assure the accuracy of the distance.

A man who should be remembered for his contributions to golf is Fred Raphael. It was Fred who, as an advertising executive, was tagged to produce "Shell's Wonderful World of Golf" and who then initiated the Legends of Golf event held at Onion Creek, Austin, Texas. That event gave the impetus needed for the Senior PGA Tour to get off the ground. It involved pairing former champions into teams. Professionals like Sam Snead, Jimmy Demaret, Gene Sarazen, Julius Boros, and Tommy Bolt showed that they could still play wonderful golf, and people wanted to see more of them.

Raphael was not a golfer when he assumed his position as the producer of the premier televised golf program in the country. Taking the game up, he was never much good, but he enjoyed the recreation. Fred was once invited by a member to play Pine Valley. Fortunately, he became friendly with Gene Sarazen and Jimmy Demaret, who provided the commentary for his televised golf matches. They encouraged him to play, and Sarazen helped out with equipment, including a huge supply of golf balls. Fred's round was one to be remembered, as he scored 154. To his credit, he counted every stroke, including penalties for lost balls.

The golf balls given to him by Sarazen were the smaller, British-sized, which were not legal in the United States. That certainly didn't make any difference to Raphael, and they gave a golfer of his talent no advantage. A while later the member who arranged for Fred to play Pine Valley phoned and said the club president had called him on the carpet because 24 British-sized golf balls had been found on the course. The member wanted to know what to tell the president. Fred replied, "Tell him to keep looking. There are four more out there somewhere."

*H*ow difficult is Pine Valley? The club hosted an invitational for some of the leading professionals during the late 1930s. That was when Pine Valley played at just over 6,000 yards, not a long course even then. In the 1937 event, Sam Snead and Jimmy Thomson were joint first at 302, a score that was 22-over par.

It is not unusual for a golfer of considerable skills to be going along in fine fashion, when all of a sudden, double figures pop up on a single hole. Cut out of sand, pine, and swamp, the original 184-acre parcel of land now consists of 623 acres. Construction began in 1913 under the supervision of George Crump. Not being a golf architect, he enlisted the help of H. S. Colt. Crump died at the early age of 46 in 1918 and never saw his dream come true. Hugh Wilson was brought in to finish the 12th through the 15th, using Crump's designs, which still existed. Wilson had gained fame for building the East Course at Merion, one of the classic courses in the United States. When Pine Valley was ready for play, it was considered the most difficult golf course in the world. Most still feel that way, as it carries the highest slope rating in the country.

Jay Sigel can also tell you how hard is Pine Valley. During 1983, he was captain of the American Walker Cup team that won at Royal Liverpool. Later in the year he won the Pennsylvania Open, successfully defended his U.S. Amateur title, and then captured the U.S. Mid-Amateur. Few would argue that he ranked among the top five amateur golfers in the world that year, if not the best.

As the season was winding down, he entered the Pine Valley Club Championship. It was a 36-hole event played from the regular tees, not all the way back as is customary in many competitions. The weather over the two days was as nice as anyone might hope for in October. Jay was 16-strokes-over par and still finished second.

A popular gentleman in the Detroit area, John Ginopolis has never claimed to be a good golfer. Still, like millions of others, he enjoys the game. He is better known for running a successful restaurant, one that is frequented by the movers and shakers in the Motor City. Whenever Frank Sinatra came to town, dinner at Ginopolis's restaurant was a priority for the star performer. At Pistons basketball games, Johnny sits in the front row; the same is true with any other sporting event. He is the kind of person everyone likes, for good reason.

When the initial Walter Hagen Invitational was held in 1967, it was a unique event for the Detroit area. The tournament attracted wide coverage by the local media. Each group played with a celebrity, and John drew Mr. Hockey, Gordie Howe. In addition to being one of the finest hockey players in history, Gordie excelled in other sports, including golf, a game in which he once qualified for the Michigan Open. Standing near the first tee, Ginopolis noticed a television crew recording the opening drives. One thing he observed was that the camera continued to focus on the golfer after the tee shot was hit, not following the ball but capturing the stroke follow-through of the participant.

Taking some practice swings at the side of the tee, he tried to visualize how Sam Snead might look from start to finish. The time came for the Howe group to start their round, and John was the first to hit. The camera rolled as Johnny made one of the sweetest swings of his improbable golf career. Unfortunately, the ball was topped, traveling only about fifty yards on the ground. That didn't fase John, who kept perfect balance and looked straight out the fairway to some distant point where a good drive would land. Howe looked at him and said, "Hey, John, the ball's right in front of you."

Through clenched teeth, Ginopolis continued his pose, replying, "I know. I know."

When Mike Souchak moved to Detroit to take over as the head professional at Oakland Hills, he invited John and Mike Lucci, the former Detroit Lions linebacker, to play a round with him at the famous course. Most of the members had not had the opportunity to meet Souchak, and when Ginopolis, Lucci, and Souchak got to the first tee, a fairly large group had assembled to watch Souchak take a swing. Mike suggested Ginopolis hit first. Any golfer about to hit the first drive is nervous, but for Johnny, it was a nightmare with the big gallery. The result was a whiff. He turned to Mike and said, "I knew this course was tough, but I didn't know it was this hard."

*J*immy Demaret said that Clayton Heafner was the most even-tempered golfer on tour: "He's angry all of the time."

Once, during the Oakland Open, the announcer mispronounced his name on the first tee. Heafner was so incensed that he walked off the course and withdrew from the tournament without hitting a single shot.

🚩

G reat care is taken by the championship committee when the pairings are made for the opening two rounds. Winners of recent majors, those who have won tour events, nonwinners, and qualifiers are usually lumped in the same categories. It has also been a practice to put past champions together, even if they are not as competitive as they were when they won the title.

When Ian Baker-Finch discovered he was paired with Arnold Palmer in the 1996 British Open at St. Andrews, he was vocal in complaining that he had to play with a "has-been." It was to be Arnold's final British Open and was recorded for golf history when he doffed his cap on the Swilcan Bridge for a timeless photograph. Playing with the man who returned the oldest of golf championships to its prior glory should have been an honor for any golfer.

Starting the opening round, Baker-Finch was introduced, acknowledged the applause, and stood over the ball for his drive. As he took his swing, a wind blew off his visor, and he made a vain attempt to hit the drive. The ball barely got off the ground, starting left. It continued in that direction, across the 18th fairway, not stopping until it was out-of-bounds. A complete miss would have brought better results. It was hard for Arnold to hide the little smile as he observed what may have been the worst drive ever hit by a past champion off the first tee.

🚩

B ill Rogers probably enjoys remembering winning the British Open at Royal St. George's in 1981 more than anything else in his career. There was an incident on the 17th hole during the Colonial National Invitational, however, that he would probably like to forget. When he reached the top of his backswing, Bill felt something pop in his wrist. With a quick reaction, he missed the ball on purpose, by at least a foot. Neither he nor his playing partner, Bruce Lietzke, knew which rule might apply, so Rogers called for a ruling from an official.

Rule 14 defines a stroke as "the forward movement of the club made with the intention of fairly striking at and moving the ball." In this case, it was obvious to those watching that Bill had not tried to strike the ball. Since the pop in his wrist occurred after Rogers had set the club at the top of his swing, he was still charged a penalty stroke. He missed the cut by one stroke.

*E*arly in 1973, Johnny Miller was playing in the Atlanta Classic; he needed a par on the final hole for a victory. It would have been his third professional win, and he wanted it badly. The hole was a fairly easy par 5, so he stood confidently on the tee.

His drive started out at the light rough and began to hook. Miller felt it was going to be in a good position for his second to the green. But there was a woman sitting in a metal seat at a point where the ball might land, and as she watched the flight of the ball, she became concerned. The lady jumped up and moved away, but she didn't take the seat with her, and that's where the gods of golf came into play.

Miller's ball hit the seat at an angle that caused it to fly about a hundred feet in the air, dead right. It came to rest four inches out-of-bounds, and the tournament was lost.

*Y*ou might expect golfers good enough to make it to the final of a national championship to be pretty accurate. That wasn't the case in the 1939 British Amateur. Between them, Alex Kyle and Anthony Duncan hit nine balls out-of-bounds during the match.

*T*here are times when golf officials are criticized for rulings. Some of the criticism is not warranted, but in one case, it seems as if the officials were in another world when they made a decision. It happened to Brett Upper, who returned the lowest 72-hole total and yet was not declared the champion. Brett was not guilty of signing for a wrong score.

No one called and said they saw him break a rule. He became a victim of circumstances.

Having won the 1990 PGA of America Club Professional Championship gave him an automatic invitation to play in the 1991 British Club Professional Championship. In addition, the former tour player also received an exemption to play in the PGA Championship and World Series of Golf. It should have been a most enjoyable trip, but it turned into a disaster.

Upper played brilliantly in the final round. He was the only competitor to score under par, with the result that he edged Scotland's Billy McColl by one stroke. That's when the committee met, making a ruling that may have been the worst ever made. They stated that he was not a member of their association, so he could not be declared the champion even though they had invited him to participate. McColl was declared the champion, given the trophy with his name engraved on it and a year's free use of an automobile. He also received an invitation to play in the 1991 American event. Brett did receive the winner's check, but he was never recognized as champion of a tournament he actually won.

*B*efore embarking on a successful career as a professional golfer, which included 82 LPGA victories, Mickey Wright was a student at Stanford University. Mickey was arguably the finest woman golfer of all time and possibly had the best swing of any golfer in the history of the game, man or woman. No less an authority than Ben Hogan said that of her swing.

One of the classes she took while in college was golf, and her final grade was a D, barely passing and certainly not with honors. Later admitting to being a bit of a smart aleck, Mickey said she probably deserved the low mark she was given by Mrs. Brown, who never won a golf tournament of any consequence.

*A*t the 1932 PGA Championship at the Keller Course in St. Paul, Minnesota, there was one match that looked as if it was going to end early. Al Watrous was nine up on Bobby Cruickshank with 13 holes to play. Watrous was a fine player; he won the 1922 Canadian Open and finished second to Bobby Jones when the amateur won his first Open title at Royal Lytham in 1926. Al conceded a par putt to Bobby, which was not that easy, and the hole was halved. Then Cruickshank began a run of 11 consecutive one-putt greens. The lead started to dwindle, and when Wee Bobby made a long one on the 18th, they were all-even.

On the fifth extra hole, Al was on in two about 20 feet from the hole, but he three-putted. Bobby sank a six-footer, and what appeared to be a rout turned into one of the big disasters in the history of the PGA Championship, possibly because of one conceded putt.

The runner-up in that PGA Championship to Olin Dutra was Frank Walsh. The PGA media guide that year stated, "Frank is a long driver down wind."

One PGA Championship that had a strange twist occurred in 1941 at the Cherry Hills Club in Denver, Colorado. The finalists were Byron Nelson, the defending champion, and Vic Ghezzi. Even though Byron was three up with nine to play, Ghezzi began a birdie barrage to finish all-even. They halved the 37th, and it looked as if the same thing would happen on the 38th.

Both hit good drives, and their seconds were just short of the green. Each hit chips to about four feet from the cup, with Nelson an inch or two away. He lined up the putt, concentrating on the line, and stroked the ball. On his follow-through, his putter head touched Vic's ball, and Byron was given a one-stroke penalty. That gave Ghezzi his only major title.

Andra Kirkaldy, a colorful golfer from St. Andrews who was named the Honorary Professional for the R&A, once missed a one-inch putt on the Foreman's Hole during the second round of the 1889 Open at Musselburgh. Andra carelessly tried to play it with one hand. The marker asked if he had tried to putt the ball, and Kirkaldy replied, "Yes, and if the hole was big enough I'd like to bury myself in it."

YOU KNOW IT'S BAD WHEN THEY NAME A BUNKER AFTER YOU

A fine Scottish golfer who eventually made his way to America was Willie Campbell. He would be better known had he won the British Open Championship, but that wasn't to be, primarily because of a bunker at Prestwick's 16th hole. Prestwick had been lengthened to 18 holes from the original 12 in 1883. The next year the club again hosted the Open, and that's when Willie took four shots to get out of the bunker and lose the championship that appeared to be his. To this day, the bunker is called "Willie Campbell's Grave."

A nother short putt was missed in the British Open 92 years later on the 14th hole at Royal Birkdale, which did have an influence on the outcome of the championship. Tom Watson was trying to win his fifth title, but it wasn't a walk in the park.

Hale Irwin was on the green in regulation during the third round, and his approach putt stopped within a couple of inches of the hole. Thinking about the birdie that got away, Hale did something that many golfers have done before and since. He tried to knock it in with the sole of his putter. Much to his surprise and dismay, Irwin hit the ground with the back flange, and the putter blade went over the ball for what amounted to a whiff.

In the final round, Hale played well, only to finish one stroke behind Watson. What might have resulted in a play-off never occurred because of a careless lapse of concentration.

While one can only guess what the outcome of the British Open might have been if Irwin had holed his putt, there was one incident when the final standings were definitely affected because of a missed two-footer.

Leo Diegel was the professional golfer who adopted a strange putting stroke because of the problems he had with the short club. This was back when no one dreamed of having a long putter to solve putting woes. Leo tried everything to improve his performance on the green. Unfortunately, it didn't help him in the 1933 Open Championship at St. Andrews.

Both Denny Shute and Craig Wood had already posted 292, which would result in a play-off the next day. Diegel knew he needed two putts on the final hole to tie and also to qualify for the play-off. He hit his first putt, which ended up only two feet from the hole. The next should have been routine for a man who already owned two PGA crowns. The result, however, was a complete miss. That dropped Leo to joint third and offered no chance to add his third major title.

During the first round of the 1974 English Open Amateur Stroke Play at Moortown, Nigel Denham hit his approach a bit too strongly on the final hole. That might be a mild way to state it. The ball bounced up the steps and into the clubhouse right through an open door. It hit a wall and finally stopped in the men's bar, about 20 feet from the windows. It was determined that Nigel's ball was still in play, as the clubhouse was not out-of-bounds.

He opened the window and pitched the ball to within 12 feet of the cup. Denham was congratulated on his shot; but several weeks later the R&A ruled that he should have been given a two-stroke penalty for opening the window. They said the clubhouse was an immovable obstruction and no part of it should have been moved. So, if that ever happens to you, hit the pitch shot a bit harder than Nigel did, because the glass is bound to slow up the ball a little.

One of the sad stories in golf occurred in 1973, but the name of the lady has never been revealed. Dick Sarta, the professional at Preakness Hills Country Club in Wayne, New Jersey, related the incident, protecting the innocent or victim, as the case may be.

Playing in a women's club tournament, a member came to the final tee in the 72-hole competition with a 24-stroke lead over her nearest rival. The last hole was a 125-yard par 3 over a small pond, and she had no problem with it in the previous three rounds. Not so this time. She swung 14 times, and the ball came to rest in the water after each tee shot. Finally, the 15th cleared it, and she holed out for a 31. Good-bye trophy and more than a dozen golf balls.

Not long for a par 5, the 13th at Augusta National has nevertheless been the scene of a few interesting incidents. One occurred in 1953 during the playing of the third round of the Masters. Johnny de Forest hit his approach shot into the bank of the creek in front of the green. After looking at it, he decided he could play the ball from its position rather than take a drop and the penalty stroke.

Carefully, he removed one shoe, a sock, and rolled up his pants to above his knee. He then placed his left foot on the bank and his right in the water. There was only one problem. He had removed the shoe and sock from the wrong foot, much to the delight of the gallery.

In 1977, Tsuneyuki Nakajima became the youngest Japanese PGA champion in history. He was rewarded with an invitation to play in the Masters the following year. Nakajima eventually became known to golfing fans around the world as "Tommy," although he was still Tsuneyuki when he made his first trip to Augusta.

He was even par that day as he came to the Azalea Hole. Unfortunately, he had scored an 80 in his opening round. In order to make the cut, Tommy was going to have to make a few birdies, so maybe an eagle on the 13th would make his task a little easier. Trying to hit a long drive, Nakajima hooked it into the water, took a drop, and hit his next shot only about 90 yards. Then he hit his fourth in the creek in front of the green. Thinking he might be able to hit out of the water, Tommy took a swing, and the ball came down on top of his shoe. That resulted in a two-stroke penalty. Now, the total was seven. Handing the club back to his caddie so it could be cleaned, after which it was dropped in the hazard, caused another two-stroke penalty. He was successful on the next swing, although the ball went over the green. From there in, it was routine—a chip and two-putts for a 13, thus breaking the record high in the Masters for one hole set by Frank Walsh in 1935, when he had scored a 12 on the 8th.

The press asked if Tommy would come to the interview room, and being a gentleman, he agreed. When asked if he lost his concentration, he replied through an interpreter, "No, I lost count."

*H*aving recorded a 13 on one hole in a major had to be a nightmare for Nakajima. Surely something like that was not going to happen again and certainly not in the same year. He would find out that lightning can strike twice.

Tommy entered the British Open, which was held that year at St. Andrews. He was having a good championship. Starting the final round, Nakajima was only one stroke behind Greg Norman, but he three-putted the first hole and went downhill from there. By the time he got to the 17th, he was no longer in contention; but he still hit two excellent shots to reach the lower level of the green in regulation. Tommy putted, then watched in horror as the ball picked up speed as it went left, into the Road Bunker. The bunker is deep, and the green slopes away from it. A delicate sand shot was required to make sure the ball didn't continue onto the road. Three times he swung, and three times the ball failed to make it over the lip by inches. Finally he was able to get out on the fourth try, and he then two-putted and made a nine on the hole after reaching it in regulation figures.

While the bunker is still officially known as the Road Bunker, the St. Andrews caddies christened it "The Sands of Nakajima."

$\mathcal{M}$aybe there's something about the Road Hole and golfers from Asia. During the 1992 Dunhill Cup, which consists of team competition between different nations, Nam-Sin Park was one of the members of the South Korean contingent. He hit a drive that looked as if it was out-of-bounds, so he hit another. When the round was over, Christy O'Connor Jr. reported to officials that his opponent didn't announce that he was hitting a provisional ball in English. There was one large problem. The South Korean didn't speak the language. It didn't make any difference to the officials. Park was still disqualified, which led to a victory for the Irish team.

$\mathcal{A}$nother golfer, who was invited in the interview room at Augusta like Nakajima even though he had not recorded a stellar round, was Seve Ballesteros in 1988. He would have preferred that one question had not been asked. A writer inquired as to how Ballesteros four-putted the 16th, and Seve said, "I miss the hole. I miss the hole. I miss the hole. I hole it."

$\mathcal{T}$hose having had the opportunity to see Tommy Bolt play consider him one of the better shot makers of all time. He could maneuver the ball left to right, hit it high or low, and invent a shot when it was needed. Bolt had the reputation of also being the most celebrated club thrower in golf. In reality, Tommy didn't throw clubs that many times, but he made the most of that reputation. He would explain that he had perfected the throw so that the club always went down the fairway and toward where he had hit the shot, so as not to waste time picking it up. In those days of limited prize money, anything a golfer could do to make himself more attractive to the fans was a plus and could result in some extra cash for exhibitions and endorsements. What is not generally known is that Tommy's anger was usually reserved for himself. In reality, he was a most pleasant man with a great many friends and a very generous person.

After he won the U.S. Open in 1958 at Southern Hills, there were the usual number of offers for Tommy to participate in exhibitions, and every sponsor wanted the reigning U.S. Open champion to play in their tournament. The PGA had passed a rule that golfers could not receive appearance money, but that pretty much applied to the American tour, and there were ways to circumvent those rules.

Bolt was asked to play the Caribbean Tour the winter after his important victory. To get name players, tournament directors almost had to guarantee some money, since the purses on that tour were smaller than those in the United States. There was great appeal in playing in those warm-weather locations, and it could make for a wonderful family vacation. Bolt was signed to give exhibitions in such places as Bogotá, Colombia; San Juan, Puerto Rico; and Caracas, Venezuela. It just happened that those clinics coincided with the dates of the tournaments to be held in the same locations. Of course, travel expenses were included. While it was not appearance money, it amounted to the same thing.

The club-throwing reputation preceded him, even in the Caribbean, and Bolt wasn't about to disappoint the galleries. At one clinic he finished hitting shots and explained that golf was really a simple game, and everyone could enjoy playing regardless of age or ability. To prove his point, he asked his son to come to the practice tee and show the people what his father had taught him. With that, the young boy grabbed a club and threw it down the range.

There was a previous incident that added to his nicknames of "Terrible Tempered Tommy" and "Thunder Bolt." When Bolt played in the Motor City Open at Red Run, in Michigan, his caddie was Lincoln Jackson. Linc eventually became a golf professional himself, gaining the moniker "Big Bear" because of his size. But, back in 1952, Jackson was a lean youngster and a good athlete, excelling at all sports. The two hit it off very well during the practice rounds; Bolt was impressed with Jackson's knowledge of the game and the course. Then the tournament began.

The opening hole was a par 5, not overly long and very definitely a birdie hole for the talented players in the tournament. Bolt was a great admirer of Ben Hogan. He worked hard to perfect a slight fade on all of his shots, just as Hogan had done. He believed it could be controlled better than a hook, and like his idol, he spent countless hours on the practice tee working toward that end.

Tommy was hitting an approach to the green, which was guarded on the left by a tree. A great many golfers tried to position the second shot on the right side of the fairway to take the tree out of play and give a better angle to the hole. Bolt's shot started toward the right side of the green. As soon as he saw the beginning flight of the ball, he knew it would miss the green, since it was going to fade.

When the shot flew off the club face, Linc laid down the bag and walked forward to pick up the divot. Intent on the flight of the ball, Tommy didn't see his caddie. All he could think of was how he had hit the shot wrong, missing the birdie opportunity, and he began to get angry with himself. Bolt did what came naturally to him. He threw the club directly down the fairway, following his own instructions of always throwing toward the target. There was only one problem. Linc was in the way. The caddie bent down, picked up the divot, and started back so it could be replaced. As he looked up, there was a club coming just to the right of his head.

Without a moment's hesitation, Linc reached up and plucked the club out of the air by grabbing the shaft, never missing a step. As he walked back, he cleaned the face of the club, put the divot in the scarred earth, stepped on it, picked up the bag, and replaced the club without a single word. It was almost as if the sequence had been choreographed by some dance instructor. The gallery couldn't believe what it had just seen and began to laugh. The red began rising up Tommy's neck. It was probably a combination of being concerned that he could have hurt his caddie and that he was also upstaged by a teenage boy. When Bolt finished the hole, making a par, there still was no discussion about the incident, although the gallery was still buzzing.

On the second tee, Tommy hit his drive right down the middle of the fairway, looked at Linc, and flipped the club into a nearby tree, saying, "Catch that one, wise ass."

During his American tour of exhibitions in 1900, Harry Vardon entered the U.S. Open at the Chicago Golf Club in October, resulting in a victory by this British golfing hero. On the final hole, the championship was well in hand, and he made a careless jab at a putt no longer than six inches. He missed the ball completely, then took a proper stance and holed the putt. When the championship concluded, he still had a margin of two strokes over his nearest opponents, but Vardon was embarrassed at his carelessness.

Richard Boxall, an English professional, had experienced some pain in his left leg while he was competing in the 1991 Open, but with such an important championship at stake, he continued on and dismissed the irritation. As he walked on the ninth tee, he was only two strokes behind the leader.

Then it happened. Boxall hit his drive and collapsed on the ground. He had broken his tibia and had to be taken to the hospital in an ambulance.

Move over, John Daly. During the second round of the 1992 Texas Open, Carl Cooper wanted to get his tee shot as close to the green on the 456-yard third hole as possible. After all, that's a formidable two-shotter. His drive carried about 300 yards, a distance that would make most golfers happy. The ball hit an asphalt cart path on the downslope and took a huge bounce. It continued down the path beyond the 5th green and then past the sixth tee, ending up near the 12th green.

The ball finally stopped because of a chain-link fence. An unofficial measurement placed the tee shot at 787 yards. Cooper might have been impressed with the length but not the final result. He recorded a double bogey and missed the cut by two strokes.

After Frank Beard finished writing his book *Making the Turn,* the publisher was anxious to get it into the stores and on the shelves. After all, Frank had collaborated on one 22 years earlier, in 1970, a chronicle of his year on the PGA Tour, which sold very well. The 1992 book dealt with his experiences and observations on the PGA Senior Tour.

There was only one problem. In the publisher's haste to get it to the stores, the first 5,000 copies had a full-color photo on the dust jacket of Tommy Aaron—not Frank Beard.

There was another printing error that happened when John Feinstein's *The First Coming: Tiger Woods: Master or Martyr* was published in 1998. The photograph used for the cover was printed backward, making Tiger a left-hander.

HOW CRAIG STADLER'S PANTS COST HIM $37,333

Never known as a fashion plate, Craig Stadler once tried to keep a pair of slacks from being soiled, and it cost him dearly. He hit a shot under a pine tree on the 14th hole during the 1987 Shearson Lehman Brothers Andy Williams Open. After looking at his options, Craig laid a towel on the ground to kneel on so he could hit the next shot. Not much was made of the incident until highlights of the third round were being aired on television on Sunday.

The telephones began to ring questioning whether Stadler had broken Rule 13-3, which states, "A player is entitled to place his feet firmly in taking a stance, but he shall not build a stance." Officials reviewed the tape and decided he had indeed done just that. Since Craig had turned in his scorecard the previous day, it meant he had to be disqualified for signing an incorrect scorecard.

Unfortunately, he wasn't informed of the decision until he had completed the final round, thinking he had tied for second place and won $37,333. Instead, Craig received nothing.

There was a bit of poetic justice to the story. The tree became diseased, and it was decided that its removal was necessary in 1995. Stadler had the honor of helping to cut it down. There was no report about the slacks he wore for the occasion.

*A*nother tree caused a disastrous 9 on the scorecard for Arnold Palmer during the 1967 Bing Crosby National Pro-Am at Pebble Beach, and it was also on the 14th hole. Going for the green in two, Arnold hit the tree and the ball went out-of-bounds when it bounced the wrong way. Dropping another, he again hit the large pine with the same result.

That night, there was a violent storm and the tree was toppled. Arnold has always had a lot of admiring fans, but he never knew Mother Nature was one of them.

*T*he highest score ever posted in the U.S. Open was recorded by J. D. Tucker in 1898 at the Myopia Hunt Club. The unfortunate golfer shot 157 in the first round. The course was no pushover that year. Over the four rounds of the championship, the average score was 90.97.

*W*ith the possible exception of the Home Hole at the Old Course, perhaps the most photographed in the world is the 16th hole at Cypress Point. From the championship tees, it measures 233 yards across an inlet of the Pacific Ocean, with the green situated on a small peninsula. When the wind is blowing in the golfer's face, it can make a difficult tee shot almost impossible. For shorter hitters, there is an area to the left of the green that can be used as a target so the player can lay up and then pitch to the green in hope of saving par. When Cypress Point was used as one of the courses for the Bing Crosby National Pro-Am, the 16th always ranked as the most difficult hole on the PGA Tour.

Ed "Porky" Oliver, a leading professional in the 1940s, once recorded a 16 on the hole with five shots in the water. Henry Ransom found his ball playable on the beach, if it could really be called playable. He finally picked up after attempting to hit it up the sheer cliff to the green. After his last shot ricocheted off the rocks and hit Ransom, he told his caddie to pick it up. "When they start hitting back at me, it's time to quit," he said. Without hitting one shot in the water, another professional, Hans Merrill, made 19 when his ball landed in one of the dreaded ice plants, which look so innocent but are impossible to play out of when a ball lands in them.

*G*ranting exemptions into major championships without a golfer's having to go through qualifying rounds has become routine. Usually those selected are past champions who may be beyond their prime or someone who had been inactive for a period of time because of an injury. At times, the exemptions cause controversy but for the most part are accepted by golf fans.

In 1941, Nelson Rockefeller, later to become governor of New York and Vice President, made a special request of the USGA to include two Brazilian golfers in the U.S. Open field. They had set sail for the United States but didn't make it in time for the qualifying rounds. His intervention, plus appeals from the Brazilian Golf Federation, finally got them into the championship at Colonial Country Club. One of the golfers was Walter Ratto. Whether he deserved an exemption was answered with his opening tee shot. Ratto hit a tree with the ball, and it bounced back over his shoulder, behind the first tee. His playing partner asked, "Am I up, or are you away?" The Brazilian returned scores of 90 and 100.

Golfers waiting for a starting time at a public course have been known to grumble because there were too many players. Even a private club member gets upset when calling for a Saturday morning tee time, only to find that the earliest spot available is noon.

Take heart. It could be a lot worse. Consider that the typical golf club in Japan might have 2,800 members with only one course on which to play. Next, take the case of Ken Mizuno. In February 1992, he was arrested by Japanese authorities on charges of evading $44.4 million in taxes. It seems that Mr. Mizuno sold some memberships to Japanese golfers so they could tee it up at Ibaraki Country Club, northeast of Tokyo. He wasn't happy selling 2,800 memberships at anywhere between $13,950 and $54,260. He sold 52,000 memberships to the club. Now, that could make for a very long wait on the first tee.

Dr. Sherman Thomas of Washington, D.C., got goosed on the golf course in 1979 and didn't like it one bit. As he was about to putt, a goose honked, causing him to miss. Dr. Thomas became so enraged, he clubbed the goose to death. It resulted in his being brought to trial and fined $500.

Professional golfers once staged a strike at the 1929 Orange Free State Championship in Bloemfontein, South Africa. One player, Archie Toss, was not a member of the PGA, so 13 other competitors refused to play. Tournament authorities declined the association professionals' demands to disqualify him, since Archie had paid his own expenses to get to the site from Cape Town. Finally, three of the protesting professionals agreed to participate, and the tournament was staged with Toss the winner in a very small field.

🚩

*A*nother strike occurred at the 1978 Dutch Open, with circumstances much like those in South Africa. The European Tournament Players' Division (ETPD) got concerned about all of the Americans who were entering European events. Many of them were tourists, not golfers who played on tour, but tourists who were wearing white shoes and carried cameras. They were in Europe to see the sights and play an occasional round of golf. What could be better than entering a tournament? The argument was that the quality of play was not very high for tourists of that type, and they cluttered the field, depriving some European professionals of the opportunity to participate.

An agreement was finally reached between the ETPD and the Dutch Federation to allow only qualified Americans to play in their championship. It included PGA members and the top 15 nonqualifiers from the PGA Tour school. The accord seemed simple enough. Few regular American PGA members entered European tournaments, and if a professional wasn't good enough to qualify for the American PGA Tour, chances were that he wouldn't offer too much competition.

The Dutch Federation, however, sent out ten sponsor's invitations, as had been their custom for the previous 59 years. Three of those invitations went to Bobby Risch, Kurt Cox, and Scott Simpson. They were Americans who would not normally have been eligible under the new pact. The Dutch considered them special invitees and not subject to the agreement they had with the ETPD. The European professionals didn't agree with that decision and issued a strike notice.

The tournament began with the three Americans, six amateurs, and a few Dutch club professionals. After the first round, the two groups got together again, agreeing that the championship would start anew and be a 54-hole event. Two of the stipulations were that if one of the three invited Americans won, he could not be called the Dutch Open champion. Any money he won would not be paid by the ETPD but by the Dutch Federation. As it turned out, an American who had joined the strike against his fellow countrymen, Bob Byman, won the title.

The 1987 Senior Tournament Players Championship went into the record books as the first over-50 tournament won by Chi Chi Rodriguez. The unsung hero, however, was Al Chandler. On the 15th hole, Al hit his second shot near an oak tree where he twice missed the ball completely as he was trying a chip shot. Finally on the green, Chandler carelessly whiffed for the third time as his putter passed over the ball on a short tap-in. Three complete misses on one hole by a golf professional.

Playing in the 1993 International, Dennis Trixler missed short putts on the first and second holes. He told his caddie that he was going to switch to his driver on the next hole. Following his approach, Trixler pulled out the Big Bertha and holed a 35-footer from the fringe. On the next 10 holes, he made six birdies and thought he might have found the answer to his putting woes.

Alas, it didn't turn out that way. Dennis tried using it again during the first round of the Greater Milwaukee Open; he had 35 putts and shot 76. It was back to the conventional putter after that.

Jackie Pung, a professional from Hawaii, shot 298 in the 1957 U.S. Women's Open at Winged Foot, apparently the winner over Betsy Rawls. There was only one problem. She had scored a 6 on the fourth, but her marker put down a 5 for the hole. Jackie's total for the round, 72, was correct, and there was never any question about cheating. The penalty for such an infraction is disqualification.

Members of Winged Foot came to her rescue. While they couldn't replace the trophy, nor change the record, a collection was taken and Jackie was presented with $2,520. That was more than the $1,800 Betsy received for being the champion. When a member was asked why they took up the collection, he replied, "After all, she did win."

Rules have caused the downfall of other golfers as well. In most cases, the contestants know them pretty well, but there are times when an infraction can cause a problem that even goes beyond a couple of strokes or disqualification.

Acting as a referee in the CPC Women's International, John Laupheimer was assigned to a group that included Alice Dye, Mary Everard, and Julia Greenhaigh. On the fourth hole, Julia asked Mary to mark her ball, which was in a direct line between her position and the hole. Mary marked as requested and threw the ball to her caddie, who cleaned it and returned the ball to the player after Julia had played her shot. There was one major problem. The ball had not been on the putting surface, and cleaning it was not permitted according to Rule 23-2. It resulted in a stroke penalty.

Mary was not aware of what had happened until John told her on the way to the next tee. To put it mildly, she was upset with the ruling when she was informed and refused to talk with the referee for the remainder of the round. It would have been bad enough had the penalty been called by any other person, but Mary and John had been married just a few months before. So much for wedded bliss.

Sawgrass doesn't need any help to be a difficult golf course, but during the 1977 Tournament Players Championship, the wind began to blow and made it much harder rather than merely difficult. That tournament probably draws the strongest field of the year, but the players were humbled during the second round as the winds were coming from the west at 30 to 40 miles per hour.

J. C. Snead had already hit to the green on the fourth hole when a gust lifted his plantation hat and sent it rolling on the brim like a wheel. Snead watched helplessly as it turned over and over, eventually hitting his ball. The result was a stroke penalty, which contributed to his 76. Still, that score was three better than the average that day for the best professional golfers in the world.

T. C. Chen, the only golfer to make a double eagle in U.S. Open history, seemed to have things in hand as he played the final round in 1985 at Oakland Hills. As he walked on the fifth tee, he enjoyed a four-stroke lead and was playing steady golf. His approach to the green was hit with a 4 iron and was at least 30 yards off-line. It was the first indication that things might get interesting.

It landed in the heavy rough among some trees. T.C. still had a clear shot, but he didn't quite get to the green, and the ball remained in the ever-present U.S. Open rough, about a yard short of the putting surface. From there, he hit a wedge, not once but twice. On the follow-through, Chen clipped the ball again, incurring a penalty stroke. Now he was laying five and was still not on the green. His chip was a bit bold, and after two putts, he recorded an 8 for the hole. Stunned by what had happened, T.C. bogeyed the next three holes, and from four ahead, he found himself three behind. Andy North went on to win the championship; but T.C. added to golfing lore, as such a shot is now known as "hitting a Chen."

*P*iloting a single-engine airplane, David Hughes was spraying for mosquitoes over the 12th hole at the Fort Washington Golf Club in Pinedale, California. Naturally, the plane was low, flying about 80 feet above the fairway. Suddenly, he saw a golf ball come up over the nose; before he could react, it crashed through the windshield and hit his helmet, just above his right temple.

The ball flew out the open right window. David had some cuts, but he managed to land the airplane without a further mishap. There was no report as to what happened to the golf ball, but the course was sent a bill for $312 by the Consolidated Mosquito Abatement District of Fresno County for damages.

*B*obby Jones certainly became a legend in golf, but early in his career, the real legend was Harry Vardon, winner of six British Open championships, in addition to the 1900 U.S. Open. Jones was paired with him in the 1920 U.S. Open at Inverness.

In the second round, they came to the seventh hole, and both hit well-positioned drives. Vardon, slightly away, hit a run-up that finished close to the hole. Jones decided to pitch his ball, choosing a niblick. Instead of the shot coming off as he planned, it was topped and ran over the green into a bunker.

Embarrassed, Jones walked with Harry to the next tee and said, "Mr. Vardon, did you ever see a worse shot than that?"

Vardon, a man of few words, replied, "No." End of discussion.

A golfer named Clayton Moyer once made a bet he could one-putt every green during a nine-hole round. Everything went according to plan for eight holes. On the ninth, he had a 30-foot chip to put himself close, but he chipped it in. Moyer lost the bet, however, because he didn't actually one-putt all nine greens.

*D*apper Jimmy Demaret, who pioneered bright colors in golf apparel, loved playing in the desert, as his record indicates. He twice won both the Phoenix and Tucson opens. His second title at Phoenix came in 1950 but only after a little help from the rules chairman, Bob Goldwater. If the name sounds familiar, it's because he was the brother of Barry Goldwater, the senator from Arizona who ran for the presidency in 1964.

Jimmy drove into some orange trees on the final hole, and the ball remained in one of them. Goldwater let Jim shake the tree until the ball fell. Demaret then hit a wedge on the green and made par, beating Sam Snead by one stroke.

It could have been three Tucson victories for Demaret instead of two. He got to the final hole at El Rio Golf Club, needing a 4 to win with a closing 66 one year. Jimmy proceeded to hit five shots out-of-bounds, taking a 14.

*A*mong the legendary teachers of the game was Tommy Armour, the Silver Scot. Armour emigrated to the United States from his native Scotland after World War I, following service in the army. In his younger days, Tommy was known as the Black Scot, but the years and the color of his hair changed that.

His summer job was as head professional at Medinah, Illinois, but he spent the winters at Boca Raton, Florida, giving lessons to those who could afford them. He was charging $50 for a half hour of instruction in the 1950s, when other professionals were happy to be making $5 for the same amount of time. Much of it was based on Armour's reputation as a great teacher. With a record that included winning the British Open, U. S. Open, and PGA Championship along with a general feeling that he was one of the best iron players who ever lived, golfers felt fortunate to hear his words of wisdom at any price. He was in such great demand that time slots had to be booked weeks in advance.

When Armour gave his lessons, it was in a different manner than those given by other golf professionals. He was not a hands-on teacher. Tommy would sit at a table, under a large umbrella, usually with a Tom Collins in hand, and observe the player, offering advice as the lesson progressed. Seldom would he rise to adjust the golfer's grip or to show the proper swing plane.

One golfer staying at the hotel was able to arrange a lesson with Armour. Arriving at the appointed time, he introduced himself to Armour, who asked, "What's your handicap?"

"Seven," replied the golfer.

"Go ahead and hit some shots for me," instructed the teacher.

The golfer went over to the pile of balls and began to hit shots, being careful to do everything he had learned in prior lessons from other professionals. This went on for about 15 minutes, but Armour had not offered one comment or piece of advice. Seeing his $50 flying away, the golfer finally turned to Tommy and asked, "What do you think?"

Armour looked at him and replied, "You must be one hell of a putter."

*I*mmediately following his victory in the 1927 U.S. Open, Tommy Armour entered the Shawnee Open in Pennsylvania. Two titles in succession were not to be, as he stood on the 17th tee and hooked ball after ball out-of-bounds. Somehow he lost count and had either a 21 or a 23 on the hole. Since he wasn't sure of the exact score, Tommy had to settle for the 23.

*O*ne of the finest ball strikers in the history of golf was Dave Hill. He worked hard on his game and could maneuver the ball left to right, right to left, high, or low. Dave wore his heart on his sleeve and was also outspoken. After playing in the 1977 Ryder Cup Matches at Royal Lytham & St. Annes, for example, Dave announced that he would never return to England. He was upset with the partisanship shown by the British fans, who would cheer poor shots by the Americans, acting more as if they were at a football game than a golf match.

When he was inducted in the Michigan Golf Hall of Fame, he became upset with a playing companion during the pro-am portion of the day prior to the induction ceremonies. On the 18th hole, he hit a mediocre drive and asked his partner, a longtime member of the club, what he should hit for a second shot on the par 5. It resulted in a blind third shot for Hill, something he hated. That evening, another inductee was Wilfrid Reid, the man who had designed the course at the host club. Accepting the honor was Wilf's grandson, Pete Devaney. In his acceptance speech, Pete explained how his grandfather had designed the layout around the 18th hole, considered the signature hole for the course. When the time arrived to induct Dave, he accepted the honor and then told the audience how terrible a hole the 18th was with its blind shot to the green.

Exempt from qualifying for the 1973 U.S. Open at Oakmont, Hill played a practice round that lasted only four holes. He walked back to the clubhouse, packed his clubs, and headed home. He informed the press that he felt the best he could do was to have four or five three-putt greens in each round on the quick surfaces and didn't want to face that possibility.

That decision may have been caused by Dave's behavior at Hazeltine National Golf Club in the 1970 championship won by Tony Jacklin. The Thursday round had been played in difficult conditions, with Jacklin scoring 71 to take the first-round lead. The weather wasn't as bad for the second round, and Hill returned a 69, placing him in the hunt. He was invited to the press tent. Instead, Dave had lunch and with it a few drinks. One of his business partners, Belford Wallen, who lunched with him, encouraged Dave to go for an interview with the press, and eventually he did just that.

Hill gave the customary hole-by-hole account of his round, and then one of the writers asked him how he found the course. Dave responded that he was still looking for it. The rest of the writers saw an opening, and questions began coming from all parts of the press tent. One of the queries was, "What did Hazeltine lack?" Dave answered, "Eighty acres of corn and a few cows."

Everyone forgot, or didn't care, who was leading the U.S. Open. The stories all centered around Hill's criticisms. The USGA didn't do anything, but the PGA stepped up, in the person of commissioner Joe Dey, and fined David $150 for statements not in the best interest of the association. Like other fines that had been imposed on him, Dave didn't flinch. He merely paid it. One of the ironies of that championship was that when Hill received his second-place check, it was unsigned. He had to return it to the USGA for a signature so it could be cashed.

*T*here are a lot of superstitious people in sports and especially in golf. Players have been known to only mark their ball on the green with a "lucky" coin, wear the same color shirt for the final round when that shirt had been worn to win a previous tournament, or never change a golf ball following a birdie, to name just a few.

One golfer who could not be placed in that category was Helen Bopp of Phoenix. She decided to play golf on Friday, February 13, 1981, at the

Villa De Pax Golf Course. On the 13th hole, she took a swing and broke her arm. That may have changed her attitude toward superstitions.

*I*n Malaysia, there is a select group of people who make their living as *bomohs*, or rain doctors. For the 2000 Malaysian Open, the tournament hired one to keep the rain away at a cost of 200 *ringits*. That translates to about $60. In the third round, there was a downpour that halted play, and the bomoh forfeited his fee.

MISTAKEN IDENTITY

*T*he *Burlington County Times,* printed in New Jersey, ran an advertisement in 1979 for a movie. The ad read, "*Going South*—Jack Nicklaus." The actual star of the film was Jack Nicholson.

A college tournament that has grown in stature through the years is the National Minority College Golf Championship. One of the favorites each year has been Jackson State, led by coach Eddie Payton. The golf teams that participate are from predominately black colleges, although the teams may have Caucasian players.

Ironically, the 1999 championship resulted in a team's not being able to play—the University of Texas–Pan American. The team consisted of Hispanics, and the Black College Coaches Association voted not to accept its entry, even though the college was 88 percent Hispanic. Not knowing of the decision until he was already at the tournament site, coach John Garcia had his team play in an unofficial capacity. Had the scores counted, UTPA would have finished second to Bethune-Cookman College, and Manuel Inman would have had the best total for the individual crown.

As it turned out, Bethune-Cookman fielded a team made up of golfers from Australia, Canada, and Great Britain, not one of whom was a minority golfer. Still, the team qualified under the rules.

*A*fter some outstanding rounds, including a course record equaling 63, Greg Norman led the 1996 Masters by six strokes over Nick Faldo, his closest pursuer. The wheels came off during the final round, though, with Norman shooting a 78 to Faldo's 67. It included a stretch of four holes where Greg went from a three-stroke lead to a two-stroke deficit. The six-stroke lead was the largest for any golfer who lost a major championship on the last day up to that date. It also marked the sixth time that Norman had a lead going into the final round of a major and didn't emerge as the champion.

*A*mateurs have always been a part of the Masters. Including them was very important to Bob Jones, a lifetime amateur. At one time, the field included many more nonprofessionals than in recent tournaments. For example, all of the members of the U.S. Walker Cup team were invited, including alternates. One of them in 1954 was Billy Joe Patton from North Carolina, who had been an alternate on the team the previous year.

Career amateurs were familiar with him, but Billy Joe was not necessarily known to the rest of the golfing world, even though he had been victorious in the North-South Amateur. Certainly no one would have listed him as one of the favorites to contend for the Masters.

Surprisingly, Patton tied for the first-round lead with Dutch Harrison, then took it by himself after 36 holes. At the end of the third round, however, he had relinquished the lead to none other than Ben Hogan. But that changed on the sixth hole of the last day, when Billy Joe found the cup for an ace. All of a sudden, he was in front of Hogan and Snead, the two most noted golfers in the field. As he walked on the 13th tee, he was tied with the two legends. His drive was perfect, enabling Patton to go for the green with his second on the short par-5 hole.

Patton did just that, hitting a 4 wood. Unfortunately, the ball hit on the right side, rolled over the bank and into Rae's Creek. He elected to take a drop and eventually holed in seven. After a birdie at 14, Billy Joe again found water on the next, and that was the tournament. He finished one stroke behind both Snead and Hogan. Had it not been for the bold shots over water on both par 5s, Patton might have gone down in history as the only amateur to win the Masters.

Known for his quick wit as a television golf announcer, Gary McCord didn't exactly own the PGA Tour during the 15 years he toiled against the best golfers in the world. While he later took some time off from his broadcasting career and was victorious on both the NIKE and Champion tours, he was never able to cash in with the big boys.

That led Gary to order a vanity license plate that read "NOWINS."

One of the favorites in the 1919 U.S. Open at Brae Burn was "Long Jim" Barnes, who was the first American PGA champion. Paired with him for the opening round was Willie Chisholm. It appears that this was the only start Willie had in the U S. Open, since his name cannot be located among the records for any of the other championships. If it was his only open, Willie made the most of his appearance. He wasn't exactly scaring any of the other competitors as he walked on the eighth tee, a 185-yarder over a deep ravine, at the bottom of which was a small brook with some large boulders just beyond the water. For members of Brae Burn, it wasn't the favorite hole on the course, as they had to climb "cardiac" hill to get to the green. For the U.S. Open, the golf committee graciously built a bridge so players could easily walk from tee to green.

Chisholm had just made a double bogey on the fifth and a triple at the next, which was actually a bit of an improvement over his first four holes. It's probably superfluous to say that Barnes had the honor, but he did, and Jim hit an iron to the green. Willie selected his club, hitting it a little fat. Fortunately it carried over the creek, although it came to rest a few inches in front of one of the boulders.

Walking down to the ball, Willie decided to hit a niblick for his next shot. Jim Barnes took up a position in the middle of the bridge to watch the next shot, or shots, as it turned out. Chisholm took a swing and hit the rock. The next attempt brought the same result, as did the third. Eventually Willie realized the club was going to disintegrate before the rock, so he decided to chip out to the side. Two tries and he was able to accomplish his goal.

Following a little more bad luck, Willie made it to the green, where he proceeded to three-putt. Since Chisholm had been playing the hole for the better part of 30 minutes, he was not sure what his score was and asked Jim for some help. Barnes told him the total was 18, a record high for a single hole in the U.S. Open up to that time.

"Oh, Jim, that cannot be so," replied Willie. "You must have counted the echoes."

*W*illie's record high score on one hole stood unchallenged for 19 years until the U.S. Open was held at Cherry Hills in 1938. The man who established the new standard was Ray Ainsley from Ojai, California.

Running in front of the 16th green was a little stream with some fast-moving water, and that's where Ray's second shot landed. He tried to hit the ball from the water with little success until it finally stopped against a sandbar in the stream. Wanting to make sure he got it out this time, Ainsley gave it a little extra. Actually, it was quite a bit extra, as the ball flew past the green and into some bushes.

Eventually he was able to get it on the putting surface, where he holed out for a 19. When asked why he hadn't taken a penalty stroke from the water, he informed the press that he thought he had to hit the shot from where it lay. Not knowing the rules cost him some additional strokes, but it did get Ainsley in the record books.

*B*oth Chisholm and Ainsley had their "big" holes in a major. John Daly picked the Bay Hill Invitational in 1998 to record a high number. On the final day of the tournament, competitors had to play 36 holes because of weather problems on Thursday and Friday. Playing the back nine first in the last round, Daly came to the sixth hole (his 15th) at 2-under par. The crescent-shaped hole is perhaps the most memorable at Bay Hill. Water adjoins the 543-yard par 5 on the left side from tee to green. It's a matter of biting off as much as you dare from the tee.

Daly tried to hit his tee shot on a line that required a 275-yard carry. The ball landed in the water, so John walked to a point where it had first crossed the hazard and dropped a ball to play his third shot, this time selecting a 3 wood. The next five shots also found the water. As he hit ball after ball, spectators began to call out *Tin Cup,* referring to the movie of the same name in which Kevin Costner played a driving-range pro and did a similar thing on the final hole of the U.S. Open. Daly's sixth attempt cleared the hazard but was buried in the bank, so he had to take a drop, resulting in another penalty stroke.

By this time, he was lying 14. John hit a 6 iron that hit some rocks next to the green and caromed into a bunker. From there, he hit out and two-putted for an 18.

John wasn't trying to just hit the ball and get the hole over with. After each water shot, he aimed a bit farther to the right, but the ball would hook more than the previous shot. Even with the disaster, Daly had 85 for the round, beating two other professionals. For the tournament, he won $4,720. Had he made a par on the hole, it would have resulted in a 285 total, good for $28,000.

*T*he 18 recorded by Daly didn't come close to the official record for the highest total on a single hole on the PGA Tour. The way it happened still brings chuckles to Dave Hill. During the second round of the 1966 Thunderbird Classic, Hill scored a 10 on the 18th hole. His marker, Gardner Dickinson, recorded an 8. Dave looked at the card and put down the 10, but he forgot one important thing. He failed to cross out the 8 in the space for the hole. Dave signed the card and officially had 108 on the 18th, for an 18-hole total of 178. It could have been worse if Dave had marked the 10 after the 8. In that case, the score would have been 810. The recorded total was 98 strokes higher than he had actually scored for the round, but since the card was official, the score stood. David didn't make the cut.

Perhaps Hill was trying to set a new all-time record for the most strokes ever taken on a single hole. While he was able to do that for the PGA Tour, he didn't come close to matching Mrs. J. F. Meehan.

Playing in the Shawnee, Oklahoma, Invitational for women in 1913, she came to the 16th hole, which measured a mere 130 yards. Her husband accompanied her, probably to offer encouragement. He was a bit dismayed when her drive found the river instead of the green. Now, she was playing a special ball. It floated. The ball went with the current, away from the green.

Her hubby saw a boat, helped the missus into it, and began to row after the ball. A bit more than a mile away, the ball came to rest on some ground, enabling her to begin the long trek back. Going through woods and underbrush, either she or her husband kept meticulous count. When she holed out, it was for a 166, a record that will most likely stand forever.

Playing in a record 44 consecutive U.S. Opens, Jack Nicklaus had as much experience with golf rules as any professional golfer. It's also well known that he's a great family man, taking pride in his children and supportive of his sons seeking golf careers. So it wasn't unusual for him to offer to caddie for son Gary in the 1983 qualifier for the U.S. Open. After all, what could be a better experience than to play in the championship with your son in the field?

Jack forgot one thing as a caddie. He somehow miscounted the clubs in Gary's bag. There were 15, and that was one too many. The result was a four-stroke penalty. It wasn't the first time that Jack made a mistake as a bag toter. The previous year, he caddied for Jackie and couldn't locate his errant shot on the first hole, causing a penalty as well.

*T*rying to follow in the footsteps of the greats, Walter Danecki decided to enter the 1965 Open. Walter was a mail sorter from Milwaukee, Wisconsin, who played mostly on weekends on a municipal course. When filling out his entry form for the Open, he had to indicate whether he was an amateur or a professional. He decided he wanted the pot of gold and marked down that he was a professional.

The idea was to combine a vacation in Great Britain and play in the Open at the same time. The entry was filed and accepted by the R&A. Of course, that didn't mean Danecki was automatically entered in the Open. He had to go through qualifying rounds at Hillside, not far from Birkdale, where the championship proper was to be conducted.

His first round was 108. The R&A officials thought he would withdraw and even arranged for a substitute to play the second round in his place. But Walter showed up on the tee, saying he wasn't a quitter. His opening round drew some attention, and he gained a fairly large gallery. After opening with 7-7-8, Danecki settled down and made two bogeys in succession. His good playing was not to last long, however, and when he completed his round in 113 for a total of 221, he missed qualifying for the Open by 70 strokes.

*T*he following year, the R&A put in more stringent requirements, being careful to scrutinize the entry forms. They must have become a bit lax by 1976, when they accepted an entry from Maurice G. Filtcroft. A 46-year-old crane operator, he had just taken up golf 18 months before. His entry indicated he was an unattached professional from Barrow-in-Furness.

Qualifying was held at Formby, in the Liverpool area. When he completed his round, it was 121 strokes, 49-over par. He admitted that some of his scores were approximations, but he did make one par of which he was proud. That came on the 14th. By that time, he had abandoned using woods, teeing off with a 3 iron, because three was his lucky number. His tee shot flew into the rough, from where he recovered before sculling a 9 iron that rolled within three feet of the cup.

The British press had a field day with him, and Maury gave some memorable quotes like, "I did not think I was ready for the Open Championship, but my wife persuaded me to play." Filtcroft resembled Marty Feldman, the television comedian and played the round with mail-order golf clubs. With photographers anxious to preserve the incident on film, Maury just slightly smiled, stating, "If I'd known my picture would be taken, I'd have put in my teeth."

*F*iltcroft didn't stop there. On at least four other occasions, he posted an entry, even using different names. In 1983, for example, he entered as Monsieur Gerard Hoppy, professeur de golf, in Switzerland. He was escorted off the course by the not-too-happy officials. Five years before, Maurice managed to get in nine holes during the qualifying round. He agreed to withdraw if he received a refund of his entry fee. In 1980, he also got in nine holes, but he couldn't talk the R&A into a refund when they told him he was through for the day.

*J*ust making the cut in the Masters is something to remember. Unfortunately, when Charles Kunkle Jr. did it in 1956, his best rounds were behind him. In the final round, he shot a 95—the highest completed score over 18 holes in Masters history.

*A*t times, geese are a great problem at the Oakmont Country Club in Santa Rosa, California. Anyone who has played on a course that has some of these birds can attest to the fact that they can be very messy as well as bold.

Charles Schulz was a frequent player at Oakmont. Of course, he was famous for the *Peanuts* comic strip and all of the items associated with the popular feature. An avid golfer, Schulz used the game as a subject of his comic strip many times. He also used animals such as Snoopy and Woodstock in his strips as well, so seeing geese on the course probably made him feel right at home.

In 1992, he was playing with Dean James, the head professional at Oakmont, when he spied a number of the honkers down the eighth fairway. Schulz hit a good drive, which, after about three bounces, hit a goose. It didn't hurt the bird, who seemed to jump up and then settle down to feed again, but it might have caused the artist to lose a couple of yards. Schulz turned to James and said, "I knew I should have yelled quack."

*B*eing close to the brass ring but not being able to win is a frustration suffered by many outstanding golfers. Making it into a play-off means some very good golf was played, but losing results in second place and a disappointment.

When it comes to losing play-offs, the record belongs to a surprising name. The professional with the most play-off losses in PGA Tour history is Ben Hogan. He participated in 20 play-offs and came away empty 12 times. Losing 11 times in 25 play-offs was Jack Nicklaus. Arnold Palmer, Ray Floyd, and Gary Player each lost 10 play-offs, with Gary successful only three times.

Ben Crenshaw probably hated them more than anyone. In total, he was in eight play-offs on the PGA Tour and never won.

*G*olfers have been known to use four-letter words to describe bunkers, or sand traps, as they are more commonly called by those not adhering to proper golf terminology. There is a famous one, however, that does officially have a four-letter name, the Hell Bunker on the long 14th at the Old Course, St. Andrews.

It has been the downfall of many players through the years and probably will continue to be as long as the game is played at St. Andrews. Perhaps the best-known victim was Gene Sarazen during the 1933 Open Championship.

Gene had won the year before at Prince's, and the victory meant the world to him. If he could successfully defend the championship, he would join a select group, but Hell Bunker did him in. As he was playing the hole, his second was hit a bit thin and ended up in the bunker, which seems to be wider than some hamlets in Scotland. Trying to do more than simply escape from the bunker, Gene buried his next shot under the lip and, after two more mighty swings, finally got the ball out. He recorded an 8 for the hole and missed the play-off between Craig Wood and Denny Shute by one stroke.

A close friend and business associate, Dick Holthaus, and I have played golf together in a great many different states. He was a member of Bellerive in St. Louis and was certainly used to playing difficult courses. I invited him to join me at Indianwood on one of his business trips to Michigan. The course was designed by Wilf Reid and resembles Shinnecock Hills but with moguls, knee-high rough, and plenty of sand bunkers. Except for a few trees, a golfer might feel the course being played was a seaside links.

After we finished the round, Dick turned to me and said, "I've been in more bunkers than Eva Braun."

*T*he Spanish Travel Office tried to cover all of the possibilities in a phrase book issued for tourists. It gave the word "leche" as a suitable swearword to be used when playing golf.

*P*aired together in the final round of the Argentine Open, Vicente Fernandez and Eduardo Romero forgot to exchange the official scorecards given to them on the first tee. Each recorded the other's score on his own card, signed them, and then discovered the awful truth. Both were disqualified, preventing Romero from tying Jim Furyk, who was declared the champion.

During the 1940s, Wilburn Stackhouse was a regular player on the PGA Tour. He was nicknamed Lefty, although he played golf right-handed, but the fame he attained in the game was from his temper. Most of his outbursts came about as a result of his desire to enjoy the spirits that came from a bottle. It was not unusual for Lefty to reach the destination of a golf tournament, begin drinking, and miss his starting time for the first round. That didn't stop him from driving on to the next site and repeating the process.

While some tournament golf was played during the war years, the schedule was much reduced and purses cut. Usually, purses were paid in War Bonds instead of cash. With the country at war, attendance at the events was not up to the numbers attained in the late 1930s. The man who ran the tour was Fred Corcoran, who would do whatever he could to swell the gate. On occasion, that meant inviting celebrities who had nothing to do with the game of golf, a forerunner to the celebrity pro-ams experienced today.

For the Knoxville Open, Fred invited Sergeant Alvin York, the most decorated American soldier in World War I and a national hero, to attend and watch the tournament. York, a native of Kentucky, just might mean a few additional people in the gallery. The war hero had never seen a golf tournament. He stood near the ninth green with Corcoran as Stackhouse was making his way up the fairway. A small field had entered the tournament, so there would be no cut and everyone who finished was assured of some prize money.

True to form, Lefty had been nipping as he went around the course. The combination of the heat and the liquor made it difficult for him to walk, let alone hit a golf ball. As he trudged toward the green, Lefty staggered and fell. He got up to take a few more steps, only to fall again. This time, the effort to rise was just too much, and he remained on the ground, unable to continue. York turned to Corcoran and said, "I never knew golf could be so strenuous." Stackhouse, of course, left for the next tournament without any prize money.

Bill Ezinicki and Jack Thompson hold the record for frustration in the U.S. Open. They have both qualified to play in the championship nine times, but neither has ever made the 36-hole cut.

Playing in the 1992 Men's Senior Club Championship at Indianwood in Lake Orion, Michigan, Jim Van Brunt had no problem hitting a 9 iron on the green on the short 10th hole at the New Course. The ball ended up on the upper right-hand corner, about 30 feet from the cup, which was cut near the lower left portion of the green that day. Up to this time, Jim hadn't exactly been challenging the course record, but he was certainly on his way to qualifying for match play if he continued playing that round, and the one scheduled the following day, in the same manner as he had toured the front nine.

An eight-handicapper, Jim had always been a bold putter, and that may have been his undoing. His first putt slipped by on the right, settling five feet beyond the hole. He stood there as his playing partners tapped in for pars after their first putts. He wasn't too concerned, as he had been making five-footers all day. Jim charged his par putt, and it went five feet past the hole again. The next missed the hole on the low side, and he was facing a three-footer for a double bogey. Perhaps he overadjusted, because this time, the ball missed the hole on the high side, stopping two feet beyond.

It was a simple little thing, but his fifth putt hit the top of the cup and spun left, never seeming to stop in spite of the slow pace of the ball after it had been struck. The ball continued until it got three feet past the hole. Now poor Jim had used up five putts and still wasn't in the cup. By this time, the other three golfers couldn't believe what was happening. Van Brunt had been putting with confidence before he reached the 10th, and his stroke didn't seem any different now. There wasn't one snicker among the golfers.

Jim tried to charge the next putt, which was slightly uphill, but he missed it on the low side. Again, it went three feet past. His seventh putt slid past the high side, finishing two feet beyond the hole. He then hit, in his opinion, the one bad putt on the green. He left his eighth putt short. The tap-in was for a 10, including nine putts.

After the ball settled in the cup, Jim reached in and tried to throw the offending sphere in a pond only about 60 feet away. The ball missed the pond.

There was a happy ending, however. Jim recorded a 94 that day; but on Sunday, he scored 74 and made it into the play-off for match play. Each time Van Brunt passed one of the members who played with him that day, they simply looked at each other and laughed. Not one word had to be said. They knew why they were laughing.

The city council in Gwelo, Zimbabwe, closed the Mkoba Golf Course in 1982. The official reason for closing it was summed up in a statement—it caused "brutality in the bunkers and fun on the fairways." Now, there has to be more of a story behind that pronouncement.

Rules are made to be followed in the game of golf. No other sport has a rule book as thick as the one prepared by the governing bodies. Even with the length, another book exists about the decisions on the rules, which is even larger. Arguments and even fights have been the result of their interpretation.

Waiting to tee off in the 1975 Walker Cup matches at St. Andrews, Bill Campbell was hitting some putts on the practice green adjacent to the first hole. While he was doing that, he looked up and saw that John Grace, his partner in the match, had just hit his drive off the tee.

Campbell immediately went to the official who was refereeing the match and informed him that he had hit a practice shot after Grace had hit, thus breaking a rule. They were penalized by the loss of the hole and went on to lose the match. Of course, Campbell knew the rules in this case, and the integrity of the game was upheld by a true gentleman.

*T*ommy Armour is credited with first using the term "the yips" when trying to explain the putting problem of not being able to take the club back to begin the stroke. He had no explanation as to why it happened, simply saying, "When you've got 'em, you've got 'em."

A classic example did not involve two great players in the golf history books, but two amateurs playing for the club championship of the Memphis Country Club. On the final hole, Hunter Phillips was one down with a three-foot putt to even the match, sending it to extra holes. It had a pretty severe break, so Phillips surveyed it carefully. On two separate occasions, he was ready to hit the putt but backed away to again look at the line. Then, he reached down, picked up the ball, offering his hand to his opponent. He said, "You've got the match. There is no way I could make that thing."

*F*ollowing a practice round for the 1992 U.S. Open, Ian Woosnam said he wasn't overly fond of Pebble Beach, feeling there were too many blind shots. Nick Faldo disagreed when he was told about Ian's comments. He pointed out that the 5-foot 4-inch Woosnam was closer to the ground than he was and that Ian had a lot of blind shots on most golf courses.

*T*he evening before the final round of the 1983 Buick Open, Isao Aoki decided to have Chinese food for dinner. When he finished the meal, he opened his fortune cookie, which had a message that read: "You will take a trip to the desert." Sure enough, the next day Isao twice hit bunkers that resulted in bogeys, and he lost the tournament by one stroke.

*U*ntil the all-exempt tour was introduced, there was a ritual known as Monday qualifying on the U.S. tour. Only the top 60 money winners from the previous year could count on starting any tournament they wished to enter along with a select group of those who were granted lifetime exemptions for having won the PGA Championship.

Golfers who had completed 72 holes in the previous tournament, plus special invitees chosen by the sponsors, joined the exempt players. The other spots in the field were contested for by the "rabbits," or "dew sweepers," who played on Monday. There was probably more pressure in that 18-hole qualifier than in the tournament proper, and it wasn't cheap.

The qualifying rounds were generally held in the same city as the tournament, although usually at different courses. If a player missed the cut at the Phoenix Open and the next event was the Doral, he would have to travel to Miami to see if he was good enough to qualify. He had the same cost for an airline ticket as the golfer on the exempt list. Chances were pretty good he wasn't invited to play in the Wednesday pro-am unless something very unusual happened. Since the qualifier was on Monday and the pro-am on Wednesday, it meant the only time he could practice on the tournament course was Tuesday. The entire procedure didn't make it easy for a young man to make it to the list of top 60 money winners.

In 1974, Mike Reasor was one of the pros facing the dreaded Mondays. The week before, he had made the field at the Monsanto Open, surviving the cut to qualify for the Tallahassee Open. While he was not among the leaders, opening rounds of 73 and 71 meant he would be playing on the weekend at Tallahassee and not have to face Monday qualifying the following week.

Then, on Friday, he went horseback riding and ran into a tree. The result was some badly torn muscles in his left shoulder. Mike couldn't use that arm, which is pretty serious for a golfer. There was one other major problem. To avoid the Monday qualifier, the rule read that the golfer had to complete 72 holes in the previous tournament, not just make the cut. Undaunted, he went to the course and competed on Saturday, using only his right arm. The score was 123, but Mike was back on Sunday. He improved by nine strokes, firing a 114. He didn't collect any prize money, but he did qualify for the Byron Nelson Golf Classic the following week. Sadly, the muscle tear didn't improve, and Reasor had to withdraw from that event, so it was back to Monday qualifying.

*M*ike Reasor's record in a PGA-sponsored event stood until 1992. Senior Chick Evans had scored 71-76 in the 54-hole Vantage during 1992. In the second round, Chick, who is not related to the famous amateur who won the 1916 U.S. Open, hurt his shoulder. It meant the 76 he shot in the second round was really quite an accomplishment. The next day, the shoulder was really giving him trouble. If it hadn't been a tournament, Chick would never have thought of playing on Sunday. In order to receive a check, he had to finish the final round and complete the tournament. Gamely, he toured the course using a 7 iron and putter, unable to take the club back more than halfway. Firing a 70 on the front nine, Evans came back in 56 for a final round of 126. By completing the tournament, he did receive $1,000.

*M*aking the 36-hole cut is important for professionals because today it means an automatic paycheck. Doug Ford, the 1953 PGA and 1957 Masters champion, continued to play on the tour using his life-time exemption well past his playing prime. Between 1975 and 1978, Doug missed the cut in 54 consecutive tournaments, the all-time record for frustration.

"*I*f you three-putt the first green, they'll never remember. But if you three-putt the 18th, they'll never forget." —*Walter Hagen*

*I*ssy Undwin was playing in East London, South Africa, without having too much luck. Through the first 13 holes, he lost 13 golf balls. If nothing else, he was consistent, because he hit his last ball into a pond for the 14th lost ball. Sure that his luck would change, he asked his playing partner if he could borrow a ball. The friend obliged, tossing one to

Issy. He muffed the catch, and the ball went into the pond as well. Feeling it might not be his day, Issy walked in.

A similar incident happened to Dave Anderson when he went out for a round of golf with some friends in Syracuse, New York. He was just beginning to take up the game and probably would have preferred to play a course a bit less demanding than the one his friends selected. It had a great many water hazards, and they took their toll on Dave, who had lost 17 balls in the water as he walked on the final tee.

Happy that there was no water on the hole, Anderson put a ball in the washer, a circular model. As he turned the handle, it came off. Everyone worked on the ball washer, but to no avail. Dave lost the 18th ball in the water, too.

R ecording two holes in one in the same round may not be an everyday occurrence, but it happens often enough that it is no longer big news except in particular circumstances. The feat was accomplished in 1949, when the sectional qualifier for the U.S. Open was held at Plum Hollow. Ray Maguire, the head professional at nearby Birmingham Country Club, was playing his second round of the day and not necessarily challenging for the lead or even for a qualifying spot. Then lightning struck. Maguire aced the 5th hole, and his game improved after that. He made another hole-in-one on the 14th, marking the only time a golfer in USGA competition aced two holes in the same round.

Unfortunately, Ray Maguire lost in a play-off to Max Evans for the final qualifying spot. To add insult to injury, he had to make a hurried telephone call to his wife to drive to the club with enough money so he could buy the customary round of drinks. In fact, Ray bought two rounds of drinks.

D etermination? Playing at Willow Run Golf Club near Milwaukee, Wisconsin, Vicki Knaack took a sip of some iced tea on the 17th hole, and suddenly she felt a burning sensation in her chest. She was rushed to the hospital, where it was discovered that she had swallowed a wasp, which had stung her esophagus. She returned to the golf course to finish and posted a 95. It was the last round of the year, she explained, so she wanted to finish.

The relationship between the touring and club professionals belonging to the PGA of America has not always been amiable. At times, it was outright hostile. Such was the case in 1969, when there was a battle regarding the control of the PGA Tour. Some events were shunned by the stars of the day and deemed unofficial tournaments, even those dating back many years. For example, Tommy Aaron won the Canadian Open, but it is still listed in the record books as an unofficial victory even though only the U.S. Open and the Western Open have longer histories in North America.

The tournament that stands out, however, was the 1969 Michigan Golf Classic held at Shenandoah in suburban Detroit. The metropolitan area had successfully staged such events as the Western Open, PGA Championship, and the U.S. Open in addition to a regular stop, the Motor City Open, which was considered one of the most appealing on the tour. The Detroit area boasted such champions as Ben Hogan, Lloyd Mangrum, and Cary Middlecoff. Attendance had always been high, and there was no reason to think the Michigan Golf Classic would be any different when planned. Problems began to surface when a number of the name professionals boycotted the event. With the lack of stars, fans stayed away. It was reported in one newspaper that the best decision that week was made by Doug Sanders, who withdrew after nine holes.

The tournament went on as scheduled, without large crowds, and it ended in a tie between Homero Blancas and Larry Ziegler. Larry won in a sudden-death play-off for his first-ever tour victory. When it was over, the professionals were told that there wasn't any money in the bank to pay the competitors. The presentation ceremony that is a custom at PGA Tour events was not held. The only people to receive money were the caddies.

Ziegler was philosophical about the circumstances, as the victory gave him an exemption on the PGA Tour that was more important than the money. Eventually, the golfers did receive their checks, but from the PGA and not the sponsors. What concerned Larry was that he never received the official trophy to remind him of his initial win. Later, a golf fan had one made up and presented it to Ziegler, but it wasn't the same as having the original, a finely designed award that resembled the trophy given for winning the World Series. The sponsor had the trophy in an attic for a number of years. Several inquiries were made about the possibility of giving the original to the champion, but the sponsor refused, not wishing for any further publicity about the tournament. In time, he dismantled the trophy. After his death, the sponsor's daughter delivered another trophy to Larry, but it was not the same as having the original. The tournament was commonly referred to as the "Mother Hubbard Open" ever since, because the cupboard was bare.

*H*eading to the tenth hole at Irem Temple Golf Club in Wilkes-Barre, Pennsylvania, R. J. Bachman didn't hit his best drive of the round, but it certainly turned out to be the most memorable tee shot he ever hit. It headed directly for the club's crowded swimming pool and hit directly on the posterior of a sunbathing woman—Bachman's wife.

*A*t the beginning of the 1998 season, the PGA Tour passed a rule that all amateurs playing in the pro-ams were required to wear spikeless shoes. However, the professionals could continue to use spikes.

*A*lmost everyone who watches golf on television knows about the island hole at the Tournament Players Club in Ponte Vedra, Florida. With the exception of a path, the green is surrounded by water. Even though it is a short hole, the professionals have dropped their share of new balls in the drink. In fact, it was reported in 2002 that 150,000 balls are hit in the water on this hole each year. With about

40,000 rounds played there annually, that's an average of 4 balls per golfer. The 17th hole proved to be the pivotal hole in a bizarre tournament in 1985.

The editors of *Golf Digest* decided to try to find "America's Worst Avid Golfer" and asked for nominations. A total of 627 individuals had been nominated, but it came down to four contestants. They were Jack Pulford of Moline, Illinois; Joel Mosser from Aurora, Colorado; Kelly Ireland, who "played" in Tyler, Texas; and Angelo Spagnolo, a grocery store manager in Fayette City, Pennsylvania. Try to memorize those names, and if you ever play in or around those cities, don't get behind them on a golf course.

The Tournament Players Club was set up to be as difficult as possible, with tees back and pin placements that would have cost Dave Hill a few thousand in fines after giving his opinion about them. All four golfers—Pulford, Mosser, Ireland, and Spagnolo—were trying as hard as they could not to finish last. After a practice round, officials thought that if one of the competitors could shoot about 140, he would be the winner. There were no predictions about what would be the worst score. Still, this was about "America's Worst Avid Golfer," and we should concentrate on the man who took the title. The outcome was finally decided on the 132-yard island, or 17th hole.

Angelo made Kelly wait on the tee for about an hour as he tried to negotiate his way on the green. Spagnolo whiffed three times, which was actually a little better than the 27 balls he hit in the water. It turned out that the 132 yards was actually out of his range. Finally, Spagnolo dropped a ball on the cart path, proceeding to putt his way to the green. Once there, Angelo three-putted for a 66. Deane Beman, the commissioner of the PGA Tour, said the cart path would be named "Angelo's Alley." When he finished with a 22 on the final hole for a final score of 257 for 18 holes, it locked up the highest score by 49 strokes.

Think about what he accomplished. His 257 for 18 holes was the equal to the score registered by Mike Souchak for a full 72 holes and the record at that time for the lowest total ever in a PGA Tour event. Of course, Mike played 72 holes. If Angelo had entered that same tournament, someone pointed out, he would have missed the cut by the 14th hole of the first day.

The cut came after 36 holes. In all, the four golfers did not hit one green in regulation, nor did they make a par. There was one bogey to go with eight double bogeys and 63 "others." The four golfers' combined score was 836.

*P*erhaps the most tragic end for a gifted golfer was the one experienced by Johnny McDermott, the U.S. Open champion in 1911 and 1912. Not only was he the youngest to ever win the championship and the first American, but he was the only teenager to do so. He is still listed as the youngest to ever win what is now considered part of the U.S. PGA Tour. Slightly built, McDermott got his start in golf as a caddie in the Philadelphia area. He became a professional in 1909 when only 17 years old.

Confident of his game, Johnny issued a challenge to any professional in Philadelphia for a home-and-home match, an announcement that was made in the newspaper. Accepting the challenge was Jimmy Campbell, and he was soundly trounced by McDermott. The following year he entered the U.S. Open for the first time and almost won it at the age of 18. Finishing in a tie with Alex Smith and his brother, Macdonald, Johnny lost the play-off, but he publicly stated that he would win the next year, and he did.

In 1913, Harry Vardon and Ted Ray were in the United States for their series of exhibitions and to play in the U.S. Open at The Country Club, Brookline, Massachusetts, which became known as the site of the championship won by Francis Ouimet, another former caddie who surprised the golfing world by defeating the great British golfers. There was one other tournament in which the English golfers played, the Shawnee Open. Because they were entered, as well as the leading American professionals, the press attended in large numbers. For the last two rounds, Johnny was paired with Alex Smith, as they were the two leaders. McDermott was up to the task, shooting 70 and 74 for a 293 total and an eight-stroke victory. Vardon and Ray finished fourth and sixth, respectively. Receiving his gold medal and prize money at the presentation ceremonies, Johnny McDermott was encouraged to give an acceptance speech.

McDermott was not an educated man. His life was golf, not school. He was highly confident in his ability to the point where he was probably a brash youngster and certainly proud to be an American. A statement was made that when the U.S. Open was held at The Country Club, he would make sure the British would not take the trophy across the Atlantic. Upon being told that he shouldn't have made such a remark, Mc-Dermott apologized to the British professionals, but the damage was done. Before long, newspapers carried an account of the incident, followed by magazine articles. Johnny received a scathing letter from the president of the USGA indicating that they might not even accept his entry for the U.S. Open at The Country Club even though he was the defending champion.

It was the beginning of the end for McDermott, still only 21 years old. He was not the same confident professional when he played at Brookline and shortly after went into a shell. He did finish fifth in the 1913 British Open at Hoylake and tied for ninth in the 1914 U.S. Open, but the magic was gone. Eventually, he was admitted to an asylum for the insane in Pennsylvania in 1916. On occasion, he would play a casual round of golf, but his results were the results of the best player in the country. McDermott lived out his days in the asylum and at times with his sisters in the family home. Johnny was able to attend the U.S. Open at Merion, Ardmore, Pennsylvania, in 1971, but he was escorted out of the pro shop because of his shabby clothes. Only Arnold Palmer recognized the former champion and paused to greet him.

There is no telling what might have happened in his golf career, because it was snuffed out all too soon. What we do know is that Johnny McDermott was the first great American-born golfer; some golf historians think he was the equal of Bobby Jones or any other golfer who played the game.

*I*n 2003, Richard Evans was playing a match against Mark Evans, who was not related. On the third hole at Glynhir Golf Club in Ammanford, Wales, he aced the 189-yard par 3; Mark mentioned to his opponent that there was probably no reason to play the hole, but Richard told him, "Give it your best shot." Mark did just that and also scored a hole in one.

Why would this be a part of the "Failures" chapter? Well, at the next hole, the golfers hit drives into the trees, and both lost their golf balls.

The inscription on Joe Kirkwood's tombstone reads:

Tell your story of hard luck shots,
Of each shot straight and true,
But when you are done, remember, son,
Nobody cares but you.

BIBLIOGRAPHY

Almost Straight Down the Middle. Chris Plumridge. Herts, England: Queen Anne Press, n.d.

The Australian and New Zealand Golfer's Handbook. 5th ed. Edited by Muir Maclaren, A. H. Reed, and A. W. Reed. Sydney, Australia: n.d.

Believe It or Not—That's Golf! George Houghton. London: William Luscombe, 1974.

The Book of Golf Disasters. Peter Dobereiner. New York: Harper & Row, 1983.

The Bulletin. Edited by Bob Labbance. Cleveland, OH: The Golf Collectors Society, Inc., 2002.

Centel Western Open Program. Edited by Gary Holloway. Western Golf Association, 1991.

Champions Tour and PGA Senior Tour Media Guides. Ponte Vedra Beach, FL: various years.

Classic Golf Courses of Great Britain and Ireland. Nick Edmund. Boston: Little, Brown and Company, 1997.

Come Swing with Me. Doug Sanders with Larry Sheehan. Garden City, NY: Doubleday & Company, 1975.

The Crosby: Greatest Show in Golf. Dwayne Netland. Garden City, NY: Doubleday & Company, 1975.

Davies' Dictionary of Golfing Terms. Peter Davies. New York: Simon & Schuster, 1980.

Down the Fairway: The Golf Life and Play of Robert T. Jones, Jr. Robert T. Jones Jr. and O. B. Keeler. New York: Minton, Balch & Co., 1927.

Eighteen Stakes on a Sunday Afternoon. Geoffrey S. Cornish. Worcestershire, England: Grant Books, 2002.

The Encyclopedia of Golf. Nevin H. Gibson. New York: A. S. Barnes and Company, 1958.

Fifty Years of Golf: My Memories. Andra Kirkaldy. New York: E. P. Dutton and Company, 1921.

The First Coming: Tiger Woods, Master or Martyr. John Feinstein. New York: Ballantine Books, 1998.

Five Lessons: The Modern Fundamentals of Golf. Ben Hogan with Herbert Warren Wind. Drawings by Anthony Ravielli. New York: Barnes, 1957; Trumbull, CT: Golf Digest/Tennis, Inc., 1985.

A Game of Golf, a Book of Reminiscence. Francis Ouimet. Boston: Houghton Mifflin, 1932.

The Golden Era of Golf. Al Barkow. New York: St. Martin's Press, 2000.

Golf at the Presidio. Art Rosenbaum. San Francisco, CA: Presidio Golf Club, 1994.

Golf Begins at Forty. Sam Snead. New York: The Dial Press, 1978.

Golf Digest. Trumbull, CT: various dates.

The Golfer's Handbook, 1968 Edition. Edited by John B. Duncan. Glasgow, Scotland: 1968.

The Golfer's Handbook, 1975 Edition. Edited by Percy Huggins. Glasgow, Scotland: 1975.

Golf Facts. Ian Morrison. London: Quarto Publishing, 1993.

Golfiana. Edited by Charles C. Dufner. Edwardsville, IL: various dates.

Golf in Britain. Geoffrey Cousins. London: Routledge & Kegan Paul, 1975.

Golf Is a Funny Game, But It Wasn't Meant to Be. Ken Janke. Ann Arbor, MI: Momentum Books, 1992.

The Golf Journal. Far Hills, NJ: United States Golf Association, various dates.

Golf Resorts of the World. Brian McCallen. New York: Harry N. Abrams, Inc., 1993.

Golf's Lighter Side. Edited by Chris Plumridge. Oxford, England: Lennard Publishing, 1989.

Golf: The Major Championships, 1987. David and Patricia Davies. Haywards, Heath, UK: Partridge Press, 1987.

Golfweek. Winter Haven, FL: 1992.

Golf World. Trumbull, CT: various dates.

The Greatest Game Ever Played. Mark Frost. New York: Hyperion, 2002.

The Great Golf Courses of Canada. John Morand. Toronto, Ontario: Warwick Publishing, 1993.

Harvey Penick's Little Red Book: Lessons and Teachings from a Lifetime in Golf. Harvey Penick with Bud Shrake. Hingman, MA: Wheeler Pub., 1992.

The International Tournament Program, Volume IV. Edited by Kaye W. Kessler. Castle Pines, CO: The International, 1989.

Just Let Me Play: The Story of Charlie Sifford, the First Black PGA Golfer. Charlie Sifford with James Gullo. Latham, NY: British American Publishing, 1992.

Keepers of the Green. Bob Labbance and Gordon Witteveen. Ann Arbor, MI: Ann Arbor Press, 2002.

Life Is Sweet, Brother. Bernard Darwin. London: Collins, 1940.

Links Lore. Peter F. Stevens. Dulles, VA: Brassey's, Inc., 1998.

Links of Life. Joe Kirkwood. Oklahoma City, OK: 1973.

Making the Turn: A Year inside the PGA Senior Tour. Frank Beard with John Garrity. New York: Macmillan, 1992.

The Masters. Furman Bisher. Birmingham, AL: Oxmoor House, Inc., 1976.

Masters Journal, 1993–2001. Edited by John R. McDermott. New York: NYT Special Services, 1993.

The Memorial. Edited by Ken Bowden. Norwalk, CT: Sports Marketing Group, 1980.

The Open. Peter Alliss with Michael Hobbs. London: William Collins Sons, 1984.

The Oxford and Cambridge Golfing Society. Edited by Peter Bathurst and John Behrend. Worcestershire, England: Grant Books, 1997.

Pebble Beach Golf Links. Neal Hotelling. Chelsea, MI: Sleeping Bear Press, 1999.

PGA Tour Media Guide. Ponte Vedra Beach, FL: PGA Tour, various years.

PGA TOUR PARTNERS. Minnetonka, MN: PGA Tour Partners Club, various dates.

Playing the Like. Bernard Darwin. London: Country Life, 1934.

Presidential Lies. Shepherd Campbell and Peter Landau. New York: Macmillan, 1996.

Records of the Masters Tournament, 1934–1982. Augusta, GA: Augusta National, Inc., 1982.

Reminiscences of the Links. A. W. Tillinghast. Edited by Richard C. Wolffe Jr., Robert S. Trebus, and Stuart F. Wolffe. Springfield, NJ: TreeWolf Productions, 1998.

The Rules of the Green. Kenneth G. Chapman. Chicago: Triumph Books, 1997.

St. Andrews and Golf. Morton W. and John M. Olman. Cincinnati, OH: Market Street Press, 1995.

St. Andrews, Home of Golf. James K. Robertson. Cupar, Fife, Scotland: J. & G. Innes, Ltd., 1967.

The Story of American Golf. Herbert Warren Wind. New York: Alfred A. Knopf, 1948.

The Story of Muirfield Village and the Memorial Tournament. Paul Hornung. Columbus, OH: Golden Bear Publishing, 1985.

Thirty Years of Championship Golf. Gene Sarazen. New York: Prentice-Hall, 1950.

The Truth about Golf and Other Lies. Buddy Hackett. New York: Doubleday and Company, 1968.

Under the Lone Star Flagstick. Edited by Melanie Hauser. New York: Simon & Schuster, 1997.

Unplayable Lies. Fred Corcoran. New York: Duell, Sloan and Pearce, 1965.

The U.S. Open—Golf's Ultimate Challenge. Robert Sommers. New York: Atheneum, 1987.

U.S. Open Program—1991. Edited by John McDermott. Chaska, MN: Hazeltine National Golf Club, 1991.

U.S. Open Program—2000. Edited by Robin McMillan. Pebble Beach, CA: Pebble Beach Golf Links, 2000.

U.S. Open Program—2001. Edited by Robin McMillan. New York: U.S. Open, United States Golf Association, 2001.

The Walter Hagen Story. Walter Hagen. New York: Simon & Schuster, 1956.

A Wee Nip at the 19th Hole. Richard Mackenzie. Chelsea, MI: Sleeping Bear Press, 1997.

Win and Win Again. Curtis Strange with Kenneth Van Kampen. Chicago: Contemporary Books, Inc., 1990.

The World Atlas of Golf. Pat Ward-Thomas. London: Mitchell Beazley Publishers, 1976.

INDEX